RANDOM HOUSE

LARGE PRINT

ALSO BY JOSEPH J. ELLIS
AVAILABLE FROM
RANDOM HOUSE LARGE PRINT

AMERICAN CREATION:
Triumphs and Tragedies
at the Founding of the Republic

HIS EXCELLENCY: George Washington

First Family

First Family
Abigail and John

JOSEPH J. ELLIS

RANDOM HOUSE
LARGE PRINT

For Ellen, my Abigail

CONTENTS

Contents

Contents

PREFACE

My serious interest in the Adams family began twenty years ago, when I wrote a book about John Adams in retirement, eventually published as **Passionate Sage.** I had a keen sense that I was stepping into a long-standing conversation between Abigail and John in its final phase. And I had an equivalently clear sense that the conversation preserved in the roughly twelve hundred letters between them constituted a treasure trove of unexpected intimacy and candor, more revealing than any other correspondence between a prominent American husband and wife in American history.

I moved on to different historical topics over the ensuing years, but I made a mental note to come back to the extraordinarily rich Adams archive, then read all their letters and tell the full story of their conversation within the context of America's creation as a people and a nation. The pages that follow represent my attempt to do just that.

The distinctive quality of their correspondence, apart from its sheer volume and the dramatic character of the history that was happening around them, is its unwavering emotional honesty. All of us who have fallen in love, tried to raise children, suffered extended bouts of doubt about the integrity of our ambitions, watched our once youthful bodies betray us, harbored illusions about our impregnable principles, and done all this with a partner traveling the same trail know what unconditional commitment means, and why, especially today, it is the exception rather than the rule.

Abigail and John traveled down that trail about two hundred years before us, remained lovers and friends throughout, and together had a hand in laying the foundation of what is now the oldest enduring republic in world history. And they left a written record of all the twitches, traumas, throbbings, and tribulations along the way. No one else has ever done that.

To be sure, there were other prominent couples in the revolutionary era—George and Martha Washington as well as James and Dolley Madison come to mind. But no other couple left a documentary record of their mutual thoughts and feelings even remotely comparable to Abigail and John's. (Martha Washington burned almost all the letters to and from her husband.) And at the presidential level, it was not until Franklin and Eleanor Roosevelt occupied the White House that a wife exercised an influence over policy decisions equivalent to Abigail's.

It is the interactive character of their private story and the larger public story of the American founding that strikes me as special. Recovering their experience as a couple quite literally forces a focus on the fusion of intimate psychological and emotional experience with the larger political narrative. Great events, such as the battle of Bunker Hill, the debate over the Declaration of Independence, and the presidential election of 1800, become palpable human experiences rather than grandiose abstractions. They lived through a truly formative phase of American history and left an unmatched record of what it was like to shape it, and have it happen to them.

As I see it, then, Abigail and John have much to teach us about both the reasons for that improbable success called the American Revolution and the equally startling capacity for a man and woman—husband and wife—to sustain their love over a lifetime filled with daunting challenges. One of the reasons for writing this book was to figure out how they did it.

First Family

CHAPTER ONE

1759–74

"And there is a tye more binding than Humanity, and stronger than Friendship."

KNOWING AS WE DO that John and Abigail Adams were destined to become the most famous and consequential couple in the revolutionary era, indeed some would say the premier husband-and-wife team in all American history, it is somewhat disconcerting to realize that when they first met in the summer of 1759, neither one was particularly impressed by the other. The encounter occurred in the parlor of the pastor's house in Weymouth, Massachusetts, which happened to be the home of Abigail and her two sisters. Their father was the Reverend William Smith, whom John described in his diary as "a crafty designing man," a veteran public speaker attuned to reading the eyes of his audience. "I caught him, several times," wrote John, "looking earnestly at my face." Like most successful pastors, he was accustomed to being the center of attention, which apparently annoyed John, who described Reverend Smith prancing across the room while gesturing ostentatiously, "clapping his naked [?] sides and breasts with his hands before the girls."[1]

Abigail, in fact, was still a girl, not quite fifteen years old to John's twenty-four. She was diminutive, barely five feet tall, with dark brown hair, brown eyes, and a slender shape more attractive in our own time than then, when women were preferred to be plump. John was quite plump, or as men would have it, stout, already showing the signs that would one day allow his enemies to describe him as "His Rotundity." At five feet five or six, he was slightly shorter than the average American male of the day, and his already receding hairline promised premature baldness. Neither one of them, at first glance, had the obvious glow of greatness.

John's verdict, recorded in his diary, was that he had wasted an evening. He was courting Hannah Quincy at the time—some say that she was actually courting him—and his first reaction was that neither Abigail nor her sisters could measure up to Hannah. They seemed to lack the conversational skills and just sat there, "not fond, nor frank, not candid." Since Abigail eventually proved to be all these things, we can only conclude that this first meeting was an awkward occasion on which the abiding qualities of her mind and heart were obscured beneath the frozen etiquette of a pastor's parlor. And besides, she was only a teenager, nine years his junior, not even a legitimate candidate for his roving interest in a prospective wife.[2]

To say that "something happened" to change their respective opinions of each other over the next three years is obviously inadequate, but the absence of documentary evidence makes it the best we can do. John had legal business in Weymouth that involved the status of the pastoral house occupied by the Smith family, which meant that he was literally forced to interact with Abigail. And he accompanied his then best friend, Richard Cranch, who was courting (and eventually married) Mary Smith, Abigail's older sister. This, too, prompted interactions. And his flirtatious relationship with Hannah Quincy ended in a mutually declared romantic truce, which made John, once again, eligible.

Time was also a factor. The difference between a fifteen-year-old girl and a twenty-four-year-old man seemed a chasm; the difference between eighteen and twenty-seven was much more negotiable. Though it seems too easy to say, chance and circumstance provided them with the opportunity to talk with each other, to move past the awkwardness of a stuffy Weymouth parlor, thereby initiating a conversation that lasted for almost sixty years.

But talk by itself was not sufficient to explain their mutual attraction. The letters that began to flow back and forth between them late in 1761 contain some explicit expressions of powerful physical and sexual urges, so that the picture that emerges depicts two young lovers conversing about Shakespeare's sonnets or Molière's plays in between long and multiple kisses, passionate embraces, and mutual caresses. Their grandson Charles Francis Adams, who published the first comprehensive edition of their correspondence nearly a century later, was either too embarrassed or too much a prisoner of Victorian mores to include any of their courtship correspondence. Here is a sample of what he chose to censor. John to Abigail, addressed to "Miss Adorable": "By the same token that the bearer hereof [JA] satt up with you last night, I hereby order you to give him, as many kisses, and as many Hours of your company after nine o'clock as he pleases to demand, and charge them to my account."[3]

Or John to Abigail, explaining that a sudden storm had prevented a trip to see her at Weymouth: "Yet perhaps blessed storm . . . for keeping one at my distance. For every experimental philosopher knows, that the steel and the magnet, or the glass and the feather will not fly together with more celerity . . . than somebody . . . when brought within striking distance—and Itches, Aches, Agues, and Repentance might be the consequences of contact in present circumstances."[4]

Then Abigail to John, proclaiming that their

mutual attraction was visceral as well as intellectual: "And there is a tye more binding than Humanity, and stronger than Friendship . . . unite these, and there is a threefold chord—and by this chord I am not ashamed to say that I am bound, nor do I [believe] that you are wholly free from it."[5]

The inevitable "did they or didn't they" question is impossible to answer conclusively, though their first child, named Abigail, was born eight and half months after their marriage, just barely within the bounds of propriety. But the fact that they were strongly tempted is beyond question, and a crucial indication that their affinity was not solely cerebral. For both of them, love entailed a level of intimacy that no conversation could completely capture and required a physical attraction. And they both felt it. If Abigail referred to it as "the third chord," we might shift the metaphor and describe it as an emotional affinity that made unconditional trust between them a natural act.

One of the distinctive features of their extraordinary correspondence over a lifetime—more than twelve hundred letters—was also present from the start, namely, the tendency to banter playfully about serious subjects, thereby creating a certain ambiguity as to whether the issue at stake was cause for concern or laughter. For example, in a note to Abigail's sister Mary, John jokingly claimed that Abigail was rumored to have a crush on the recently coronated British monarch, George III, and that "altho my allegiance has been hitherto inviolate, I shall endeavor all in my Power, to foment Rebellion." (Little did he know that his joke would become a prescient prophecy.) Or there is Abigail's mock criticism of John that then concludes with a double-edged compliment:

> You was pleas'd to say that the receipt of a letter from your Diana always gave you pleasure. Whether this was designed as a compliment (a commodity I acknowledge that you seldom deal in) or as a real truth, you best know. Yet if I was to judge a certain persons Heart by what the like occasion passes through a cabinet of my own, I should be apt to suggest it as a truth. And why may I not? When I have often been tempted to believe that they were both cast in the same mold, only with this difference, that yours was made with a harder mettle, and therefore is less liable to an impression. Whether they both have an eaquil quantity of steel, I have not yet been able to discover, but do not imagine that either of them are deficient.[6]

Abigail was apparently more than half serious when, a few months before their wedding, she asked

John to deliver on his promise "and tell me all my faults, both of omission and commission, and all the evil you either know or think of me." John responded with a mock "catalogue of your Faults, Imperfections, Deficits, or whatever you please to call them." She was, he observed, negligent at playing cards, could not sing a note, often hung her head like a bulrush, sat with her legs crossed, was pigeon-toed, and to cap it off, she read too much. Abigail responded that many of these defects were probably incurable, especially the reading, so he would have to learn to live with them. The leg-crossing charge struck her as awkward, since "a gentleman has no business to concern himself with the leggs of a lady."[7]

The letters exchanged during their courtship (1761–64) provide the first and fullest window into the chemistry of their relationship, but it would probably be wrong to presume that the correspondence accurately reflected the way they talked to each other when together. Letter writing in the eighteenth century was a more deliberative and self-consciously artful exercise than those of us in the present, with our cell phones, e-mail, and text messaging, can fully fathom. The letters, of course, are all we have to recover the texture of their overlapping personalities. While they constitute a long string of emotional and intellectual pearls unmatched in the literature of the era, they were also self-conscious performances, quasi-theatrical presentations that were more stylized and orchestrated than real conversations. There are some things, in short, that we can never know for sure about their deepest thoughts and feelings, even though they are among the most fully revealed couples in American history.

Two essential ingredients in their lifetime literary dialogue were clear from the start: first, Abigail, despite the lack of any formal education, could match John with a pen, which was saying quite a lot, since he proved to be one of the master letter writers in an age not lacking in serious contenders; second, there was a presumed sense of psychological equality between them that Abigail expected and John found intoxicating. She was marrying a man who loved the fact that she was, as he put it, "saucy," and he was marrying a woman who was simultaneously capable of unconditional love and personal independence. They recognized from the beginning that they were a rare match. There were so many topics they could talk about easily and just as many things they did not have to talk about at all.

The wedding occurred on October 25, 1764, in the same parlor of her father's house in Weymouth where they had initially found each other so uninteresting. In her last letter to John before the wedding, Abigail asked him to take all her belongings, which she was forwarding in a cart to their new home in Braintree. "And then Sir, if you please," she concluded, "you may take me."[8]

DOWRIES

What did each of them bring to the marriage? Well, most basically, John brought sixty acres of land and a small house that he had inherited from his father, who died in 1761. Abigail brought a cartload of furniture and a household servant, who was partially paid for by her father. By the standards of New England at that time, these assets, though hardly massive, were not meager. They were starting off with more material resources than most newlyweds.

What about their respective bloodlines? On this score Abigail brought more status than John. Her mother was a Quincy, a name that rested atop the Braintree elite; the family eventually had the town named after them. Their mansion at Mount Wollaston was the closest thing to a baronial estate outside of Boston. Her father was a Harvard-educated minister, while John's was a farmer and shoemaker without a college education.

But this discrepancy was a bit deceptive, because Deacon Adams, as he was called, was a respected local leader who, at one time or another, had held every office in the Braintree town government. Moreover, as John made a point of emphasizing in his autobiography, the Adams family could trace its lineage back to 1638, making it one of the most long-standing families in Massachusetts, a venerable if not particularly prominent line.[9]

That said, when John graduated from Harvard in 1755, he was ranked fourteenth out of twenty-five students, a ranking based solely on family status rather than academic achievement. (Academically, by the way, he was one of the top three students in his class, and the status-based system of ranking became a casualty of the American Revolution.) There is indirect evidence to believe that Abigail's mother opposed the marriage, convinced that her daughter was marrying down and could do better. Such social calibrations were swept away by Abigail's uncompromising insistence that she had found her man and was determined to have him.[10]

In terms of providing for a family, John's prospects were excellent. He had that Harvard degree, had studied with some of the leading lawyers in the colony, had passed the equivalent of the bar exam in 1761, and had begun to develop a reputation as one of the up-and-coming attorneys in the Boston area. Indeed, he had chosen to delay marriage until he was twenty-nine, three or four years later than the norm for males in New England at that time, in order to ensure that his income could provide for a wife and family.[11]

Abigail brought equivalently sturdy strengths. From early childhood she had been exposed to the mundane but essential duties of managing a household. Though the Smith family had four servants, two of them slaves, all the daughters were required to perform the cooking, cleaning, spinning, and gardening duties that were expected of a New England wife. She could manage servants, to be sure, but she could also perform the various tasks they were assigned alongside them, to include maintaining a permanent fire in the fireplace for cooking, scouring heavy kettles and pots, feeding and killing chickens, and performing elemental carpentry repairs of cabinets and cupboards. In a pinch, she could also split logs for the fire.[12]

Then there were the less tangible assets that both brought to the union—the ambitions, insecurities, obsessions, excesses—all the mental and emotional ingredients that had begun to congeal in their respective personalities. John had nine more years of experience to distill, and the fact that he began keeping a diary soon after graduating from college means that the record of his interior life as a young man is much fuller than anything we have for Abigail. Many New Englanders of the time kept diaries, but most of them are about the weather. When John recorded which way the wind was blowing, however, he was usually being metaphorical, referring to the gusts surging through his own soul.[13]

In one sense John's early diary entries are reminiscent of an introspective tradition as old as New England Puritanism. He was forever making lists of daily tasks to perform, books to read, ways to discipline his day. But he invariably failed to meet his own standards. One day, for example, he vowed to rise before sunrise but then slept until seven o'clock and, as he put it, "Rambled about all Day, gaping and gazing." He kept imposing moral tests on himself that he consistently failed. Instead of reading his law books one day, he spent all his time "in absolute idleness, or what's worse, gallanting the Girls." Like the classic Puritan diary, his was a record of imperfection.[14]

Unlike the aspiring Puritan saint, however, who was preoccupied with the question "Am I saved?" John's obsession was more secular: "What is my destiny?" In some respects this secularization of the Puritan ethic resembled the list of disciplined habits Benjamin Franklin made famous in his "The Way to Wealth," which took for granted that worldly success, not eternal salvation, was the proper goal of life. But John's introspective philosophy, if he had ever given it a title, would have been called "The Way to Virtue." Mere worldly success in terms of wealth was never enough for him; indeed, it was actually dangerous, since wealth inevitably corrupted men and nations by undermining the disciplined habits that produced the wealth in the first place. Making wealth your primary goal, as he saw it, was symptomatic of a second-rate mind destined to die rich but unfulfilled.

John's ambitions soared to a greater height, a place where fame rather than fortune was the ultimate reward. When he read Cicero's orations against Catiline out loud in front of a mirror, he confided to himself that "it opens my pores, quickens the circulation," as he imagined himself an American Cicero delivering an equivalently dramatic speech. Or when he read Shakespeare, he asked himself how he could replicate the bard's genius at creating characters he had never experienced directly: "Why have I not genius, to start some new thought, something that will inspire the World, [and] raise me at once to fame?" For a country lawyer, he was aiming very high, looking to lash himself to a cause larger than himself.[15]

One of the most consequential decisions he ever made, second only to his decision to marry Abigail, was to become a lawyer rather than a minister. Though he tortured himself with guilt-driven questions for a full year after his graduation from college, knowing that his father hoped he would choose the pulpit, the outcome was never in doubt. Once the intellectual elite of New England, the ministry had drifted to the sidelines by the middle of the eighteenth century, caught up in increasingly pedantic theological quarrels and burdened by what

John called "the whole cartloads of trumpery, that we find Religion incumbered with in these Days." He had no desire to languish in obscurity, splitting theological distinctions at night and preaching harmless homilies to parishioners on Sunday. (Abigail's father, it turns out, was a sterling example of what he did not wish to become.) He was determined to become a major player in this world, not an erudite guide to the next one. Whether she knew it or not, Abigail was marrying one of the most ambitious men in New England.[16]

He spent three years (1755–58) teaching school and reading law in Worcester. During this formative phase he let all his friends know that his teaching job was a mere way station that allowed him to support himself while he prepared for grander things, that "keeping this school any length of time would make a base weed and ignoble shrub of me." He recorded a daydream in his diary in which he imagined his classroom as a little commonwealth, casting himself in the role of dictator, a sort of Cromwell of the kindergarten:

> I have several renowned Generals but three feet high, and several deep-projecting politicians in petticoats . . . Some rattle and Thunder out A, B, C, with as much Fire and impetuosity, as Alexander fought . . . At one table sits Mr. Insipid flopping and

fluttering, spinning his whirligig, or playing with his fingers as gaily and wittily as any frenchified coxcomb. At another sits the polemical Divine, plodding and wrangling in his mind about Adam's fall in which we sinned all as his primer declares. In short my little school, like the great World, is made up of Kings, Politicians, Divines, Fops, Buffoons, Fidlers, Sycophants, Fools, Coxcombs, chimney sweeps, and every other character drawn in History or seen in the world.[17]

Finally, he began what was to become a lifelong conversation with his internal demons. "Vanity I am sensible, is my cardinal folly," he lectured himself, "and I am in constant Danger, when in company, of being led an ignus fatuus by it without the strictest caution and watchfulness over my self." He was too candid, too conspicuous in his ambition, too talkative. He would come home after an evening of conversation with the local elite at Worcester and pour out his lamentations, especially his irresistible urge "to shew my own importance or superiority, by remarking the Foibles, Vices, or Inferiority of others," which invariably alienated the very people he sought to impress.[18]

More ominously, he often felt overwhelmed by his own passions—be they vanities, ambitions, or envies—acknowledging that in those moments he was wholly out of control, like an erupting volcano. On one occasion he described his emotions as "Lawless Bulls that roar and bluster, defy all Control, and sometimes murder their proper owner." On another occasion they became thunderstorms: "I can as easily still the fierce Tempests or stop the rapid thunderbolts," he chided himself, "as command the motions and operations of my own mind."[19]

Eventually John's dialogue with his own boisterous passions informed his understanding of all politics, gradually projecting onto the world his incessant emotional turmoil and thereby envisioning all societies as cauldrons of swirling, inherently irrational drives that it was the chief business of government to control. For the time being, however, his internal eruptions, raging bulls, or violent thunderstorms, whatever one wished to call them, defied his best efforts at control. And he knew it. (His own sense of being unbalanced was one reason he made balance the beau ideal of his political philosophy.) As he saw himself, he was a gifted young man with appropriately lofty ambitions, all of which could be ambushed by his erratic, overly excitable, at times explosive instincts. "Ballast is what I want," he lectured himself; "I totter with every breeze"—though the breezes were all blowing inside himself. Whether the source of John's periodic bursts of vanity, insecurity, and sheer explosiveness was mental or physical—there is some scholarly speculation that he had a thyroid imbalance—remains a mystery. There is no question, however, that he was susceptible to swoonish emotional swings, especially when under extreme stress, and he would struggle with this problem throughout his life.[20]

Whether she knew it or not, and there is some evidence she did, Abigail's chief role as John's wife was to become his ballast. She needed to create a secure domestic environment in which he felt completely comfortable, a calm space where his harangues and mood swings were treated as lovable eccentricities, the butt of jokes that would allow him to laugh at himself. He needed to be bathed in love, to be regarded not as an emotional liability but as a passionate asset. This was obviously a huge order. As it turned out, it came naturally to Abigail.

Why that was so is difficult to document, since Abigail did not keep a diary, and few letters before her courtship with John have survived. We are therefore forced to tease out of the scattered evidence some kind of plausible glimpse of her personality at the threshold of her marriage, inevitably influenced by the much more plentiful evidence from her more mature years, then connect the dots backward to her youth.

On the one hand, we know she was raised to be

a conventional New England woman, and groomed to live the life of a traditional New England wife: marry at around twenty and produce children every two years until her fertility faded, which meant that she expected to spend her twenties and thirties either pregnant or recovering from delivering a child. She presumed that she would run the household, educate the children at least to a level of literacy, and subsume her own ambitions within the life and work of her husband. These traditional expectations were always unquestioned presumptions for Abigail, and taken together, they constitute the primary reason that she does not fit comfortably into a modern feminist paradigm.[21]

On the other hand, while her mother encouraged her to adopt the traditional female virtues of the day, her father and grandmother encouraged her instincts to be opinionated. Reading was the chief form of rebellion. Her father owned an impressive library containing most of the classics in literature, history, and religion. Her interest in Milton, Pope, Dryden, and Shakespeare became a source of pride rather than a worrisome concern. (If she had been raised in Virginia, her reading habits would have been considered slightly scandalous and her tart tongue a liability that required correction.) Although she never received any formal schooling, she was "homeschooled" more like a boy than a girl. And while she was never exposed to Latin and

Greek, she was learning to read French when she met John. Her later letters, even more than John's, are littered with literary references that reflect the habit of reading acquired in her youth.

There are also frequent references to her obstinacy and stubbornness, which her father and grandmother Quincy found endearing. She preferred her hair to be done this way, not that, or to wear this dress rather than that one. She had strong views about how to manage the servants and whether the congregation responded properly to her father's weekly sermon. And, in the end, she knew her own mind well enough to reject her mother's advice that John was not her ideal mate. This independent streak was not the result of her reading; indeed, her passion for reading was its consequence. Like a beautiful woman's beauty, it was simply there, something she came by naturally and that no one tried to stamp out. On the contrary, as Grandmother Quincy once told her, "wild colts make good horses."[22]

Logically, Abigail should have felt torn between her two sides as a traditional New England woman and a fiercely independent personality. But she did not. The apparent contradiction felt to her like a seamless continuity. She could mend a hem while engaging you in a discussion of Macbeth's fatal flaw. If that caused trouble for some people, that was their problem. One of the reasons she felt so confident about her marriage to John was that he loved the edgy combination and took great delight at the literary allusions sprinkled throughout her letters. She was simultaneously a dutiful wife and an intellectual equal, a lover and a friend, a heart and a mind.

In fact, on the heart side of the equation, Abigail was John's superior. Together with his gargantuan ambitions and overlapping vanities, he brought massive insecurities to the relationship: a nervous, excitable, at times irritable temperament rooted not so much in self-doubt—he was completely confident of his abilities—but rather in uncertainty that the world would allow him to display his talents. To be sure, John was hoping to play a bigger game on a much larger public stage, while Abigail's focus was the much smaller arena of the family. But within that orbit she was supremely and serenely confident, totally immune to the demons that bedeviled him, the even keel to his wild swings, the safety net that would catch him when he fell. In psychological terms, he was neurotic and she was uncommonly sane. His inevitable eruptions would not threaten the marriage, because she was the center who would always hold.[23]

Abigail's bottomless devotion was put on display in April 1764, seven months before their marriage, when John decided to undergo inoculation against smallpox. An epidemic was raging in

Boston, and John correctly calculated that inoculation, though risky, was much less so than catching
the smallpox in "the natural way." (In March 1764
Boston reported 699 cases of smallpox acquired in
"the natural way," causing 124 deaths.) John's letters while he was quarantined were models of
bravado—he was "as Happy as a Monk in his clois-
ter or an Hermit in his Cell."[24]

Abigail had wanted to join him so they could
undergo the inoculation process together. But John
reasoned that as long as she remained in Weymouth
or Braintree, the epidemic in Boston would not
threaten her, so the risk of inoculation was greater
than the risk of exposure. She sent him several
parcels of tobacco so that he could "smoke" the
daily letters she expected him to write, thereby
removing any contamination. "I don't imagine you
will use it all for that purpose," she joked, given his
preference for a cigar as a companion to take her
place.[25]

Though they were only engaged, Abigail
already thought of herself as his wife. "I am very
fearful that you will not, when left to your own
management, follow their directions," she cautioned, "but let her who tenderly cares for you both
in Sickness and Health interest you to be careful."
She felt guilty at not being there to take care of him.
Even though she could not visit him in quarantine,
she said she wanted to go to Boston anyway so she

could just "look at him through the window." She was completely smitten.[26]

FAMILY VALUES

Most histories of colonial America for the decade between 1764 and 1774 are framed around several pieces of parliamentary legislation that led directly to the American Revolution. The key items are the Sugar Act (1764), the Stamp Act (1765), the Townshend Acts (1767), and the Coercive Acts (1774). Taken together, they represented a policy change by the British government designed to consolidate its control over a vast North American empire acquired in the French and Indian War. Imposing a higher degree of imperial control, and expecting American colonists to help pay for it, made perfect sense from the perspective of London and Whitehall, but it was regarded by most colonists as a dramatic change in the rules of the game, most especially in its presumption that Parliament possessed the authority to tax them without their consent. What seemed so sensible to George III and his ministers was seen as tyrannical, arbitrary, and imperious by most colonists, who believed that their status in the British Empire had shifted from being equal members of the imperial family to abject subjects. And because this British legislative initiative led to the loss of its North American empire south of Canada, historians have tended to assess the effort harshly, as probably the most fatal blunder in the history of British statecraft.[27]

Abigail was hardly oblivious to these legislative benchmarks of British imperial policy, but her own benchmarks were pregnancies and births: Abigail, called Nabby, arrived in July 1765; John Quincy almost exactly two years later; Susanna, a sickly infant who lived only fourteen months, in December 1768; Charles in May 1770; and Thomas Boylston in September 1772. In effect, she was pregnant or recovering from childbirth for most of the decade. Beyond much doubt she was reading the newspapers and pamphlets that defined the terms of the emerging constitutional crisis. And as John became more and more involved in the protest movement in Braintree and Boston, we can presume that they talked together about the political issues at stake. But her primary focus, what defined her daily life, was the growing brood of children and the demanding domestic duties they created for a young mother.

John's primary focus, on the other hand, was his legal career and his gradually expanding role as an outspoken opponent of British policy. He was almost surely involved in the family chores as well—putting the children to bed, reading to them, conferring with Abigail about disciplinary decisions and the educational program appropriate for each child. On this score we cannot be absolutely sure, however, because of what we might call "the paradox of proximity," which is to say that we know most about the intimate lives of Abigail and John when they were apart and could converse only by corresponding. When they were together, the historical record of their family life is at best sketchy.

They did exchange a few letters during the first decade of their marriage, when John was on the road, handling cases from southern Maine to Cape Cod. These letters provide some slivers of evidence that John was very much an involved father. "I know from the tender affection you bear me," Abigail wrote in September 1767, "that you will rejoice to hear that we are well, and that our daughter rocks him [John Quincy] to Sleep, with the Song of 'Come pappa come home to Brother Johnny.'" When John was trying a case in Plymouth in May 1772, he expressed frustration at being absent from the family routine: "I wish myself at Braintree. This wandering itinerating life grows more and more disagreeable with me. I want to see my Wife and children every day." He claimed that whenever he was on the road, his imagination carried him back to Braintree and "our lovely Babes": "My Fancy runs about you perpetually. It is continually with you and in the Neighborhood of you—frequently takes a walk with you, and our little prattling Nabby,

Johnny, Charley, and Tommy. We walk all together up Penn's Hill, over the bridge to the Plain, down to the Garden, & c every Day." When he was home—his office was in the house—John did not have to imagine such outings, so it seems safe to conclude that interacting with the family was an integral part of his day.[28]

The division of labor within the marriage, then, was clear but not absolute. Abigail was primarily a wife and mother who focused on the household. John was primarily the breadwinner pursuing a legal career. But she was also a political confidante, and he was an active father and husband. In that sense they were both androgynous, not for any deeply ideological reasons but because neither one was comfortable denying any important dimension of their respective personalities. And the more they interacted, the more they defied rigid gender categories and completed each other.

As they were working out their new roles as husband, wife, and parents, the American colonies were being asked to work out new roles within a reconfigured British Empire. Abigail and John launched their marriage at the same time the British ministry launched its legislative initiative to impose parliamentary authority over the colonies. In fact, Nabby arrived at almost the same time that news of the most offensive parliamentary initiative, the Stamp Act, arrived in America.

In one sense this convergence was purely coincidental. But the coincidence is worth contemplating, because it permits us to recover the messier and more layered mentality of history happening, that is, as Abigail and John actually experienced it. The great public events of the time that stand front and center in the history books were only part of the story they were living, and the more private side of the story—their family life—became the lens through which they perceived and made sense of those grander events emanating from England. The prominent role that John came to play in orchestrating the opposition to British policy, a role that provided him with the revolutionary credentials that established the foundation for his entire career in public life thereafter, required great patience as well as bottomless conviction. He was ready for the role that history eventually assigned him after the marriage to Abigail in a way that he had not been before.

HISTORY CALLS

During the three years before his marriage, John began to write essays aimed at the public press. He was clearly not content to become a successful country lawyer, and the ambitions surging inside him were searching for an outlet on some larger stage. His first effort was a series of essays entitled "The Evils of Licensed Houses," none of which was ever published. This was probably for the best, since their purported point—that most taverns were dens of iniquity—was contradicted by the evidence in his diary at the time, which depicted the boisterous camaraderie of dancers, drinkers, and singers at his favorite tavern as a beguiling portrait of the human menagerie at play. Perhaps he felt guilty about his own feelings of fun, so the essays were his clumsy effort at making amends. Or perhaps he simply was telling prospective readers what he thought they wanted to hear.[29]

His next effort, which did make it into the Boston newspapers, was a series of pieces written under the pseudonym "Humphrey Ploughjogger." Mostly moral lectures on the evils of political factions and partisanship, these essays were distinctive in their style, which attempted to mimic the voice of a quasi-literate farmer with a down-home sense of humor and a rustic kind of wisdom. For example, Humphrey ridiculed "grate men who dus nothing but quarrel with one anuther and put pices in the nues paper," which, if you think about it, was a parody of himself. One could read the Ploughjogger essays as a primitive version of an American literary tradition that reached its artistic culmination in Mark Twain's **Adventures of Huckleberry Finn.** In the context of the moment, however, its significance would seem more personal. John was trying on different identities and voices as he auditioned for a role in the limelight. At the cusp of his marriage, he comes across as a painfully earnest, still unfocused young man, full of himself in several senses of the term, but still very much a work in progress.[30]

In the spring of 1764 Great Britain began to implement its new imperial strategy for the American colonies. The imperial initiative, most especially the Stamp Act (1765), was a heavenly gift for John, who had been searching for a cause of truly historic proportions, and the ministry of George III, along with the British parliament, now provided it almost providentially. Abigail and the soon-to-arrive children provided him with a family haven from the vicissitudes of the world, a comfort zone where he did not have to worry about constantly proving himself, a more stable psychological foundation for his ever-quivering ego. Not so incidentally, Abigail also offered an outlet for the long-suppressed sexual energies of a twenty-nine-year-old male. All at once he had a cause as large as an imperial crisis and a newfound confidence. The consequences were nothing short of spectacular.

The first consequence was a series of four essays in the **Boston Gazette** entitled **A Dissertation Upon the Canon and Feudal Law.** (John later made a point of mentioning that portions of this work were drafted in his Braintree study while Abigail was nursing Nabby upstairs.) His initial entry in the imperial debate—scores of others would quickly follow—**Dissertation** was perhaps the most intellectually cogent and stylistically satisfying collection of essays he ever wrote. Years later, he recalled its composition fondly, adding that "it might as well have been called an Essay upon Forefathers Rock."[31]

Many of John's subsequent contributions to the political debate were closely reasoned legalistic arguments, often of a tedious sort. **Dissertation**, on the other hand, had a sweeping and soaring quality that derived from its central premise, which was that the political cultures of England and New England were fundamentally at odds. The former was rooted in the arbitrary and coercive forms of government of the Old World, legacies of the medieval fusion of church and state. The entire history of New England since the first settlements, on the other hand, was a repudiation of this legacy, which over the course of almost 150 years had yielded political and religious institutions based on the principle of consent.

Although John began drafting **Dissertation** before news of the Stamp Act arrived in Boston, his analysis of the inherently imperious character of the British Empire eerily foreshadowed the most offensive features of the Stamp Act. He was one of the first into the fight.

Dissertation became one of the earliest expressions of what came to be called American Exceptionalism, though in John's version only New England was featured as the unique depository of an essentially consensual and participatory politics. His argument laid the intellectual foundation for the more focused rejections of Parliament's authority that he published over the next decade, because it suggested that the disagreements between the American colonies and Great Britain were deeply rooted in two fundamentally different historical experiences, and therefore were probably irresolvable. It was a rather auspicious way to launch a political career, the kind of panoramic and prophetic contribution that one might expect from someone much older. It signaled the arrival of a major presence on the Boston political scene.[32]

He followed up **Dissertation** with a more pointed attack on the Stamp Act as an illegal violation of long-standing American rights. This was **Braintree Instructions**, which he wrote at the request of the Braintree town meeting. He made three arguments, none particularly original but all rendered in a succinct and defiantly punchy style: first, that the Stamp Act was unconstitutional because Parliament was claiming a power to tax colonists that it did not possess; second, by taking this unprecedented step, the members of Parliament were the true radicals and the colonists the true conservatives; third, given the illegality of the Stamp Act, the proper way to proceed was to refuse to obey it, since, as he later put it, "it was no more binding than an Act to destroy half of our Species."

Forty towns in Massachusetts, including Boston, adopted the language of **Braintree Instructions** as the clearest and most forceful expression of their political sentiments. This made John, almost overnight, one of the most famous men in Massachusetts. And when **Braintree Instructions** was published in several London newspapers, he became one of the most infamous men in England.[33]

Abigail had almost surely assumed that she was marrying a man of potentially local prominence who might achieve a lawyerly version of her father's ministerial career at Weymouth. All of a sudden, the size of the theater and the stakes of the game had changed dramatically. We do not know how she viewed this escalation of prospects. She was nursing Nabby and about to become pregnant with John Quincy, so she already faced a demanding set of physical and emotional challenges. Now a new and at least equally demanding dimension was added to her life. She was being asked to accompany John—presumably the children, whatever their eventual number, trailing behind—as he strolled toward his appointment with destiny.

DRAWING LINES

"The year 1765 has been the most remarkable year of my life," John recorded in his diary as the year was ending. "The enormous engine fabricated by the British Parliament for battering down all the rights and liberties of America, I mean the Stamp Act, has raised and spread through the whole continent a spirit that will be recorded to our honor, with all future generations." This observation, made in the moment, turned out to be correct. American opposition to the act became the opening shot in a struggle that led to withdrawal from the British Empire, the creation of an American republic, and the ascendance of a country lawyer named John Adams to the top tier of a quite remarkable group of American statesmen, later capitalized and mythologized as the Founding Fathers.[34]

John was extremely prolific during the next decade, publishing between twenty-five and thirty essays that challenged Parliament's right to tax the colonies and, eventually, to legislate at all for them. One could argue that Abigail was equally prolific during this time, laying the biological foundation for what would eventually be called the Adams dynasty. John's political writings dominate the historical record of their lives together at this time, in part because they focus on major public issues that ended up altering the course of history, in part because of the paradox of proximity, meaning that there are very few letters offering a window into Abigail's domestic world.

One does get a few glimpses of Abigail's mentality every now and then, as when she complains to her sister that John's legal cases have made him "such an Itinerant . . . that I have but little of his company." Or when she reports that two-year-old Nabby is "fat as a porpoise and falls heavey," thereby producing a continually bruised forehead. Or when, in 1774, John is preparing to leave for the Continental Congress in Philadelphia and worries out loud to Abigail about whether to buy a new suit and how much linen to pack. On a day-by-day basis, the primary lens through which both of them viewed the world—she, of course, more than he—was the family. As a result, the more publicly oriented historical record distorts their actual experience of living through a rather propitious moment in American history at the same time as they were defining their respective roles within the marriage and founding a family.[35]

The unbalanced documentation also makes it difficult to know how fully informed Abigail was about the political debates that consumed so much of John's energy and attention. Her letters make clear that she was reading the Boston newspapers. Glancing remarks in his letters suggest that he shared his thoughts with her, read early drafts of his essays to her, and asked her advice about key decisions, such as whether to accept election to the Massachusetts legislature in 1770. (On the latter score, John mentioned in his autobiography that he "expressed to Mrs. Adams all my Apprehensions" and that Abigail, "that excellent lady, who always encouraged me, burst unto a flood of Tears" but eventually endorsed the decision to take the post.) We also know from later chapters in John's political career that Abigail was a fully informed and deeply involved political confidante, so it is plausible to read that role into this earlier chapter.[36]

The clearest evidence of her political posture comes in a letter to Isaac Smith Jr., a cousin who was living in London. "From my infancy," she wrote, "I have always felt a great inclination to visit the Mother Country as tis called, and had nature formed me of the other Sex, I should certainly have been a rover." Then she went on: "Dont you think this little spot of ours better calculated for happiness than any you have yet seen? Would you exchange it for England, France, Spain or Ittally? Are not the people here more upon an Equality in point of knowledge and of circumstances—there being none so immensely rich as to Lord it over us, neither any so abjectly poor as to suffer for the necessaries of life." Clearly, if the lines were ever drawn, she stood proudly with New England.[37]

In his published essays John was also drawing a series of lines, the chief one being between American rights and Parliament's authority, but not until the end of the decade, in 1774, was he prepared to contemplate drawing the ultimate line that severed the connection between the colonies and the British Empire, and even then he was reluctant to cut the cord with the Crown. As we have seen, the argument first advanced in **Dissertation** implied that the history of New England had created a fundamentally different set of political assumptions and institutions from those operative in England. And much later in his life he claimed that, at least in retrospect, the argument made by James Otis in the writs of assistance case in 1761, in which Otis denied the right of Parliament to sanction searches of Massachusetts homes, foreshadowed the eventual break. (Adams was present in the courtroom for Otis's presentation, later describing himself as "a short, thick Archbishop of Canterbury" and Otis as a more impressive orator than Patrick Henry.) However, throughout the late 1760s and early 1770s John's political agenda was not American independence, but getting the British ministry to come to its senses in order to recover America's historic status within the empire.[38]

Under the pseudonym "Clarendon," he emphasized that it was the British constitution that guaranteed the rights of all Englishmen, establishing as a principle of law that the British Empire was "not built on the doctrine that a few nobles or rich commons have a right to inherit the earth." The Stamp Act was, by this reasoning, clearly a violation of "those ancient Whig Principles" and therefore no more binding on any true Englishman than some crazed pronouncement by the local drunk.[39]

In late 1766 and early 1767 John published eleven essays, using multiple pseudonyms, to engage "Philanthrop," who was really Jonathan Sewall, one of his Harvard classmates and closest friends. (Sewall had once proposed that they undergo inoculation together so that their constant banter would prevent boredom.) Sewall's specific goal was to defend the governor, Francis Bernard, for his endorsement of the Stamp Act. His larger goal was to warn that organized opposition to Parliament's authority was treasonable, and would lead inexorably to a break with Great Britain that would produce only anarchy and ruin in the colonies. Despite the fact that John continued to treat Sewall as a friend, he vilified Philanthrop as an "old Trumpeter . . . spewing out venomous Baillingsgate." And John countered the threats of social chaos by arguing that if it ever came to an open breach with Great Britain, the vast bulk of the Massachusetts citizenry would rally to the cause in a decidedly orderly fashion. The British, in short, had much more to lose than the Americans.[40]

John's other major effort, a series of eight essays

published in the **Boston Gazette** early in 1773, focused on what was to become a trademark issue for the remainder of his political career—the essential role of an independent judiciary. His specific target was a proposal to have the salaries of Massachusetts judges paid by the Crown. The larger target was the entire system of patronage emanating from the governor's office, now occupied by Thomas Hutchinson, which made all judicial appointments a corrupt bargain with the devil.[41]

In two senses, this debate was intensely personal for John, at times obsessively so. First, Hutchinson became the chief embodiment of British corruption and condescension even though he was a native New Englander who had written the authoritative history of Massachusetts. "Mr. Hutchinson never drank a cup of tea in his life," John observed much later, "without Contemplating the Connection between that Tea, and his Promotion." When a visitor once asked him what he thought of Hutchinson, John was even more hostile: "I told him I once thought that his Death in a natural Way would have been a Smile of Providence . . . and the most joyful News to me that I could ever have heard." When John wanted to imagine the most tyrannical and corrupt features of the British Empire, the face he saw was Hutchinson's. It was an early manifestation of what became a prevailing pattern throughout his political life, namely, to personalize the opposition by focusing his hostility on a single figure, who then became a wholly vile and contemptible creature worthy of permanent enshrinement in the Adams rogues' gallery. Hutchinson was eventually joined there by Thomas Paine, Benjamin Franklin, and Alexander Hamilton.[42]

Second, in 1768, soon after John moved Abigail and the family to a house on Brattle Square in Boston—the move proved temporary—he received a highly lucrative offer to become judge advocate in the Admiralty Court, one of those patronage plums that would set him up for life, but at the price of his subsequent silence on all the salient arguments about Parliament's authority. The offer came from his old friend Jonathan Sewall, who had recently accepted the post of attorney general, an obvious sellout in John's judgment. He rejected the offer immediately, but he began to realize that he was making life-altering decisions with huge consequences for his family on the basis of his political convictions, which, no matter how heartfelt, could very well lead to his professional and personal ruin. "I have a Zeal at my Heart for my country," he confided to Abigail, "which I cannot smother or conceal . . . This Zeal will prove fatal to the fortune and Felicity of my Family, if it is not regulated more than mine has hitherto been."[43]

There is no record of Abigail's ever urging John to trim his political sails in order to protect the future of the family, or to accept a lucrative offer that would have compromised his political integrity. In fact, there is no evidence that she gave the matter any thought at all. Her husband had to do his duty as he saw it, and while she was an opinionated and independent-minded woman, her duty as a wife was to support him. "I must entreat you," John pleaded with her, "my dear Partner in all the Joys and Sorrows, Prosperity and Adversity of my Life, to take a Part with me in the Struggle." The plea proved unnecessary. Abigail never entertained doing anything else.[44]

The most severe test, which she passed with flying colors, occurred in 1770, when John was asked to defend the British soldiers who had fired on and killed six members of a Boston mob that was harassing them with taunts and snowballs. John agreed to take the case for two reasons: first, he believed that it was important to demonstrate that even vilified "Lobsterbacks" could get fair treatment in Massachusetts, despite the highly politicized atmosphere; second, he thought that the so-called massacre had been manipulated by Samuel Adams and the leadership of the Sons of Liberty for political purposes. "Endeavors had been systematically pursued for many months, by certain busy characters," he observed, "to excite Quarrells . . . between the Inhabitants of the lower class and the Soldiers, and at all risques to inkindle an immortal hatred between them." Rather than a dramatic example of British tyranny, which he was on record of opposing so passionately, the Boston Massacre was, in truth, "planned by designing Men," and the real victims were the British soldiers.[45]

This was obviously a politically unpopular posture, and John made a point of consulting with Abigail before going forward. She concurred that the mob had been instigated, so that John's decision to defend the British troops was the virtuous course regardless of the political fallout. She was, at the time, recovering from the death of Susanna, her third child, and pregnant with Charles, her fourth. So she was emotionally immersed in some rather dramatic events of her own, but still fully capable and willing to accompany John on a dangerously unpopular course.[46]

Eventually Captain Thomas Preston, the British commanding officer at the scene, was found not guilty, along with all but two of the British soldiers, who had their thumbs imprinted as punishment for a lesser charge. John's fear that his successful defense of the British soldiers would create implacable enemies proved wrong—the word "out of doors" was that John's political credentials were beyond reproach and that his conduct had the approval of Sam Adams, the leader of the Sons of Liberty, who had probably orchestrated the events leading up to the massacre in the first place. Indeed, John's reputation soared, and he was elected to the

Massachusetts legislature a few months later by a comfortable majority, the epitome of the passionate patriot, now with personal integrity to boot.

CROSSING THE
RUBICON TOGETHER

By the early 1770s John had reached the conclusion that the likelihood of a political reconciliation with Great Britain was remote in the extreme. The British ministry was committed to a strategy of American subjugation to Parliament's authority, and he could find no realistic reasons to believe that it would come to its senses before producing a permanent rupture in the British Empire. "I see that there is not Wisdom, Justice, and Moderation in the Mother Country," he observed to Isaac Smith Jr. in 1771, "to desist voluntarily from such Attempts to make inroads against us." But if American independence in some form was inevitable, he did not believe it to be imminent. It was probably several decades away: "You and I shall be saints in Heaven," he predicted to Smith, "before the Times we dream of. But our grandsons may perhaps think this a canonical Prophecy."[47]

The events between 1770 and 1774 caused John to accelerate his sense of the historical schedule. In a somewhat overclever move, the British ministry removed import duties on all other commodities but retained the duty on tea at a very low rate, making it less expensive to purchase tea from Great Britain while simultaneously reasserting the principle of parliamentary sovereignty. Instead of co-opting the colonists, this provoked the Boston Tea Party (1773), a festival of raucous destruction organized by the Sons of Liberty in which a Boston mob, somewhat frivolously disguised as Indians, boarded three British ships anchored in Massachusetts Bay and tossed about £15,000 worth of tea overboard. (John was of two minds about mobs, finding the more impulsive version at the Boston Massacre disreputable but the highly organized effort that destroyed the tea wholly justifiable.) The British ministry responded by escalating the stakes, closing the Boston port to all trade, shutting down all the Massachusetts courts, and imposing martial law on the city. Massachusetts was to be made into an object lesson of what happens when colonists brazenly defy the authority of the British government.

Predictably, but interestingly, John and Abigail responded to these harsh measures in the same dramatic (one might even say melodramatic) way: "We live my dear Soul," he wrote to her, "in an Age of Tryal. What will be the consequences I know not. The town of Boston, for ought I can see, must suffer martyrdom. It must expire and our principal consolation is, that it dies in a Noble Cause." This hyperbolic tone reflected John's sense that a line had been crossed that could never be retraced. But he wanted Abigail to know that he was not despondent or depressed: "Don't imagine from all this that I am in the Dumps," he wrote her. "I can truly say, that I have felt more Spirits and Activity since the arrival of this News than I had done before for years."[48]

In John's view, the Coercive Acts had exposed the latent agenda of the British ministry for all to see. Intricate constitutional arguments about long-standing colonial rights, debates in which John had been a major player, now paled in comparison to the total and wholly arbitrary revocations of colonial rights within the empire. From the British perspective, the colonists really had none, it was now clear. John had been saying that this was the unspoken assumption of the British ministry for ten years. The Coercive Acts proved that he had been right. Abigail concurred completely.[49]

This placed them on the cutting edge of radical thinking within Massachusetts, and much further ahead of public opinion in the rest of the colonies, which remained wedded to the hope for a peaceful reconciliation. Both of them had come to see the imperial crisis as an all-or-nothing choice between American independence and slavery, with all efforts at a split-the-difference compromise nothing more than a seductive illusion. As John put it to Abigail:

"And the Question seems to be, whether the American Colonies are to be considered as a distinct Community so far as to have a Right to judge for themselves, when the Fundamentals of their Government are destroyed or invaded?" This was a defiant, even treasonable, position, which was one reason he asked her to "keep these letters chiefly to yourself." He also asked her to "put them up safe, and preserve them," for they provided "a kind of picture of the Manners, Opinions, and Principles of these Times of Perplexity, Danger, and Distress." One of the reasons that so many of their letters have survived is that they both recognized, early on, that they were living through a truly propitious moment likely to find a prominent place in the history books.[50]

In June 1774 they were apprised that John had been selected as one of four Massachusetts delegates to the Continental Congress. Accepting that appointment constituted a major public statement about his political loyalties, and Jonathan Sewall pleaded with him to refuse the offer, warning that attending the Continental Congress would brand him as a traitor and destroy his legal career. Remembering the poignancy of that moment many years later, John recalled his response: "I answered that I knew Great Britain was determined on her systems, and that very determination determined me on mine; that he [Sewall] knew I had been constant and uniform in opposition to all her measures; that the die was now cast; I had passed the Rubicon; swim or sink, live or die, survive or perish with my country was my unalterable determination."[51]

Abigail was equally resolute. There was no question that John had to go to Philadelphia. Their minds were so perfectly aligned on that score that no discussion was necessary. There was also no question that she was perfectly competent to manage the farm and four young children, aged two to nine years, while he was away. The conversations were about details: What clothing should he pack? What horse should he take? Before he left, they needed to purchase more fertilizer for their fields, John insisting on "Mud Flatts or Creek Mud . . . mixed with Dust and Dung." It was the kind of privileged conversation that could occur only between two soul mates knowing they were entering a new chapter in their lives and their marriage, tending together to the details because the larger issues required only nods and glances.[52]

John departed from Boston on August 10, 1774. An aspiring novelist could work wonders with the scene. The four Massachusetts delegates boarded a well-appointed coach in full view of five British regiments encamped on Boston Common. They were preceded by two white servants, well mounted and armed, followed by four black slaves dressed in livery, two on horseback and two footmen. It was a motley mix of royal splendor, military power, social deference, and racial inferiority, all traveling together on a mission to oppose British tyranny. Though there were no women in the picture, Abigail was lurking in the background, cheering, worrying, and praying for John's safe return.[53]

CHAPTER TWO

1774-78

"My pen is always freer than my tongue, for I have written many things to you that I suppose I never would have talked."

THOUGH THERE WAS no way of knowing it at the time, John's departure for Philadelphia launched a new chapter in the marriage that paralleled a new chapter in American history, soon to be called the American Revolution. For the next four years, Abigail and John would be apart much more than they were together. (And for the six following years, when John was in Paris, except for one brief return to Braintree, they were completely separated.) From a historian's point of view, the geographic distance between them proved a godsend, for it reversed the paradox of proximity and created a flood of letters that provide unprecedented access to their private thoughts and feelings. From Abigail and John's perspective, distance put their partnership to a new test, one that it eventually passed with flying colors, ironically exposing their most private intimacies in letters designed to close the distance.

Indeed, Abigail claimed that she was more forthcoming in her letters than she would have been in face-to-face conversations: "My pen is always freer than my tongue," she wrote in 1775, "for I have written many things to you that I suppose I never would have talked." John concurred. Sitting at his writing desk almost forced him to delve deeper into the murmurings of his mind and heart, but he was not as capable of expressing them. "If I could write as well as you," he confessed, "it would be so, but, upon my word, I cannot." This was high praise, and most scholarly commentators on the correspondence agree.[1]

Context, as always, is crucial. From 1774 to 1778 John was mostly in Philadelphia, making himself into one of the most prominent and outspoken advocates of American independence in the Continental Congress and eventually the rough equivalent of secretary of defense during the first three years of the war. The rules established by the congress forbade him to write about the ongoing debates, and his daily schedule of full sessions with the entire congress, as well as multiple committee meetings in the evenings, left little time for personal matters. He was at the center of the proverbial wind tunnel during one of the most dramatic and consequential moments in American history. The extraordinary number of letters he managed to write to Abigail is testimony to his need for some sliver of private space where he could unburden himself to the person who knew him better than anyone else on the planet.

Abigail was up at Braintree, managing the farm with a few hired hands and raising four young children. She regarded her duties as a domestic version of John's public service, a sacrifice justified by the political crisis through which they were all living. Abigail, in fact, was in much greater physical danger than John, in part from the proximity of the British army in Boston, in part from the smallpox epidemic that raged throughout eastern Massachusetts.

Like John's, her days were crowded, not with crucial affairs of state but with the daily duties of a single parent attempting to hold a family together amid pitched battles (e.g., Bunker Hill) and rampant contagion. She, too, sought solace in a private space that she called "my closet." She found such a space in her aunt's home in Boston during a visit in 1776. "In this Closet are a number of Book Shelves," as she described it to John, "and a pretty little desk or cabinet where I write all my Letters and keep my papers unmolested by any one."

Her Braintree house lacked such a "closet," so she had no place where she could escape the duties and demands of the day, read letters from John, and write her own in splendid isolation. Like Virginia

Woolf over a century later, Abigail felt the urge for a room of her own, where her thoughts and feelings were not defined or confined by her dominant roles as a wife and mother. As she put it, "I always had a fancy for a closet with a window which I could peculiarly call my own."[2]

LETTERS AND POSTERITY

It requires a truly imaginative leap for us to comprehend the more deliberative character of letter writing in the eighteenth century. It took two or three weeks for letters to travel between Braintree and Philadelphia, so they often crossed, meaning that the political or emotional crisis that prompted the letter had been resolved before the response arrived, like a message from the past. As a result, letters were less an ongoing conversation than a time-bound exchange of ruminations, more thoughtful and self-consciously composed than our Internet communications, but also less interactive.

John was more outspokenly frustrated by this intractable reality than Abigail: "Is there no way for two friendly souls to converse together although the bodies are four hundred miles off?" he asked. "Yes, by letter. But I want a better communication. I want to hear you think or to see your thoughts." In his mind, letters could not replace the shared routines and rhythms of family life that he had come to depend upon as the foundation for his own emotional balance: "I want to take a walk with you in the garden, to go over to the common, the plain, the meadow. I want to take Charles in one hand and Tom in the other, and walk with you, Nabby on the right hand and John upon the left, to view the cornfields, the orchards, etc." Letters were important, to be sure, but they were not an adequate substitute for the emotional ballast of daily domestic interaction.[3]

He tended to write in the early morning, before the congress met, she in the evening, after the children were put to bed. Since John was prohibited from writing about the political debates, his early letters focused on the sights and sounds of Philadelphia, which had surpassed Boston as the largest and most cosmopolitan city in the American colonies. Here, for example, is his colorful response after witnessing a Catholic Mass for the first time: "I have this day been to a Romish Chappell. My Inauguration is so full of holy Water, Crossings, Bowings, Kneelings and Genuflections, Images, Paintings, Crucifixes, Velvet, Gold, but above all Musick. I am amazed that Luther and Calvin were ever able to break the Charm, and dissolve the Spell." There is a stream-of-consciousness character to many of John's letters, where strings of nouns (and sometimes verbs) gushed onto the page in a kind of verbal explosion that was more a barrage than a coherent collection of sentences.[4]

Abigail's letters tended to be longer and more self-consciously crafted. Initially, Abigail complained that John's letters were too brief and read like hastily written memoranda: "All the letters I receive from you seem to be wrote in so much haste, that they scarcely leave room for a Social feeling," she scolded. "They let me know you exist . . . , but I want some sentimental Effusions of the Heart." He needed to know, she apprised him, that his letters arrived in Braintree like testimonials from the battlefront: "You would laugh to see them [the children] all run upon the sight of a letter—like chickens for a crumb, when the hen clucks. Charles says 'Mar, what is it, any good news?' " All his letters were apparently read out loud at the dinner table.[5]

The main reason that so many of their letters survived from this time is that John, early on, decided that they should make copies. "I have now purchased a Folio Book," he wrote in June 1776, "in the first page of which . . . I am writing this Letter, and intend to write [i.e., copy] all my Letters to you from this Time forward." He urged Abigail to do the same thing, claiming that "I really think your Letters are much better worth preserving than mine."[6]

Making copies of all their letters was a tedious chore. And their crowded schedules soon overwhelmed their best intentions. John's insistence that they try to do it was rooted in his keen sense that they were living through a defining chapter of American history that subsequent generations of their descendants would find instructive. But beyond his own family, he realized that the preservation of their correspondence would document their role in resolving the imperial crisis, not just for the Adams family but for all posterity. He understood the historical significance of his moment. If the movement for American independence succeeded, and if a written record of his prominence in that movement was preserved, his place in the American pantheon was assured. These very private letters, then, were written with one eye on a very public audience, which John called posterity, and which ultimately means us.

PHILADELPHIA STORY

Before arriving in Philadelphia, John had envisioned the Continental Congress quite grandly as "a School of Political Prophets ..., a Nursery of American Statesmen." He imagined an American equivalent of the Greek and Roman orators and hoped that he would fill the role of the American Cicero. His private ambitions were palpable and gargantuan. And so far providence had somehow shaped events to accommodate them. The British ministry had created a political crisis in its effort to reform the British Empire, thereby providing the script for an epic historical drama. The Massachusetts legislature had elected him as a delegate to the Continental Congress, thereby placing him on the great stage. Now all he needed to do was play his appointed role and ensure his secular immortality.[7]

From the outset, this uncharacteristically romantic vision encountered several formidable obstacles. The first hint of the clash between his expectations and political reality took the form of his realization that the delegates from the other colonies were not like Greek or Roman statesmen, but rather self-important provincials who lacked his understanding of the monumental issues at stake. Patrick Henry was the exception, but the other members of the Virginia delegation seemed determined to deliver endless soliloquies that floated above the fray like inflated balloons.[8]

His diary entries on fellow delegates were often highly critical. Roger Sherman of Connecticut was "Rigid as a starched Linen . . . Awkward as a junior Batchelor or Sophomore." Benjamin Rush of Pennsylvania, destined to become a lifelong friend, came across as "too much of a Talker to be a deep Thinker. Elegant, not great." John was obviously measuring himself against the competition for prominence within the congress, so his personal assessments should be read as highly opinionated verdicts that shed more light on his own urge to become a dominant player than a detached appraisal of his colleagues. But beyond his own psychic twitchings, his frustration with the quality of debate within the congress had roots in a larger political problem: "Tedious, indeed, is our Business," he complained to Abigail. "I have not been used to such ways."[9]

What confounded John was the fact that political opinion in Massachusetts had moved much further toward the prospect of American independence than in the other colonies. This made eminent sense, since only Massachusetts had been placed under martial law and made to suffer the indignity of occupation by the British army. But what was a mainstream position in Boston was regarded as extremist in Philadelphia. The entire Massachusetts delegation, John included, were seen as dangerous radicals: "We have been obliged to act with great Delicacy and Caution," he explained to Abigail, "to keep ourselves out of Sight, and to feel pulses, and Sound the Depths—to insinuate our Designs and Desires by means of other Persons." For the main goal of the vast majority of delegates was not defiance, but reconciliation. And these moderates lived in constant fear that the same incendiaries who had tossed the tea in Boston Harbor might provoke an incident with the British troops that would escalate the crisis to a political point of no return.[10]

The ideological convictions that John brought to Philadelphia were fundamentally incompatible with the agenda of the moderates. From the start of his political participation as a critic of British policy, John had described England and New England as two separate political cultures with different histories and contradictory values that could never be wholly reconciled. In his published writings for the **Boston Gazette** and his correspondence with friends on both sides of the looming divide, he did not describe Britain's efforts to consolidate its American empire as misguided blunders by uninformed policy makers in London and Whitehall. Instead, he viewed the legislative assault by Parliament as a conscious plot designed to deprive American colonists of their rights as British citizens, to transform them into abject subjects or, worse, slaves. His conspiratorial mentality meant that it was impossible for him to view a tragic figure like Thomas Hutchinson as anything but a vile sycophant. It also meant that he regarded any policy of reconciliation based on the belief that the British would come to see the error of their ways as a naive pipe dream.

Abigail's perspective was equally, perhaps even more, nonnegotiable. Though she was surely influenced by her husband's opinions, her experience as a woman gave her views on British policy a more floridly moralistic tone and an almost operatic voice.

In addition to her conversations with John, her correspondence with two other women, Catharine Macauley and Mercy Otis Warren, who just happened to be the two most intellectually prominent female critics of British policy in the English-speaking world, gave her convictions a distinctive edge.

Macauley was an Englishwoman whose multi-volume **History of England** became a kind of Bible for political dissenters in England and America. She depicted all of English history as a struggle between liberty and tyranny. The cause of the American colonies, then, should also be the cause of every liberty-loving Briton. It was the forces of light against the forces of darkness, with no ambiguous hues and shades to complicate the story—what came to be called "Whig history" in its purest form.[11]

Mercy Otis Warren was an American version of Macauley, sister of John's political hero, James Otis (who, unfortunately, was going mad), a resident of nearby Plymouth who became one of Abigail's closest confidantes. Warren also saw the Anglo-American conflict in highly moralistic terms, wrote several propagandistic plays populated by British villains and virtuous Americans, and eventually wrote a three-volume **History of the American Revolution** that John found deficient because it failed to give him the leading role he thought he deserved.[12]

In her correspondence with Macauley and Warren, Abigail tended to defer to their superior status, imitating their melodramatic tone and bombastic categories. "The only alternative which every American thinks of is Liberty or Death," she wrote to Macauley, "for we are invaded with fleets and Armies." The letters to Warren mimicked the same hyperbolic style: "Our only comfort lies in the justice of our Cause . . . O Britain, Britain, how is thy glory vanished—how are the annals stained with the Blood of thy children." Intricate constitutional questions were irrelevant within this framework, since the core issue at stake was a question of power, and the British were obviously prepared to exercise that power arbitrarily. If for John that meant slavery, for Abigail it meant physical violation, in short, rape. These were the ultimate ignominies for a man and a woman, so in that sense John and Abigail agreed that the British ministry was committed to a course that justified their most primal fears. The conversation John encountered at the Continental Congress—with its emphasis on accommodation, compromise, and reconciliation—lacked altogether the emotional dimension of his and Abigail's deepest convictions.[13]

Abigail's perspective never changed, and her location within striking distance of the British army in Boston gave her physical fears for herself and her family a palpable edge. Though John's perspective never really changed either, his location in the Continental Congress forced a shift in tactics. The moderates seeking reconciliation dominated the dialogue there, and while he thought them misguided—as he told Abigail, they were "waiting for a Messiah who will never come"—he gradually and grudgingly realized that most of the colonies were politically unprepared to contemplate secession from the British Empire. "But America is a great, unwieldy Body," he explained to Abigail. "Its Progress must be slow. It is like a large Fleet sailing under Convoy. The fleetest Sailors must await the dullest and the slowest."[14]

He played no role whatsoever in the congress's expression of solidarity with the plight of Massachusetts or the creation of a Continental Association to adopt nonimportation agreements until the Coercive Acts were revoked. His membership in the Massachusetts delegation required him to avoid any appearance of partisanship on these issues.

But he was a major player in drafting the Declaration of Rights and Grievances. It called for the restoration of the political status of the American colonies "at the end of the late war" (1763). This meant that the colonial assemblies, not Parliament, should legislate "in all cases of taxation and internal polity" but consent to Parliament's regulation of trade "out of mutual interest to both countries." While John believed that such an arrangement could work—over a century later it became known as the British Commonwealth—he also believed that the likelihood of the British ministry's accepting this scheme was remote in the extreme. In that sense, he was drafting a document that was not designed to reach an accommodation with Great Britain, but rather to expose the futility of all such efforts.[15]

Whatever his motives, John's mastery of the constitutional arguments made him a conspicuous presence in the Continental Congress. (He later claimed, somewhat defensively, that his political stature at that moment was never exceeded because of the enemies he made later on.) When the Continental Congress adjourned in January 1775, he returned to Braintree and immediately began work on a series of essays entitled **Novanglus,** which appeared in the **Boston Gazette** from January until April.

These were tedious, overburdened, excessive displays of legalistic learning that exposed John's undisciplined, Vesuvian style, which seemed dedicated to overwhelming the opposition with a lava flow of words. But **Novanglus** was also the first publication to defend the position of the Continental Congress, which he had helped to draft, rejecting Parliament's authority not just over taxation, but over all colonial domestic policy. It was not a novel constitutional position for John, but it was a significant clarification of the American argument. Despite his impulsive temperament, he had managed to make himself one of the most prominent leaders of the moderate American cause, even though he never believed that it had the remotest prospect of succeeding. He was now publicly recognized as a major player in the Continental Congress.[16]

FAMILY VALUES, AGAIN

In May 1775, when John returned to Philadelphia for the Second Continental Congress, he was effectively leaving his family in a war zone. A month earlier the incendiary incident that the moderates in congress had long feared occurred at Lexington and Concord. John believed that the casualty reports in the Boston press—295 British dead or wounded at the end of the day—were probably exaggerated. There was no doubt, however, that the political crisis had escalated to a military conflict, and its epicenter was the Boston area. "I am concerned for you and our dear babes," he confided to Abigail. "In Case of real Danger, fly to the Woods with our children."[17]

The sense of fear and guilt he felt—should he leave the congress to be with his wife and "babes"?—only intensified a month later when he read these words from Abigail: "The Battle began upon our intrenchments upon Bunker Hill, at Saturday morning about 3 o'clock and has not ceased yet and tis now 3 o'clock Sabbeth afternoon . . . How many have fallen we know not—the constant roar of the cannon are so distressing that we cannot Eat, Drink or Sleep."[18]

Abigail had actually taken John Quincy, then eight years old, to view the battle from the top of Penn's Hill. They witnessed from afar the Pyrrhic British victory, achieved at the cost of a thousand casualties, nearly half their attack force. (Back in London, one retired British officer observed that a few more triumphs like Bunker Hill would lead to the annihilation of the British army.) John's public reaction was political, for the blood spilled reinforced his long-standing argument that reconciliation with Great Britain was highly unlikely. But his private reaction was emotional. What was he doing four hundred miles away in Philadelphia, safely ensconced, while his beloved Abigail and four young children were hunkered down within earshot of a major battle?

Little John Quincy never forgot what he saw that day. And in his reminiscences many years later, as a very old man, he recalled the abiding sense of fear that his mother and siblings lived under for several weeks because of British foraging parties and various bands of marauders taking advantage of the lawless conditions. (When he attended the dedication of the Bunker Hill Monument in 1843, he expressed only loathing for the main speaker, President John Tyler, a "slave monger" whose presence represented a desecration of the values that true patriots had died for.) Abigail played down the danger in her letters to John, but he recognized the risks she was running: "It gives me more Pleasure than I can express to learn that you sustain with such Fortitude, the Shocks and Terrors of the Times," he wrote. "You are really brave, my dear, you are a heroine." She responded with a verbal kiss: "Adieu my Dearest Friend, and always believe me unalterably yours."[19]

It soon became clear to John that the greatest threat to his family was not the British army but disease, chiefly smallpox and dysentery. In addition to seven thousand British troops garrisoned in Boston, there were twelve thousand American militia, soon to become the Continental Army, encircling the city in what came to be called the Siege of Boston. The unsanitary conditions created by two army encampments exacerbated the preexistent smallpox epidemic, then added a particularly lethal version of dysentery to the toxic mix. "Our House is an hospital in every part," wrote Abigail, "and such is the distress of the neighbourhood that I can scarcely find a well person to assist me in looking after the sick." Within a two-week period, eighteen people died in Braintree. "A general putrefication seems to have taken place," Abigail reported, "and we cannot bear the House only as we are constantly cleaning it with hot vinegar."[20]

Abigail's primary posture toward her role as single parent was stoic acceptance: "Here I serve my partner, my family and myself, and enjoy the Satisfaction of your serving your Country." But this convenient formulation—a neat division of labor between public and private duties—had never accurately described the way the Adams family actually worked. Abigail had strong political opinions about American policy, and John had domestic responsibilities, especially the education of the children, that played an important role in broadening and balancing his volatile personality. But now, as the threats of war and disease came at Abigail and her little brood in waves, she could not help but feel pangs of resentment at shouldering these burdens alone: "Our Country is as if it were a Secondary God," she complained to Mercy Otis Warren. "It is to be preferred to parents, wives, children, Friends and all things, the Gods only excepted." There were some dire occasions, and this happened to be one of them, when family responsibilities should trump public service. She needed John now more than did those delegates at the Continental Congress.[21]

John's response was a combination of empathy and evasion: "My best wishes and most fervent Prayers attend our little Family," he explained. "I have been banished from them, the greatest part of the last Eighteen Months, but I hope to be with them more, in Time to come." The chances of that occurring, in truth, were remote in the extreme, in great part because those two armies perched near Braintree represented a dramatic escalation of the imperial crisis that made a recess of the Continental Congress impossible even to imagine. On another occasion he raised the possibility of moving his family to Philadelphia. This was a logistical impossibility for the foreseeable future, as John himself acknowledged: "Let me please myself with the Thought however."[22]

Though she never said it outright, and would have chastised herself afterward for doing so, Abigail felt that, given the circumstances, John's highest duty was to his family, and to her, rather than his country. He saw it differently: "From my earliest entrance into Life, I have been engaged in the public Cause of America. And from first to last I have had upon my Mind, a strong Impression, that things would be wrought up to their present Crisis. I saw from the Beginning that the Controversy was of such a Nature, that it would never be settled, and every day convinces me more and more." In short, now that his political prediction of an inevitable break with the British Empire was coming true, and now that the crisis was entering its climactic phase, history was calling him to play a major role in the final chapter of the story, and that call took precedence over all others. The combination of patriotism and ambition was seamless in his soul.[23]

Abigail understood her man's paradoxical urges

better than anyone else alive, so instead of challenging his choices, she eventually endorsed them. If he could not join her, then he should carry the American colonies where they needed to go more effectively than any other member of the congress. "Let us separate, [for] they [the British] are unworthy to be our Brethren. Let us renounce them and instead of supplications . . . let us beseech the almighty to blast their counsels and bring to Naught all their devices." This was exactly what John wanted to hear.[24]

Whatever strains John's prolonged absence put on the marriage, Abigail was an emotionally stable, psychologically sophisticated adult who understood the sacrifices that love required. Her four children, however, were going through formative stages of their own development. And the elemental fact was that their father was not present during most of that time. Though he frequently decried the situation himself, John's public duties made him an absentee parent.

There is a reason, rendered available by hindsight, to notice this fact. For we know what happened to all the Adams children, and it is not an attractive story. Charles died young from alcoholism; Tommy also drank his way through a dreary life; Nabby married badly and was forced to leave her husband to live with her parents before succumbing to breast cancer. John Quincy, of course, the apple of John's eye, was a huge success, arguably the greatest secretary of state in American history and the first son to follow his father as president. But even John Quincy, for all his intellectual sophistication and political achievement, was not a happy man, lacked the emotional spontaneity of his father, and seemed to regard laughter as an unnatural act. Given this prevailing pattern, which is truly heartbreaking to know as one reads John and Abigail's parental observations as their children were growing up, the salient question is unavoidable: Did the absence of a father stunt their emotional growth?

This question is ultimately unanswerable because, as every parent can testify, you can never know. Your best efforts often fail, and some children flourish despite your worst efforts. In John's case, effort was not the problem; distance was. He was physically and emotionally unavailable to his children. The correspondence that has survived suggests that John made a concerted effort to remain a reliable presence in his children's lives, but they came to regard him as a quasi-mythical figure, a faraway father of bottomless virtue and rock-ribbed patriotism whose moral probity and political courage set a standard that they, especially the boys, could never match. If he had been living at home, they would have witnessed his human foibles and failures. But he was not.[25]

One of the earliest letters from John Quincy,

written when he was seven years old, documents the emotional problem: "I have been trying ever since you went away to learn to write you a letter," the boy began. "I shall make poor work of it, but Sir, Mamma says you will accept my endeavors, and that my duty to you may be expressed in poor writing as well as good. I hope I grow a better Boy and that you will have no occasion to be ashamed of me." For the very reasons alluded to in the letter, it was never sent. Abigail explained why: "Master John is very anxious to write . . . , but he begs me to make his excuse and say that he has wrote twice before, but it did not please him well enough to send it." Given his father's heroic stature at that moment in John Quincy's mind, nothing he could write would suffice.[26]

Throughout the remainder of John Quincy's quite extraordinary career, his father embodied a combination of public and personal probity that verged on the superhuman. John made the matter worse by constantly reminding John Quincy that he was a gifted child who would disappoint him if he somehow squandered his talent, an appropriate warning to a young adult, but an emotional millstone for a ten-year-old.

A parent who is present only in the form of letters was almost destined, despite his best efforts, to be misunderstood. When John took time from his crowded schedule to write letters of personal encouragement to John Quincy, Charles, and Nabby, he felt that he had done his domestic duty. He had not written Tommy because, at age five, he did not think Tommy could read. But Tommy did not see it, or feel it, that way. As Abigail explained: "It would have grieved you if you had seen your youngest son stand by his Mamma and when she delivered out to the others their letter, . . . he stood in silent Grief with the Tears running down his face . . . Pappa does not love him he says so well as he does his Brothers, and many comparisons were made to see whose Letters were the longest."[27]

As soon as John learned of this episode he wrote Tommy a long letter, reiterating his love and apologizing for his failure to recognize that his mother read all letters out loud to all the children. But this episode illustrates the difficulty of sustaining a close emotional relationship with his children from a distance. Abigail periodically dropped her stoic mask and expressed her frustration with his prolonged absences: "Our little ones, whom you so often recommend to my care and instruction, shall not be [in]sufficient in virtue or probity if the precepts of a mother have their desired Effect," she observed somewhat testily, "but they would be doubly enforced could they be indulged with the example of a Father constantly before them."[28]

For his part, John acknowledged an abiding sense of guilt about his inability to perform his fatherly duties. "It is a cruel Reflection, which often comes across me," he admitted, "that I should be separated so far, from those Babes, whose Education and Welfare lies so near my Heart." His only compensation was to imagine the scene—he repeated the same mental picture in several letters—of all his children walking with him across the fields of Braintree, hand in hand. But the scene took place only in his imagination.[29]

Most of the time, John explained his separation from the day-to-day life of the family as a patriotic sacrifice rendered necessary, and therefore justified, by his public duties in the Continental Congress. (Abigail frequently closed her letters with the line "All the children send duty.") On one occasion, however, he wondered out loud if the patriotic rationale might be an excuse that masked his deeper motive, which was a quest for personal fame and a prominent place in the history books. If so, he lectured himself, he needed to conquer such impulses: "Let the Cymballs of Popularity tincle still. Let the Butterflies of Fame glitter with their Wings. I shall envy neither their Musick nor their Colours."

Such unequivocal assertions were often a sign that John could cope with conflicting commitments only by denying their existence. Moreover, he tended to worry more about the effect his separation from family had on his own life, lamenting to Abigail that "the loss of our Company and that of my dear Babes for so long a time, I consider as a Loss of so much solid Happiness." Abigail, on the other hand, tended to worry about the effect the absence had on the children. There is at least some reason to believe that she had cause for concern.[30]

REVOLUTIONS AND EVOLUTIONS

Looking back thirty years later on his role in the Second Continental Congress, John sounded quite vain: "I was incessantly employed through the Whole Fall, Winter, and Spring of 1775 and 1776 during their Sittings and on Committees on mornings and evenings . . . and unquestionably did more business than any other Member of that House." This claim sounds excessive to our ears, but it was historically correct. In what would prove to be a long and illustrious political career, his leadership role in the Continental Congress would be his most defining and shining moment. He really was, as one of his fellow delegates described him, "the colossus of independence."[31]

One reason for his growing prominence in the Second Continental Congress was that, more than any other delegate, he seemed to know where history was headed. As we have seen, from the beginning he had predicted that the underlying dispute with Great Britain was inherently irreconcilable. "We shall be convinced that the Cancer is too deeply rooted," he warned, "and too far spread to be cured by anything short of cutting it out entirely." And events kept aligning themselves with his prophecies. The bloodshed at Lexington, Concord, and Bunker Hill undermined the argument of the moderate faction in congress that an open break with Great Britain must be avoided at all costs. John could now claim that it had, in fact, already occurred.[32]

The valiant stand of the Massachusetts militia units at Bunker Hill, and the ruinous losses suffered by the British, also undermined the moderates' argument that war with Great Britain was unthinkable because the British army was invincible. After Bunker Hill, John liked to quote a comment by the Reverend John J. Zubly, the Swiss-born delegate from Georgia. During the Reformation, Zubly observed, the Catholics enjoyed the support of the pope and all the monarchs of Europe: "But as to them Poor Devils the Protestants, they had nothing on their Side but God almighty."[33]

George Washington was not quite God, though Abigail's first impression suggested that, at least as a physical specimen, he was the closest approximation she had ever seen. John had nominated Washington to assume command of the American forces outside Boston, soon to be called the Continental

Army. "You had prepared me to entertain a favorable opinion of him," Abigail wrote, "but I thought the one half was not told me." John's choice of Washington to head the Continental Army was the first in a series of three selections destined to have enormous consequences for American history. (The other two were Thomas Jefferson to draft the Declaration of Independence and John Marshall to head the Supreme Court.) Given his own pulsing ambitions, it is ironic to note that three of his greatest contributions were decisions to cede power to others.[34]

Sitting as she was within cannon range of the battle raging around Boston, it was difficult for Abigail to understand the reluctance of the Continental Congress to recognize that the war for American independence, though not officially declared, had already begun. The decision of the congress to refer to the British army in Boston as "ministerial troops" instead of "royal troops," meaning George III did not really know the battle was occurring, struck her as a preposterous illusion. John concurred, adding that the moderate desire to cling to the prospect of reconciliation was "as Arrant an Illusion as ever was hatched in the Brain of an Enthusiast, a Politician, or a Maniac." But, he told Abigail, "though I have laugh'd at it—scolded at it—griev'd at it—even ripp'd at it—it is vain to Reason against such Delusions."[35]

Eventually the hope of the moderate faction in the congress for conciliation was exposed as a complete fantasy by no one less than George III himself. In February 1776 John received reports that the British ministry was conferring with several Germanic principalities to provide mercenaries for the looming invasion of North America, designed to crush the American rebellion in the bud. "By Intelligence hourly arriving from abroad," John joked, "we are more and more confirmed that a kind of Confederation will be formed among the Crowned Skulls, and numbskulls of Europe, against Human Nature." News of the Prohibitory Act arrived at about the same time, revealing that the king had declared the colonists beyond his protection, outlawed them as rebels without any rights, and confiscated all their property in Great Britain. It would take another five months for the Americans to declare their own independence, but George III had already declared his independence from them. This is why, years later, when John was asked if he had done more than any other person to foster American independence, he declined the honor in favor of the British monarch himself.[36]

On the question of American independence, then, in terms of both its inevitability and desirability, John and Abigail were perfectly synchronized, and several steps ahead of popular opinion. But they disagreed about what American independence, once achieved, should actually look like. Abigail launched the debate with a series of pointed questions: "If we separate from Britain, what Code of Laws will be established? How shall we be governed to retain our Liberties? Can any government be free which is not administered by general stated Laws? Who shall frame these Laws? Who will give them force and energy?"

At the end of this political barrage, she dropped her inquisitory tone and recovered her voice as a wife and mother: "Our Little ones send duty to pappa and want much to see him. Tom says he wont come home till the Battle is over—some strange notion he has got into his head." In her mind and in her letters, the public affairs of state and the private family imperatives blended seamlessly.[37]

Abigail's questions rather presciently framed the debate that would dominate the deliberations of American statesmen throughout the postwar years. The seminal issue was whether separation from the British Empire would lead to the creation of a viable nation-state empowered to make laws for all the former colonies–cum–states. The Continental Congress was currently functioning as a provisional national government. But these were emergency wartime conditions. What happened after the war was won? (If it was lost, well, no answers were necessary or relevant.) Would secession from the British

Empire be followed by American nationhood, or by some loose confederation of sovereign states destined to go their separate ways after tossing off British rule?

John's answers to these questions were never delivered in person to Abigail, but published for all to see as **Thoughts on Government** in April 1776. Despite being regarded as a radical on the independence issue, John was a staunch conservative when it came to designing the framework for an indigenous American government.

In **Thoughts** he recommended that each state adopt a constitutional blueprint creating three branches of government—executive, legislative, and judicial—in which the principles of separation of powers, a bicameral legislature, and an independent judiciary were the most distinctive features.[38]

Although these features became hallowed ingredients in the federal Constitution eleven years later, it is important to recognize that John was proposing an outline for republican government at the state, not the national, level. Abigail's questions about a prospective national identity surely made logical sense, but to raise them at this time, he warned, was politically suicidal, because the controversies they were certain to provoke would destroy the fragile consensus for independence slowly emerging in the Continental Congress.

The same pattern held in another exchange

between Abigail and John in the spring of 1776, initiated by what is probably the most famous letter Abigail ever wrote. This time the letter began rather than ended with domestic news: the British army had just evacuated Boston, removing the most palpable threat to the family; but smallpox was still virulent, and she needed to decide about inoculation. Then came this: "And, by the way, in the new code of laws which I suppose it will be necessary for you to make, desire you will remember the ladies and be more generous and favorable to them than your ancestors. Do not put such unlimited power in the hands of husbands. Remember, all men would be tyrants if they could. If particular care and attention is not paid to the ladies, we are determined to foment a rebellion, and will not hold ourselves bound by any laws in which we have no voice or representation."[39]

John responded on the assumption that Abigail was being playful, which she was, but also on the mistaken assumption that she was not serious. All men knew that women were the real tyrants within the household, he joked, and he had no intention of exchanging the tyranny of George III for what he called "the despotism of the petticoat." As for Abigail's "extraordinary Code of Laws," he concluded, "I cannot but laugh."[40]

Yet Abigail was not laughing. She apprised Mercy Otis Warren of her recent letter to John, reporting that "he is very saucy to me in return for a list of Female Grievances which I transmitted to him." After John bantered back with some colorful testimonials to his wife's own "sauciness," she had the last word. "But you must remember that arbitrary power is like most other things that are very hard," she concluded defiantly, "and notwithstanding all your wise laws and maxims, we have it in our power, not only to free ourselves, but to subdue our masters, and, without violence, throw your natural and legal authority at your feet."[41]

While Abigail's argument about women's rights proved to be a couple of centuries ahead of its time, her recognition that the very arguments her husband was hurling at Parliament and the British ministry had latent implications that undermined all coercive or nonvoluntary systems of arbitrary power called attention to the Pandora's box that John and his colleagues in the Continental Congress had opened. (Probably in jest, Abigail suggested to Mercy Otis Warren that they jointly file a petition to the congress that they were being governed without their consent.) If one took seriously the argument of the American opposition, the belief in natural rights and popular consent spread like a virus to all parts of the body politic. In addition to the rights of women, clearly slavery, as well as the property qualification to vote, must be ended if America's revolutionary agenda was to be applied consistently.

In subsequent correspondence Abigail continued to press for expanded rights for women: "If we
mean to have Heroes, Statesmen and Philosophers,"
she insisted, "we should have learned women,"
because mothers would be most responsible for
educating the rising generation. And that, in turn,
meant that women should enjoy the same educational advantages as men. "The world, perhaps,
would laugh at me," she told John, "but you know I
have a mind too enlarged and liberal to disregard the
Sentiment." Belatedly grasping that his wife meant
business, John scrambled to find common ground.
"Your Sentiments of the Importance of Education in
Women," he wrote, "are exactly agreeable to my
own." That conclusion followed naturally from
being married to a woman like Abigail.[42]

But once he went beyond the private parameters
of his own outspoken wife, John thought the implementation of a wholly egalitarian political agenda
in one fell swoop a catastrophic political mistake:
"There will be no end to it," he warned. "New
claims will rise. Women will demand a vote. Lads
from 12 to 21 will think their rights not attended
to, and every Man, who has not a Farthing, will
demand an equal Voice with any other in all Acts of
State."[43]

The conservative cast of John's mind caused
him to regard the full promise of the American Revolution as a set of latent implications that must seep

out slowly over a long stretch of time. For her part, Abigail also relished the opportunities to remind him of the political and social consequences of his own arguments. While he conceded that Abigail's arguments made intellectual sense, and he was prepared to entertain them in their private correspondence, John's highest priority at the public level was to create a consensus for American independence. That effort needed to take precedence, because if it failed, all the other reforms would prove meaningless. Abigail's silence on this score indicated that she agreed, or at least deferred to the political wisdom of her husband.

CRESCENDO

The spring and summer of 1776 was a crowded moment, both for the still-divided American colonists and for the Adams family. At the public level, the decision by George III to reject all proposals for reconciliation and to mount a military assault—the largest amphibious force ever to cross the Atlantic to date—exposed the moderate agenda in the Continental Congress as wishful thinking. And the publication of Thomas Paine's **Common Sense**, which depicted George III as a ruffian and political criminal, enjoyed an unprecedented level of popularity, making it arguably the most influential piece of journalism in American history. As Paine put it in his electric style, "an island cannot rule a continent." Events were now moving in the direction that John had always predicted they would.[44]

The decisive moment, at least as John saw it, occurred on May 15, 1776. For on that day he proposed a resolution that all the former British colonies now regard themselves not as colonies within the British Empire, but as sovereign states within the American republic. This was not just a negative act, denouncing the authority of the British Empire, but also a positive act, announcing the arrival of an autonomous set of states, each of which should now draft a new constitution.[45]

John regarded this decision as "the most important Resolution that ever was taken in America," a de facto declaration of independence. He confided to Abigail that it was the culmination of his campaign to get the Continental Congress on the right side of history, and he was extremely proud of his role in making it happen: "When I consider the great Events which are passed, and the greater which are rapidly advancing, and that I may have been instrumental in touching some springs and turning some small wheels, which have had and will have such effects, I feel an Awe upon my Mind which is not easily described." He had entered the Continental Congress hoping to make history, and now he had actually done it.[46]

If John was making history, Abigail was witnessing it firsthand. She climbed up Penn's Hill again to view the artillery bombardment of Boston by American cannons perched on Dorchester Heights. "The sound I think is one of the grandest in Nature," she exulted, for it signaled the end of the British occupation. (Her eyewitness report to John included a humorous story circulating in and around the city that the infamous John Adams, who had been such a prominent advocate for American independence, had at last seen the light, defected to the British side, and boarded a ship for England.) A few weeks later she was atop Penn's Hill once more to witness the British evacuation of Boston: "We have a view of the largest Fleet ever seen in America. You may count upwards of 100 & 70 Sail. They look like a Forrest."[47]

John recorded a third triumphant moment in two letters to Abigail written on July 3, 1776. "Yesterday the greatest Question was decided which ever was debated in America," he declared, "and a greater perhaps never was or will be decided among Men." He was referring to the formal vote on the resolution, proposed by the Virginia delegation, advocating American independence from all forms of British authority. It had taken a long time to reach this climactic conclusion, longer than John had wished. But now even the ever-impatient and fidgety John Adams found a measure of virtue in the delay. "Time has been given for the whole People, maturely to consider the great Question of Independence and to ripen their judgments." Now that he had won, he could afford to be magnanimous.[48]

In subsequent recollections of this historic occasion, John tended to play down the significance of this formal vote and even the approval of the Declaration of Independence two days later. As he recalled it, the big decision had already been made on May 15, when his resolution to require each colony to regard itself as an independent state and to draft a new constitution accordingly had passed unanimously. That was the moment the lightning struck, and the formal vote on July 2 was merely the thunderous afterthought.[49]

But that latter-day recollection does not quite square with the second letter he wrote to Abigail on July 3. For there he joyously described the vote on independence as the truly culminating moment, the date that deserved to be celebrated as America's birthday:

The Second Day of July 1776, will be the most memorable Epocha, in the History of America. I am apt to believe that it will be celebrated, by succeeding Generations, as

the great anniversary Festival. It ought
to be commemorated, as the Day of
Deliverance . . . It ought to be solemnized
with Pomp and Parade, with Shows,
Games, Sports, Guns, Bells, Bonfires and
Illuminations from one End of this
Continent to the other from this Time
forward forever more.

John got everything right, including the fireworks
displays, but he got the date wrong because he
thought the vote on independence more symbolically significant than the vote on the Declaration
two days later.[50]

He was historically correct in his opinion, but
he did not take into account the fact that the rest of
America and the world first learned about the
momentous decisions by the Continental Congress
with the publication of the Declaration of Independence on July 4. (By the way, the delegates did not
sign the document on that day, as most history
books and the popular play 1776 claim. Most
signed in early August, but delegates were coming
and going and signing throughout the fall.) John
was actually at center stage on July 3–4, for he had
selected Thomas Jefferson to draft the document
and then had single-handedly defended Jefferson's
draft before the congress, which eventually deleted
or revised about 20 percent of the text. But once

July 4 became the acknowledged date for America's birth, credit shifted from Adams to Jefferson.[51]

This shift annoyed him for the rest of his life. He could claim, with the lion's share of the evidence on his side, that he had been the most vociferous advocate of American independence in the Continental Congress, consistently at the cutting edge of the radical camp, willing to risk unpopularity by dragging the moderate faction in the congress to a place they did not wish to go. For a man whose primal ambition was to achieve fame, the secular equivalent of immortality, the ascendance of Jefferson's reputation over his own proved too much to bear. In his old age he asked, "Was there ever a Coup de Theatre, that has so great an effect as Jefferson's penmanship of the Declaration of Independence?" The real business of American independence was a long-term struggle within the Continental Congress that John, more than anyone else, had orchestrated. By focusing exclusively on the Declaration, "Jefferson ran away with the stage effect . . . and all the glory of it."[52]

But in the summer of 1776 John was so pleased with the ultimate verdict itself, and so confident that his own role in the revolutionary process was beyond question, that none of his later laments over who would have the starring role in the history books seemed necessary. Moreover, as we try to recover his mood at this crowded moment, two other events intervened to complicate his thinking, and, it turns out, his feelings, in ways that made resting on his laurels impossible.

The first event was the arrival of the forward edge of the British expeditionary force on Staten Island. John had been appointed chair of the Committee on War and Ordnance on June 13, a position that made him responsible for all the large and small policy decisions governing the Continental Army. (Strategically, should we oppose the British invasion at New York? Logistically, where do we get muskets and powder?) Washington was coming down from Boston with a smallpox-infested army of twelve thousand men. The British force was conservatively estimated at thirty thousand, assisted by a naval squadron of several hundred ships perfectly suited to New York's coastal exposure and navigable rivers.[53]

All the recently vented patriotic sentiments made the defense of New York mandatory. But any detached assessment of the military situation made a stand at New York suicidal. And if the Continental Army made such a stand and was virtually destroyed in the process, all the uplifting arguments in the Declaration of Independence would be essentially meaningless and all the prominent revolutionaries, John included, could expect to be hanged as traitors.

Abigail later tried to comfort John with the suggestion that even if the Continental Army suffered a catastrophic defeat, he need not worry, because "a race of Amazons" would rise up to replace the fallen men. John spent most of July and August attempting to negotiate the gap between his own convictions about the worthiness of the American cause and the gathering strength of the British army and navy, which were poised to crush that cause with overwhelming force.[54]

The second event concerned Abigail and the children. On July 16 John learned that Abigail had taken the family to Boston for inoculation against smallpox. "It is not possible for me to describe," he told her, "nor for you to conceive my feelings upon this Occasion. Nothing but the critical State of our Affairs should prevent me from flying to Boston, to your assistance." He said he felt like "a savage to be here, while my whole Family is sick at Boston."[55]

As a result, July and August 1776 were two of the most politically dramatic and psychologically congested months in the history of the Adams family, mixing glory, foreboding, and trepidation in overlapping waves of emotion. In John's mind's eye he could simultaneously envision patriotic celebrations throughout the land, the largest fleet ever to cross the Atlantic gathering in Long Island Sound, and his entire family confined in quarantine amid a raging smallpox epidemic that, according to Abigail, had infected seven thousand people in and around Boston. On the latter score, the first reports were quite alarming: "Nabby has enough of the small pox for all the family beside," wrote Abigail. "She is pretty well coverd, not a spot but what is so soar that she can neither walk, stand, or lay with any comfort . . . She has above a thousand pussels as large as a great Green Pea."[56]

Subsequent reports from Abigail only got worse: "Little Charles in delirium for 48 hours. Has caught the pox in the natural way." That meant that he was at much greater risk, and Abigail warned John that he must prepare himself for the worst. "I would not have alarmed you," she confided, "but we cannot tell the Event." While this letter was in transit, John learned that Washington's army had carried the contagion down from Boston and only about half his troops were fit for duty, this on the eve of what promised to be the defining battle of the war. "The Small Pox has done Us more harm than British armies, Canadians, Indians, Negroes, Hannoverians, Hessians, and all the rest," he lamented to Abigail. And now it was threatening to carry off "my little Babes."[57]

If his correspondence is an accurate measure, John's primary concern was not the ongoing debates in Philadelphia, or the two armies gathering at New York, but rather his wife and children under quarantine in Boston. Or perhaps it is safer to say that he rocked back and forth between his draining public responsibilities and his emotional concern for the family. At any rate, he wrote Abigail almost every day, most frequently asking about "my sweet Babe, Charles, [who] is never out of my Thoughts— Gracious Heaven preserve him."[58]

Abigail was thrilled to receive such a steady stream of letters: "I know not how you find the time amidst such a multitude of cares as surround you," she exclaimed, "but I feel myself more obliged by the frequent tokens of your remembrance." Abigail described one scene in which John Quincy, whose inoculation had taken and was now perfectly healthy, returned from the post office, "and pulling one [letter] from under his Gown gave it to me, the young Rogue smiling and watching Mammas countenance, draws out another, and then an other, highly gratified that he had so many presents to bestow." In the same letter she also described Charles, "who lay upon the couch coverd over with small Pox, lifted up his head and says 'Mamma, take my Dollar and get a Horse for Pappa,' " so he could come home.[59]

By late August the two dramas seemed to be playing out along parallel lines. As the two armies faced off on Long Island, Charles's life hung in the balance: "Amidst all my Concern for the Army," John remarked, "my dear Charles is continually present to my Mind. I don't know what to think." Early reports from New York were not optimistic.

"I fear," he worried to Abigail, "that we have suffered a great deal." The truly bad news arrived a few days later. The Continental Army had suffered a devastating defeat, and the surviving remnant was retreating up the Manhattan peninsula in order to avoid being trapped there and face total annihilation. "In general," he explained to Abigail, "our generals were out generalled."[60]

But good news arrived at the same time. "Little Charles stands by me and sends Duty to Pappa," Abigail was pleased to report. His fever had broken and his recovery was now assured. John had almost lost an army, but he had not lost a son. Abigail advised him to leave family concerns to her and focus his attention on an investigation of the reasons for the American debacle at New York. She herself wanted to know what had gone so terribly wrong, adding that "if all America are to be ruined and undone by a pack of Cowards and Knaves, I wish to know it too."[61]

John desperately wanted to return home, but did not feel he could leave his post with the Continental Army in such disarray. He had been working eighteen- to twenty-hour days for over two months, his eyes were permanently bloodshot, and his sight was strained, making it difficult to read, especially at night. The emotional toll of witnessing a colossal blow to the American cause was high, and he knew better than most that Washington's army had gone through a near-death experience. The celebratory mood of early July was now replaced by the somber recognition that it was going to be a long war.

Remaining in Philadelphia, it turned out, allowed him to launch his diplomatic career. Soon after his decisive victory, the commander of the British army, General William Howe, apprised the Continental Congress that he was prepared to offer new and more acceptable terms of reconciliation that would put an end, once and for all, to the bloodletting. John made it known that he regarded such a promise as disingenuous and wanted no part of a parlay with Howe. Because of his stature in the congress, he was nonetheless selected to join Benjamin Franklin and Edward Rutledge of South Carolina to meet with Howe and hear him out. John's assessment proved to be correct. Howe had no authority to negotiate a realistic political compromise, only to grant pardons, and as John was delighted to inform him, the Americans had no need for pardons, because they had done nothing wrong.[62]

While this little episode marked John's first appearance as an American ambassador, it subsequently enjoyed considerable prominence in the history books, first for John's matter-of-fact defiance of General Howe's authority, and second for his colorful version of the story in his autobiography. As he told it, he and Franklin were forced to sleep in the same bed at a tavern in Perth Amboy, where they engaged in a spirited conversation about the window, whether it should be open or closed. Franklin insisted on the former, John on the latter, the first indication that these two giants of American independence represented two wholly distinct temperaments, as subsequent events in Paris were soon to expose.

This was one of the few occasions in his long relationship with Franklin when John had the last word, for in his old age he liked to point out that Franklin died with a bad cold, caught because he slept with the window open. He never told Abigail or anyone else about the window argument at the time, which suggests that it was one of those latter-day embellishments that Franklin, if he were alive and able to tell his own story, would have remembered differently.[63]

More substantially, John was the primary author of the Plan of Treaties, adopted by the congress in September. At the most immediate level it recognized that some kind of alliance with France, Great Britain's long-standing rival for European supremacy, should be a goal of American diplomacy. (For several months John had been urging Abigail, who knew the rudiments of French, to teach the language to all the children.) But John also insisted on inserting a paragraph that denied France any permanent holdings in North America as a reward for its prospective alliance. More strategically, the Plan of Treaties urged commercial relations with all European nations, but no binding diplomatic commitments to any foreign power. John did not know it at the time, but he had almost offhandedly defined the abiding goals of American foreign policy for the next century.[64]

By the beginning of October many of the other delegates had departed, making it difficult to achieve a quorum. But John regarded his duties as head of the Committee on War and Ordnance as compelling reasons to linger, especially with the fate of the Continental Army still unclear. About the same time, unbeknownst to John or anyone else on the American side, General Howe was deciding not to pursue Washington's remnant of an army into New Jersey, without much question the biggest British tactical blunder of the war. For if Howe had chosen to pursue Washington, the consensus among military historians is that the Continental Army was in no condition to defend itself. The destruction of the Continental Army would most probably have meant the end of the war, and American history would have flowed in a different direction.[65]

As the days passed, even John began to think that he was like the last sentry maintaining his post on a deserted battlefield. "I have been here," he complained to Abigail, "until I am stupefied." Worn down like the nub of an overused eraser, he eventually decided that he could accomplish little by hanging on: "I suppose your Ladyship has been in the Twitters, for some Time past," he chided Abigail, "because you have not received a Letter by every Post, as you used to do. But I am coming to make my Apology in Person." He cautioned her not to expect him for two or three weeks because of British patrols in New Jersey that he would have to evade. But he was coming home.[66]

STILLBORN

Because of the paradox of proximity, we know very little about what happened within the Adams family for the next three months. We can presume with some confidence that John encouraged Nabby to press on with her French, that he told John Quincy, now called Master John, that his destiny depended upon an austere devotion to his study of the classics, though mere academic learning was less important than a virtuous character, which could not be learned, only lived. As for Tommy and Charles, aged five and seven, they were too young for such injunctions. Their experience of inoculation had introduced them to hardship, the ultimate schoolroom, but for now they just needed to be good boys who listened to their mother.

But these are mere presumptions, deduced from letters John wrote later. As for Abigail, for similar reasons, we can presume she talked about John's prominent role in the Continental Congress, the fragile condition of the Continental Army, the vulnerability of the revolutionary cause, the need to remain strong at this difficult moment. These, however, are also only educated guesses based on what they wrote to each other before and afterward. The one thing we know with complete confidence is that Abigail was pregnant.

Because the etiquette of the era forbade any direct mention of Abigail's condition, John's letters back home after he returned to the congress require some interpretation: "I am anxious to hear how you do," he wrote from the new location in Baltimore. "I have in my Mind a Source of anxiety which I never had before, Since I became such a Wanderer. You know what it is. Cant you convey to me, in Hieroglyphicks which no other person can comprehend, Information which will relieve me? Tell me you are as well as can be expected." Leaving behind a pregnant wife made him feel guilty and joyful at the same time. "When I think of your Circumstances," he explained, "I rejoice in them in spight of all this Melancholy."[67]

Abigail wrote Mercy Otis Warren that she had considered asking John to stay with her, "and I know I could have prevailed, but our public affairs at the time were so gloomy an aspect that I thought if ever his assistance was wanted, it must be at such a time." A ray of sunshine broke through the gloom on Christmas night, 1776, when Washington crossed the ice-choked Delaware River despite horrible weather conditions and surprised the British garrison at Trenton, which surrendered after a spirited fight. A week later he struck again at Princeton, a somewhat larger engagement in which Washington himself led the final charge that broke the British line. Neither Trenton nor Princeton were major battles, but taken together they signaled an important psychological shift, rescuing the American cause from what had seemed like certain death. As John settled into his new quarters in Baltimore—Philadelphia was deemed too vulnerable to British attack—he could tell himself that a new life was stirring in his beloved wife and in America's prospects.[68]

"I feel you have gone to a foreign Country," Abigail complained after not hearing from John for over a month. The gossip mills were churning out all kinds of outlandish stories. Was it true that Washington had won a great victory at New Brunswick, capturing fifteen thousand British troops? (No, it was Trenton, and six hundred British prisoners.) She presumed that reports of Washington's death and John's death by poisoning were just British or Tory propaganda. But she needed to hear from him to be sure, most especially about the latter story.[69]

When his first letter arrived on March 9, 1777, it was full of distress about not hearing from her, especially because of her "delicate condition." All was fine, she assured him, and the movements inside her were "a constant remembrance of an absent friend, and excites sensations of tenderness which are better felt than expressed." Master John had told her that he had never seen anyone so fat.[70]

John explained that he was buried under paperwork, some of it grisly reports on the standard practice of Hessian troops to bayonet all American soldiers who surrendered in battle. But his biggest headache was the bizarre pettiness of so many officers in the Continental Army, who were "scrambling for rank and pay like apes for nuts." Mention of the military turned his mind to a lamentation that he was too old to serve; then that thought ricocheted to the regret that his boys were too young: "I wish my lads were old enough. I would send every one of them into the Army, in some Capacity or other."[71]

All his children were old enough to read, save perhaps Tommy, and John made a vow to write them all in March. He urged John Quincy to read history, the seminal source of "solid instruction" about human nature, beginning with Thucydides on the Peloponnesian War, eventually in the original Greek, but for now in translation, available in the family library. For poetry, he should begin with Milton's **Paradise Lost.** Nabby also received educational advice, mostly to recognize that she was expected to follow her mother's path beyond what was considered appropriate for women and should make French a special focus. Charles was not pushed as hard as John Quincy. He had the most engaging personality of them all, John told him, but what calling best fitted him remained a mystery. The military was not an option, since the war would be over before he came of age. Tommy, who was only five years old, was encouraged to consider a medical career, perhaps to do research on better ways to stamp out smallpox.[72]

Smallpox was very much on John's mind. His own family, now inoculated, was safe from the scourge, but John correctly believed that the disease was an even greater threat to the Continental Army than the British. After the Continental Congress moved back to Philadelphia in March, he went to a cemetery where two thousand fallen American soldiers were buried, the vast majority of them victims of smallpox and dysentery. "Disease has destroyed Ten Men for Us," he estimated, "where the Sword of the Enemy has killed one." Fortunately, Washington agreed with John's assessment, so it became mandatory for all new enlistees in the Continental

Army to undergo inoculation before reporting for duty. It was one of the most important strategic decisions of the war.[73]

John went into confessional mode with Abigail, suggesting that he had reached a high level of authority within the patriot camp that he could never fulfill: "I begin to suspect that I have not much of the Grand in my Compositions," he wrote. "I long for rural and domestic scenes, for the warbling of Birds and the Prattle of my Children— Don't you think I am somewhat poetical this morning?" If poetical, he was also misleading, as John himself acknowledged by adding: "is not the Heart Deceitful above all things?"

What he meant was psychologically complicated. By remaining in Philadelphia rather than with his children and pregnant wife, John worried that he was acting selfishly, allowing his political ambition to dominate his domestic responsibilities. He recognized that he was a deeply ambitious man. But he needed to convince himself, and Abigail, that "Ambition which has Power for its Object, I don't believe I have a Spark in my Heart . . . But there are other forms of Ambition of which I have a great deal."[74]

By "other forms" he meant the desire to live forever in the memory of succeeding generations, rather than the desire to accrue power and wealth in his lifetime. He was so anxious to press the point, however, because he recognized that the distinction invited suspicion. And no matter how sincere he felt about it, he was also trying to assure himself. There was therefore a constant refrain about abandoning the "infinite Noise, Hurry, and Bustle" of the Congress, the urge to escape the "lonely melancholy Life, mourning for all the Charms of Life . . . for all the Amusements that I ever had, which is my farm."[75]

John was being sincere, but Abigail knew he would never leave his post. Both of them adopted a sacrificial perspective: he would suffer pangs of guilt to serve his country; she would suffer the pain produced by the absence of her husband. Her resolve had its fleeting moments as her pregnancy progressed. She complained that she was denied the pleasure enjoyed by others, "of having their mate sit by them with anxious care during all their Solitary confinement." She wanted him home before the birth of the child in July, but she never asked or ordered him to return, because she knew that he would find it impossible to refuse, and she did not want to impose such choices.[76]

One less elliptical issue that they could agree upon without lingering ambiguity or conceit was the profiteering by merchants who hoarded goods and exploited wartime conditions. John delivered several jeremiads on this score, but Abigail was even more incensed, because she had to deal with such insufferable creatures on a daily basis to purchase provisions for her family. She was pleased to report one impromptu rebellion by the women of Boston against a particularly notorious profiteer:

> It was rumored that an eminent, stingy, wealthy merchant had a hogshead of coffee in his store which he refused to sell for under six shillings per pound. A number of females, some say a hundred, some say more, assembled with a cart and trucks, marched down to the warehouse, demanded the keys, which he refused to deliver, upon which one of them seized him by his neck, and tossed him into the cart. Upon his finding no quarter, he delivered the keys, they tipped up the cart and discharged him, then opened the warehouse, hoisted out the coffee themselves, put it into the trucks and drove off.[77]

By late spring of 1777 John was writing two letters to one of hers, trying to sustain an ongoing conversation as her pregnancy progressed. He would rise at four o'clock, write letters until six, then ride for an hour before going to his office. One morning he apparently had nothing new to say, so he copied a huge selection, over four thousand words, from a recent book by Lord Kames, **Sketches of the History of Man**, for Abigail's edification. Mostly, and as the delivery date neared even more so, he expressed the desire to be with her: "Oh that I could be near, to say a few kind Words, or shew a few Kind Looks . . . Oh that I could take from my dearest, a share of her Distress, or relieve her of the whole."[78]

The day before he wrote these words, Abigail had written him with some ominous news: "I was last night taken with a shaking fit, and am very apprehensive that a life was lost. As I have no reason today to think otherwise, what may be the consequences to me Heaven only knows." The following day, July 10, the contractions began, and she wrote him in between them over the next thirty-six hours: "The Doctor encourages me to Hope that my apprehensions are groundless respecting what I wrote you yesterday . . . and I almost wish I had not let that letter go." She mixed reports of the looming birth with remarks about the inflated cost of sugar, the need to get more seaweed as fertilizer, and the rumor—true, it turned out—that Ticonderoga had fallen to the British.[79]

John wrote her a newsy letter on July 11, the day of the birth, unaware of her precarious condition and full of speculation about the intentions of General Howe, who had just sailed out into the Atlantic with his entire army, his destination a mystery: "A Faculty of penetrating into the Designs of an Enemy is said to be the first Quality of a General," John observed. "But it is impossible to discover the Designs of an Enemy who has no Design at all." As it turned out, Howe did have a design, though an odd one. He intended to sail south to the mouth of the Chesapeake Bay, then march his troops overland through Delaware to attack Philadelphia. Fixated on the military crisis rather than Abigail's, John expressed bewilderment: "But they might as well imagine them gone round Cape Horn into the South Seas to land at California, and march across the Continent to attack our back settlements."[80]

It took two weeks for a letter to reach him with the news that Abigail had delivered a daughter, "an exceedingly fine looking Child" named Elizabeth, but that she was stillborn. A letter from Abigail herself arrived a few days later, describing the child as "a very fine Babe, and as it never opened its Eyes in this world it looked as tho they were closed for sleep." The cause of death was apparent, probably strangulation by the umbilical cord, but Abigail preferred not to put such details in a letter. After she was fully recovered, she was better able to express her sense of disappointment. Addressing John in the third person, she said that "I had pleasd myself with the Idea of presenting him a fine son or daughter upon his return . . . but those dreams are buried in the Grave, transitory as the morning Cloud, short lived as Dew Drops."[81]

The two- to three-week delay between sending and receiving a letter created awkward disjunctions. In this case, John had posted five letters to Abigail since her ordeal, and in all of them he was obsessed with Howe's weird maneuverings and the equally worrisome movement of General John Burgoyne's huge army, seven thousand strong, south from Lake Champlain into the Hudson River Valley. He was completely oblivious to, or at least said nothing about, the movements occurring inside Abigail.

When a series of letters finally arrived informing him of the stillborn Elizabeth, he felt both devastated and guilty. "Never in my whole Life," he claimed, "was my Heart affected with such Emotions and Sensations . . . Is it not unaccountable, that one should feel so strong an Affection for an Infant, that one has never seen, nor shall see?" His guilt resulted from the realization that his personal attention, which should have been fixed on the love of his life, was instead focused on British strategy. The tension between his public and private duties had never been so stark, and if this was some kind of providential test, he believed that he had failed it.[82]

Abigail used the incident to speculate on the injustice of living through historic times that imposed impossible obligations on both of them.

" 'Tis almost fourteen years since we were united," she recalled, "but not more than half that time we had the happiness of living together." Nor was that all: "I consider it as a sacrifice to my Country and one of my greatest misfortunes [for my husband] to be separated from my children at a time of life when the joint instructions and admonitions of parents sink deeper than in maturer years." John heartily concurred: "I am wearied with the Life I lead, and long for the Joys of my Family . . . If I live much longer in Banishment, I shall scarcely know my own Children."[83]

In late September a young aide to Washington by the name of Alexander Hamilton arrived in time to warn the Continental Congress of the approach of Howe's army outside Philadelphia. John told Abigail not to worry, that the delegates knew how to run away almost as deftly as the American militia, and Howe's occupation of Philadelphia would only increase the drain on his resources.[84]

At last, as both armies moved into their winter quarters, John wrote from the temporary congressional headquarters at York to announce he was coming home. Abigail told him she had dreamed that, upon his return, their lengthy separation produced a cool reception from him: "Your Dream will never come to pass," he assured her. "You can never be coolly received by me while my Heart beats and my senses remain."[85]

John had been gone from Abigail and the children for ten months, and both of them looked forward to a prolonged reunion during which they could recover their physical and emotional rhythms. But it was not meant to be.

CHAPTER THREE

1778–84

"When he is wounded, I bleed."

IT WAS LIKE a scene out of a sentimental novel. On February 13, 1778, John and ten-year-old John Quincy walked out the door of their Braintree home into the snow. Abigail was too distraught to accompany them up Penn's Hill, then down the other side to the shore of what is now Quincy Bay, where a skiff from the frigate **Boston** was waiting to begin their journey to France. Instead, she went back inside the house, put her head on the kitchen table, and began to cry inconsolably.

She had been crying for over a month, ever since word reached her that John had been selected to replace Silas Deane as a member of the American diplomatic delegation in Paris, charged with the all-important mission of negotiating a treaty to bring France into the war on the American side. She knew that patriotism obligated her to make this personal sacrifice silently, and Mercy Otis Warren pretty much ordered her to do just that. "But is it really necessary to muster up arguments to prevail with my dear Mrs. Adams?" Mercy asked rhetorically. Instead she should stop fretting and take pride in the recognition that her husband, as Mercy put it, "is the best qualified of any man on the Continent to represent the United States of America."[1]

Abigail certainly knew all the patriotic homilies by heart, but reciting them was one thing and really meaning them quite another. For she was being asked to part willingly for an unknowable length of time "with him whom my Heart esteems above all earthly things." She simply could not do it. "My life will be one continued scene of anxiety and apprehension," she predicted, an emotional reality that made it impossible "to cheerfully comply with the demand of my Country."[2]

There were several family conversations soon after the news of John's appointment arrived. Abigail's preference, despite an utter dread of an Atlantic crossing, was to accompany her husband, taking Nabby and John Quincy with them and leaving the youngest boys back home with relatives. "My desire was . . . to have run all the hazards and accompany him," she explained to a friend, "but I could not prevail upon him to consent." John had eventually decided that the risks of a winter crossing of the North Atlantic, plus the predatory presence of British frigates cruising the sea-lanes for prizes, might lead to the near annihilation of the Adams family, or capture and imprisonment in England for the duration of the war. He himself was duty-bound to run those risks, but Abigail and the children must not be part of the gamble, a decision he qualified by acquiescing to John Quincy's argument that he wanted and needed to spend more time with his father.[3]

It never occurred to John to refuse the appointment, an option Abigail probably preferred but never felt she could insist upon, knowing as she did that John would feel obliged to grudgingly concur, then hold it against her the rest of their lives. For while John was unquestionably an American patriot, he was also obsessed with claiming a prominent role as an architect of American independence, and the last thing that Abigail would ever do was to become an obstacle between her husband and his fondest dream.

What neither of them knew at the time, nor did anyone else in America, was that a week before John and John Quincy sailed, a treaty creating the Franco-American alliance had already been signed. In effect, the mission on which John was being sent had already been accomplished. And as he was to discover upon his arrival in Paris, there was very little of any diplomatic significance for him to do, except attempt to bridge the growing chasm between warring factions within the American delegation that had gathered around Benjamin Franklin on the one hand and Arthur Lee on the other.

All the anguish Abigail was anticipating as she sobbed away at her kitchen table would never have occurred if modern communications had been available. As it turned out, in the absence of any meaningful diplomatic agenda, the emotional agenda created by their prolonged separations became the main story. The diplomatic negotiations that mattered most were domestic, as distance forced John and Abigail, most especially Abigail, to confront their mutual doubts and dependencies in ways they had never done before. This proved to be the greatest strain on their marriage and "friendship" in their lifetimes.

OVER THERE

The six-week voyage was even more precarious than John had imagined. The **Boston** bucked twenty-foot waves, gale winds that ripped her rigging to pieces on three occasions, and a lightning storm that split the mainmast and incapacitated twenty of the crew. Three British frigates chased them for several days, and, in a separate action, the **Boston** engaged and captured a British merchant ship, the **Martha**. During that action John appeared beside the captain, musket in hand, prepared to join the boarding party until ordered below. A young lieutenant whom John had befriended was seriously wounded when a cannon exploded while firing a warning shot. John volunteered to hold the officer down while the ship's doctor amputated his leg. (He died a week later and was buried at sea with the remnants of the cannon lashed to his chest.) Through it all, John Quincy was a model of composure, always by his father's side, stunningly mature beyond his years, mastering French at a pace that John found he could not match.[4]

Meanwhile, back in Braintree, Abigail claimed that she was riding all the waves with them in her dreams. In March, while the **Boston** was still at sea, alarming reports circulated in the Boston press that Benjamin Franklin had been assassinated and the **Boston** captured after a fierce battle. These false rumors were not discredited for two months, leaving Abigail to draft letters without knowing whether to send them to the American embassy in Paris or the Tower in London. "Hitherto my wandering Ideas Rove like the Son of Ulysses from Sea to Sea," she lamented, "not knowing where to find you." She did not learn that her husband and son had landed safely at Bordeaux until June 18, two and a half months after the fact, and only then, ironically, from a reprinted account in an English newspaper: "I shall wait with impatience till I receive tidings from the well known hand of my dearest friend," she wrote guardedly. "O, When, When, shall it arrive? But hush my anxious heart."[5]

It arrived twelve days later, more a note than a letter, but bearing the glorious news that her husband and son were alive and well. "Shall I tell my dearest that tears of joy filled my eyes this morning at the sight of his well known hand," she gushed, "the first line that has blessed my sight during his four months absence . . . I have lived a life of fear and anxiety ever since you left me." It was almost as if she required a palpable expression of John's personality, the distinctive slant of his scrawl, before she could rest assured he was alive. Though he had landed at Bordeaux, Abigail wanted him to know that he had also, at last, landed "in the Bosom of his partner." She was now going to clutch him there more tightly than ever before, because the agonizing uncertainty of his fate had forced her to recognize, more than ever before, how completely her own life was wrapped around his.[6]

The chief problem was the Atlantic Ocean. While Abigail realized that letters to and from Paris would require months rather than weeks to reach their destination, she presumed that the flow of correspondence would resemble a delayed version of their exchange of letters when John was in Philadelphia. For several reasons, however, her presumption proved wrong.

First, the British navy patrolled the sea-lanes

and seized all correspondence on captured American and French vessels in the hopes of finding intelligence of use in the war effort. Knowing this, ship captains often threw their literary cargo overboard as soon as British frigates appeared on the horizon. Although it is impossible to know with any precision, approximately one-fourth to one-third of the letters Abigail and John wrote to each other in 1778–79 ended up on the ocean bottom.[7]

Second, John was acutely aware—Abigail thought excessively aware—that his letters could fall into British hands. "It is impossible for me to write as I did in America," he explained. "It is not safe to write any thing that one is not willing should go into all the Newspapers of the World." As a result, his letters, especially his earliest letters, tended to be short, businesslike, and devoid of just the kind of intimate expressions that Abigail craved to hear. He still felt them, he incessantly assured her, but he could not afford to put them on paper as he had in the past. Abigail thought this explanation rather lame: "The affection I feel for my Friend is of the tenderest kind, matured by years, sanctified by choise and approved by Heaven . . . What care I then for the ridicule of Britains should this testimony fall into their Hands, nor can I endure that so much caution and circumspection on your part should deprive me of the only consolor of your absence."[8]

By the summer of 1778 she was fretting out loud to friends that she had received only two letters from John, both overly concise reports that all was well, nothing more. The fretting became more heartfelt over succeeding months: "You could not have suffered more upon your Voyage than I have felt cut off from all communication with you. My Harp has been hung upon the Willows, and I have scarcely even taken my pen to write but the tears have flowed faster than the Ink." His prolonged silences were transforming her, she reported, from a naturally cheerful wife and mother to an insipid creature: "All things look gloomy and melancholy around me." Her mood worsened as winter approached, the long silences continued, and the snow built up around the house: "I would almost fancy myself in Greenland."9

Her depression eventually turned to anger, first directed at the Continental Congress for sending her husband an eternity away, then at John himself for his apparent inability to convey affection. She wondered out loud "if you have changed Hearts with some Laplander or made a voyage to a region that has chilled every Drop of your Blood." How could he have changed so much from that affectionate soul mate she had waved farewell to on that horrible day last February? Was there something he was afraid to tell her? Had he fallen in love with someone else? Or had his heart constricted into a hard inert muscle that barely beat? Were all his letters, the few of them she did receive, going to remain hastily written acts of apparent obligation, almost worse than nothing at all? If the latter was so, he needed to know that she now had resolved to adopt a minimalist style of her own, "modeled on the **very concise** Methods of my Friend."[10]

Abigail was hardly a frail creature, but the very depth of her own sense of affinity for John made her vulnerable when their ongoing conversation suddenly became a monologue. If she was his ballast, he was her alter ego, and when, for whatever reason—Atlantic storms, British cruisers, or John's temporary obliviousness—his presence was removed from the equation, she was like a graceful dancer suddenly alone on the floor without a partner.

Her momentary vulnerability helps explain the uncharacteristically flirtatious correspondence that she found herself having with James Lovell at this time. Lovell was a Harvard graduate and former schoolteacher whose zeal for the patriot cause had convinced the British that he must be imprisoned as a dangerous character. He was apparently dangerous in several senses of the term, for upon his release from prison and appointment to the Massachusetts delegation in the Continental Congress, he developed a reputation as a ladies' man with a wife and family back in Massachusetts and a series of female friends in Philadelphia.[11]

The letters they exchanged during John's absence had an official rationale, since Lovell was head of the Committee on Foreign Affairs, and therefore perfectly positioned to inform Abigail about events in Paris involving her husband. (In effect, Lovell could provide the information that John regarded as too sensitive to be included in his letters.) But Lovell's letters, and eventually Abigail's responses, defied all rules of official etiquette and became elaborate prose performances loaded with sexual innuendo, fanciful expressions of endearment, and mock distress at the other's suggestive language. This operatic style (e.g., "Amiable tho unjust Portia! doubly unjust!—to yourself and to me"), overloaded with literary references to Shakespeare and the classics, almost requires translation for a modern reader because of the double entendres and obvious mimicking of Laurence Sterne's layered sentimentalizing in **Tristram Shandy**, the novelistic rage of the moment in both Great Britain and America.[12]

Abigail even acknowledged that she was uniquely receptive to Lovell's double-edged expressions of affection. (For example, he claimed he could not stop himself from loving a woman who was so much in love with such an admirable man as John Adams.) "I love every one who Manifests a regard or Shews an Attachment to my absent Friend," she confessed to Lovell, "and will indulgently allow for the overflowing of a heart softened by absence, pained by a separation from what it holds most dear upon Earth." It also did not hurt that Lovell was writing just the kind of long, highly affectionate, and deeply flattering letters that she was demanding, but not getting, from John.[13]

Nothing "happened" between Abigail and Lovell, which is to say that the literary dalliance with a man fully prepared to give her his undivided attention never seriously threatened the unconditional love she felt for her "Dearest Friend." But the epistolary episode with Lovell did expose her emotional vulnerability, her craving for affectionate attention, and the sense of injustice she felt at being expected to accept secondary status forever to the country's call. She was not happy.

SEX, SPIES, AND THE FRANKLIN PROBLEM

If Abigail's major problem during John's eighteen-month absence was a pervasive sense of loneliness and neglect, his was quite the opposite. France and French society showered him with attention as the newly arrived embodiment of the Franco-American alliance. He was feted and fussed over from the moment that he and John Quincy landed at Bordeaux. And at one of the lavish dinner parties in his honor, he encountered for the first time the aristocratic mores of a world wholly different from anything he had experienced before.

The lovely wife of his host playfully asked him if he was descended from Adam, the first man, and if so whether he could answer a question that had always intrigued her: How did Adam and Eve, the first couple, learn to make love? Speaking no French, he blushed as he listened to the translation, then composed himself to explain that it was probably a natural act, like the attraction of magnets or a lightning strike, to which his hostess replied that it was certainly "a very happy shock." No woman talked this way in Braintree or Boston.[14]

More of the same greeted him in Paris, or more accurately in Passy, a village on the outskirts of the city, where Franklin resided in a magnificent château provided by the comte de Chaumont, which came equipped with a staff of nine liveried servants and a wine cellar of more than a thousand bottles. Franklin insisted that John move in with him—there was plenty of room, and his proximity would make doing diplomatic business more convenient. He also arranged for John Quincy to attend a nearby boarding school where his grandson, Benjamin Franklin Bache, was already a student.

Multiple dinners were quickly scheduled to introduce the new American minister to "the first people of Paris." (Franklin believed that the most important diplomatic work was done at dinner parties.) The beautiful Madame Brillon impressed John with her opinionated conversation, which resembled that of his own opinionated wife, but he was startled when she perched herself on Franklin's lap and began kissing "**cher** Papa" on the cheek. Another woman whom John presumed to be Madame Brillon's companion turned out to be her husband's mistress: "I was astonished that these people could live together in such apparent friendship without cutting each other's throats," he observed much later. "But I did not know the world."[15]

Eventually, John's view of this highly sophisticated and thoroughly promiscuous world came to resemble the response of the proverbial Puritan in Babylon. But at first he was rather bedazzled by it all: "To tell you the Truth," he confided to Abigail, "I admire the Ladies here. Don't be jealous. They are handsome, and very well educated. Their accomplishments are exceedingly brilliant." (One can only imagine Abigail's reaction when she read these words.) And while he eventually became highly critical of Franklin's flirtatious ways, initially he described them as the harmless habits of an old man playing the role of male coquette. He even joked to Franklin that he intended to apprise their supervisors back in Philadelphia that the senior member of the delegation was developing a wholly new, "lap-oriented" approach to American diplomacy.[16]

The more official version of American diplomacy in France was vested in the three-man commission of Franklin, Arthur Lee, and now John Adams. To say that the records of the delegation were in disarray would be misleading, since, as John quickly discovered, there were really no records at all, a condition that he immediately assumed was his mission to correct. This was tedious work—copying routine diplomatic dispatches, answering requests from marooned and penniless American tourists, approving prisoner exchanges—all time-consuming tasks that, so he explained, left little time to write Abigail. But the most pressing problem was the open break between Franklin and Lee, the roots of which would require the skills of a brilliant detective and a sophisticated psychiatrist to fathom. John quickly decided to make himself "an umpire between two bitter and inveterate enemies."[17]

Lee seemed the obvious source of the problem. Although his bloodlines were impeccable (he was a member of Virginia's most prominent family) and his educational credentials were impressive (degrees in medicine from Edinburgh and law from London), Lee had a disarming knack for seeing corruption everywhere. He had accused Silas Deane, John's predecessor in the American delegation, of war profiteering. And he claimed that Franklin's household was staffed with British spies, whom

Franklin, in his conspicuously oblivious style, was providing with every confidential decision the delegation reached. As a result, Lee refused to confer with Franklin, and Franklin concluded that Lee was beyond reason and redemption. John discovered that the effort to arrange a reconciliation, even to get his two colleagues into the same room to sign official correspondence, was impossible: "The Wisdom of Solomon, the Meekness of Moses, and the Patience of Job, all united in one character, would not be sufficient to qualify a Man to act in the Situation in which I am at present," he complained to Abigail, adding that "I have scarcely a trace of any of these Virtues."[18]

What John did not realize at the time was that all of Lee's apparently paranoid accusations were true. Deane was a corrupt profiteer and was eventually found guilty of that charge by the Continental Congress. Virtually the entire staff of Franklin's château were, in fact, spies, though not all British spies. Some reported to the French court, others to mercantile houses interested in obtaining government contracts. But the most dramatic revelation, so unsuspected that it took over a century for historians to discover, was that Edward Bancroft, Franklin's private secretary, was a British spy who provided weekly reports to London (in invisible ink) of every conversation within the American delegation.[19]

Though he never fully realized the extent of the

corruption surrounding him, John did recognize as early as May 1778 that he was spinning his wheels in a diplomatic swamp. In a private letter to Samuel Adams that he knew would be circulated within the Continental Congress, he proposed that the three-person commission was no longer necessary and one American minister to the French court would suffice. This had the double advantage of solving the Lee-Franklin problem without even mentioning it, and clearing the way for his own return home. For there was no question that if his advice was taken, Franklin would be appointed the sole American minister and John could cease being an absentee husband.[20]

The Continental Congress did take John's advice, but not until September 1778, and official word of its decision did not reach Paris until February 1779. Oddly, the appointment of Franklin was not accompanied by orders relieving John, who was left to stew amid rumors that he might be dispatched to Amsterdam or Vienna. "I never was in such a situation as I am now," he confessed to Abigail, "and my present Feelings are new to me," not knowing whether he should await further instructions or take it upon himself to head home on the next ship. He described himself as "wedged by the Waiste in the middle of a rifted Oak."[21]

During this prolonged waiting period the major, and surely most consequential, event was the deterioration of his relationship with Franklin. If only in retrospect, one could see this coming as far back as that evening in 1776 when they argued, albeit in a bantering way, over whether to open or close the window before going to sleep. More generally, Franklin's capacious but elusive personality seemed designed by the gods to drive a straight-ahead man like John crazy. More specifically, John had arrived in Paris assuming that he and Franklin were political equals with roughly equal revolutionary credentials. Back in America this was not a far-fetched assumption, but in France it was a preposterous illusion.

In a quite brilliant act of reinvention, Franklin the cosmopolitan, longtime resident of London had transformed himself into Franklin the original American, fresh from the backwoods complete with beaver hat and folksy wisdom. In Paris he was not just an American icon, he was **the** American icon, on a par with Voltaire as a philosopher and prose stylist, alongside the comte de Buffon as a world-class scientist. His image was everywhere— in portrait galleries, in print shops, on porcelain plates and gold-plated jewelry—the most famous and recognizable American sage of the enlightened age.[22]

Though it took a while, it was probably inevitable that John would find the Franklin phenomenon intolerable. The criticism started slowly, with snide observations about Franklin's vaunted proficiency in French, a touchy subject given his own total lack of fluency, then complaints about Franklin's slovenly work habits and the fact that he did not rise until eleven o'clock, while he, John Adams, was at his desk at dawn. One can almost sense the smoldering resentment when John described scenes of "continual dissipation" as crowds showed up daily "to have the honor to see Franklin, and to have the pleasure of telling stories about his Simplicity, his bald head and scattering straight hairs." On one occasion at the theater, a portrait of Franklin was displayed onstage during intermission, and John was so disgusted that he feigned illness and left the performance. The jealousy was palpable.[23]

The result was an embarrassing exhibition of envy that also had significant political implications for the American cause. For John had chosen—no, actually he could not help himself—to put a huge crack in a political partnership that still had some history to make.

In all respects save one, then, the mission to France had been an abject failure. Its diplomatic rationale, the treaty with France, had been accomplished before John even set sail. The separation from Abigail, in both time and distance, had generated emotional shock waves that shook her customary stoicism and produced a temporary breach in their partnership. And the working relationship with Franklin, which had performed magic in the past, was now damaged in ways that proved beyond repair.

The sole exception to this depressing pattern was the relationship between John and John Quincy, which solidified under the pressures of their dramatic adventures together, especially their Atlantic crossing, and their more mundane day-to-day interactions in Paris. John's earlier absences in Philadelphia, plus his deference to Abigail's parental authority when he was home, had allowed a gap to develop between father and son, not so much a serious misunderstanding as the absence of any deeper understanding. That gap was closed during their eighteen months together at such close quarters.

Part of the new alignment was a function of John's conspicuous pride in his precocious son. Virtually everyone who met John Quincy commented on his stunning composure and remarkable maturity. (Later on this would cause problems, since it meant that John Quincy never really had a childhood.) Both Abigail and John put enormous pressure on the boy, often in language that violates our modern sensibilities for its uncompromising expectations. "There are talents put into your Hands," wrote Abigail, "of which an account will be required of you hereafter, and being possessed of one, two, or four, see to it that you double their numbers." John could easily have written the same words, though he could not have written the words that followed in Abigail's letter: "But dear as you are to me, I had much rather you should have found your Grave in the Ocean you have crossed or any untimely death crop you in your Infant years, rather than see you an immoral profligate or a Graceless child."[24]

John tended to mix stern injunctions about diligence with self-deprecating jokes about the superiority of his son's mastery of French. (John Quincy frequently translated for him.) When they went to the theater together—the beginning of John Quincy's lifelong passion for the stage—John brought along a written version of the play in French, and John Quincy did a line-by-line translation for his father as the play proceeded, making him the teacher and his father the student. Small wonder that when Abigail began to berate her husband for failing to send longer and more intimate letters, John Quincy took his father's side: "You complain as bad or worse than if he had not wrote at all," he told his mother, "and it really hurts him to receive such letters." He crossed out and never sent the next line: "If all your letters are like this, Papa will cease writing at all." He had become his father's son.[25]

The final months in France were like lingering death. John decided in March 1779 that he could wait no longer for instructions from Philadelphia.

Plans to sail from Nantes on the **Alliance** were delayed when the ship underwent emergency repairs, then canceled altogether when John was apprised that he should accompany the new French minister to the United States, Chevalier Anne-César de la Luzerne, on the **Sensible**. It finally departed from Lorient on June 17 and arrived at Boston on August 3. John and John Quincy were deposited on the same shore of Quincy Bay from which they had departed eighteen months earlier. They walked over Penn's Hill again and into the house at Braintree. Abigail was crying again, but this time they were tears of joy.[26]

INTERVAL

We can imagine several scenes of blissful reunion: John turning his recurrent dream into reality by walking the Braintree fields hand in hand with Abigail, the children skipping alongside them; John Quincy being prodded to show off his fluency in French at the dinner table; Abigail crying with relief as she explained how marooned and lonely she had felt, but would never have to feel again.

We can imagine all these scenes, and some of them almost surely occurred, but we cannot really know because no letters between John and Abigail exist, for the obvious reason that they were together again at last. Nor did either of them write many letters at all from August to November 1779, making this the most undocumented chapter in their more than half century as a couple. Apparently, they were so busy recovering their customary rhythms of affection and interaction, filling up the emotional hole that distance had created, that there was neither the time nor the inclination to do much else.

There was one major exception, truly major because it almost offhandedly led to the most enduring political contribution of John's entire career, his drafting of the Massachusetts Constitution, which remains (with multiple amendments) the oldest written constitution in the English-speaking world still in use.

John was invited to join more than three hundred delegates at Cambridge on September 1, all charged with the task of drafting a new constitution for Massachusetts. An effort the previous year had run afoul of procedural disagreements, leaving Massachusetts, somewhat awkwardly, as the only state without a new constitution that embodied the republican principles of the American Revolution. The delegates selected a drafting committee of thirty men, which in turn selected a subcommittee of three that included John, which then proceeded to appoint him, as he put it later, "a Sub Sub Committee of one." Working alone in his study at Braintree, he single-handedly composed the new constitution in late September and early October.[27]

In retrospect, all the stars were perfectly aligned. With the possible exception of George Mason in Virginia, John was the most knowledgeable student of constitutional history in America. The advice he had offered in **Thoughts on Government** three years earlier had established his reputation on that score, and most of the new state constitutions adopted during the ensuing years had benefited from his guidance. The confidence the delegates to the Massachusetts Convention had in his competence reflected the broadly shared belief that there was an almost perfect match between John's legal and intellectual talent and the needs of what he insisted be called the Commonwealth of Massachusetts.

Moreover, the creative context was ideal emotionally as well as intellectually. John worked at home with his family around him and with Abigail available to comment each evening on the fruits of that day's work. In many of his previous (and subsequent) writings, John burdened his efforts with excessive displays of learning that verged on pedantry, long-winded asides that distracted the reader from the core message, often raising doubts that there was one. His temporary serenity amid the routinized domestic rhythms at Braintree, plus Abigail's reliable presence as nightly editor, allowed his words and ideas to flow, his verbal twitches to subside, and his occasional excesses to be silently edited out. It was another perfect match.

There were several distinctive touches to his draft constitution. "The body politic is formed by a voluntary association of individuals," he wrote in the preamble. "It is a social compact, by which the citizens unite with the whole people, that all may be governed by certain laws for the common good." The proper title for such an arrangement was not **state**, which could apply to monarchies as well as republics, but **commonwealth**, which could apply only to a government that vested sovereignty in the people as a collective. So great was John's prestige that no delegate ever questioned this decision, which made Massachusetts, along with Virginia and Pennsylvania, a commonwealth rather than a state forevermore.[28]

Moreover, unlike most of the other state constitutions, which made the executive branch a mere appendage to a quasi-sovereign legislature, John's draft created a powerful executive with an absolute veto over all legislation and a judiciary that was appointed rather than elected, serving not just a delineated term but "during good behavior."

As it turned out, the other delegates to the convention were not ready for such sweeping executive power, and modified his draft to permit the legislature to overturn a veto by a two-thirds majority. John always regarded this revision as a defacement, claiming that the preternatural fear of executive power represented an overlearning of the lessons of 1776. Unlike George III, he reminded his critics, all Massachusetts governors would be elected annually. Without an absolute veto, he feared that governors would "be run down by the legislature like a Hare before the Hunters." He lost this argument, though his insistence on a truly independent judiciary immune to popular pressure survived intact, a landmark contribution to American jurisprudence in which he took justifiable pride.[29]

More than any of the other state constitutions, the Massachusetts Constitution was a postrevolutionary document that rejected as naive some of the most hallowed assumptions of the preceding decade; it insisted upon a political framework more akin to the federal constitution adopted eight years later. Under the revolutionary glow, all projections of government power were stigmatized, so most state constitutions presumed that the chief function of government was to serve as a conduit for popular opinion: to digest and refine it, to be sure, and then to enact it. John's view of government, on the other hand, presumed that popular opinion was not a harmonious whole but a hydra-headed beast requiring orchestrated management, which meant channeling the different interests into separate constitutional compartments that would in turn police one another.[30]

In a very real sense, John's view of government was a projection onto the world of the control mechanisms necessary to subdue the powerful urges and impulses he felt surging through his own soul. More than any of the other American political thinkers of the age, he derived his most creative insights from a psychological understanding of the irrational side of human behavior. During the fall of 1779, with all his children surrounding him as he wrote, with Abigail once again present to listen and love, he reached a temporary level of mastery—all mastery was temporary in this context—over his abiding demons and self-destructive tendencies. Albeit momentarily, he found balance and proceeded to write, in record time, the most balanced state constitution in America.

But the magic of this moment ended just as he was putting the finishing touches on his draft. In early October he received official word from Philadelphia that he had been appointed minister plenipotentiary to the court of France, whose main task was to negotiate a treaty with Great Britain ending the war. Neither John nor Abigail had been expecting his appointment, and neither realized the highly contentious, almost comically chaotic, manner in which it had happened.

It represented the culmination of a long, bitter,

often bizarre debate in the Continental Congress of several months' duration. The debate had been triggered by Silas Deane's published defense of his own highly suspicious conduct while serving on the American diplomatic commission in Paris. Deane exposed the multiple machinations within the American delegation, which in turn cast a shadow of suspicion over everyone else, John included. Deane's sweeping allegations then touched off a chain reaction of highly partisan and extremely toxic debates within the congress, which are impossible to untangle because of the unrecorded backroom deals and relentless shiftings within the different camps. Henry Laurens, who presided over these debates in the congress, confessed that he himself was confounded by "the queerness of some of the queerest fellows that ever were invested with rays of sovereignty."[31]

Clearly, John's very integrity had been questioned, unfairly and quite preposterously as Laurens saw it, but with sufficient vigor that John's future role in public life was at stake. (His lifelong lament that jealous and small-minded enemies were plotting against him often has the distinct odor of paranoia, but in this particular instance they really were out to get him.) His appointment to the most significant and prestigious diplomatic post the country could offer was a clear indication that his friends in the Continental Congress had beaten back his enemies. But given the debate that had preceded that decision, so several friends warned him, it was imperative that John accept the assignment immediately and sail for France as soon as possible, lest his enemies, still lurking in the middle distance, overturn the decision.[32]

There was never even a remote possibility that John would decline. Domestic concerns, real though they were, could not compete with his craving for public distinction. As he saw it, he had played a major role in launching the war for independence, so it was only right that he should be accorded an equivalent role in ending it. On November 4 he officially accepted the appointment, promising to "devote myself, without Reserve, or loss of time, to discharge the duties of it." He intended to sail for France in eight to ten days.[33]

The only real question, then, was whether Abigail and the children would join him. Given her multiple expressions of regret at not accompanying him on the previous trip, and given the anxiety she experienced—close to clinical depression—during their prolonged separation, it seems plausible to assume that she expressed a strong preference to come along. But there is no evidence that she did; in fact, there is no evidence whatsoever of their private conversations on this sensitive subject.

A letter from John, written on board the Sensi-

ble just before it sailed, suggests that those conversations had been difficult and John had made the final decision that Abigail remain behind despite her protestations to the contrary: "Let me intreat you, to keep up your spirits and throw off Cares, as much as possible," he urged. "We shall yet be happy, I hope and pray, and I don't doubt it. I shall have Vexations enough, as usual. You will have Anxiety and tenderness enough, as usual. Pray strive not to have too much. I will write, by every opportunity I can get."[34]

She wrote him the same day, hoping the letter would arrive before he sailed: "My habitation, how disconsolate it looks! My table, I set down to it but cannot swallow my food. O Why was I born with so much Sensibility and, why possessing it have I so often been called to struggle with it?" By "sensibility" she meant her overwhelming emotional reaction to John's prolonged absence, a pent-up sense of sorrow that she had managed to control before his departure but that then came surging over her once he was gone.[35]

Clearly, they had exchanged mutual vows in the days before the voyage, he to write more frequently and expansively, she to avoid complaining when letters did not arrive in accord with his promises or her expectations. Clearly, at the parting this time, they were both brave. But most clearly of all, alone once again in the house, Abigail was miserable. If she had known that this separation would last for nearly five years, her misery might have been unbearable.

A CRUEL DESTINY

While Abigail attempted to reconcile herself to a life without love, John accepted the domestic sacrifice as the price, albeit a high one, that must be paid to earn a permanent place of prominence in American history. He attempted to reduce the domestic cost by bringing along Charles as well as John Quincy, who at ten and thirteen years of age respectively were deemed old enough to benefit from extended European exposure. His entourage also included two secretaries: Francis Dana, the senior staff member and former delegate to the Continental Congress; and James Thaxter, a Harvard graduate who had read law with John and tutored the Adams boys, the designated junior staffer.

While Abigail battled ennui in a stony, self-imposed silence, John and his entourage found themselves launched on an adventure. The **Sensible** sprang a leak two days out of Boston that forced them to limp across the Atlantic—if British frigates had discovered them, they would have been easy prey—and eventually landed on Spain's northwestern coast, a full one thousand miles from Paris. They mounted mules to scale the Pyrenees and endured smoke-filled accommodations, ever-present bed-bugs, and overbearing Catholic priests, whom John described as surviving relics of the Inquisition. The hardships convinced him that he had made the correct decision to leave Abigail in Braintree. "What would we do," he asked, "if you and all the family had been with me?" In an effort to demonstrate that she was always on his mind, he sent her a package from Bilbao that included green tea, several bolts of linen cloth, and eighteen dozen "Barcelona Han-kuffs."[36]

Once he established his extended family in Paris, John made an obvious effort to write Abigail regularly and to ensure that his letters contained the kind of personal thoughts and impressions she so craved. A tour of the Royal Gardens, for example, prompted a discourse on the double-edged character of Parisian splendor: "There is every Thing here that can inform the Understanding or refine the Taste," he observed. "Yet it must be remembered that there is every thing here too, which can seduce, betray, deceive, corrupt and debauch it." A subsequent tour of the art museums produced a meditation on the march of civilization across generations, which has since become justifiably famous: "I must study Politics and War that my sons may have liberty to study Mathematics and Philosophy, Geography, Commerce and Agriculture, in order to give their children a right to study Painting, Poetry, Music, Architecture, Statuary, Tapestry, and Porcelain." This was the man Abigail knew and loved, sharing himself over the distance the way she wished.[37]

For several reasons, however, it could not last. The correspondence he felt compelled to maintain with the Continental Congress—he was at best assiduous, at worst obsessive, in reporting back to headquarters—soon began to nudge out the letters to Abigail. "I am so taken up with writing to Philadelphia that I don't write to you as often as I wish," he confessed somewhat guiltily. "I hope you won't complain of me." She did not, at one point claiming that she did not expect to receive more than a few letters a year. Even though she did not mean it, she felt obliged to say it.[38]

Her low expectations, in fact, proved realistic. In part because it often took six months for a letter to reach her, and in part because many of John's letters were lost at sea, any kind of ongoing conversation became impossible. They suddenly found themselves in a virtually silent partnership.

Once again, this time for a much longer stretch, Abigail felt that she was a widow. On occasion she summoned up the bravado to joke about the non-negotiable powers of the Atlantic Ocean. "Several packets have been sent to Neptune," she quipped, "and I Query whether, having found his mistake, he has complaisance enough to forward them to you." But her more abiding mood was depression and despair, describing her situation as "a cruel destiny" and herself "sitting in my solitary chamber, the representative of the lonely love." One night she woke up from a dream in which John and both boys had returned to her, only to realize that it was merely a dream. "Cruel that I should wake," she reported, "only to experience a renewal of my daily solicitude," too disconcerted to write "solitude." John concurred that they could only come together in a dream: "What a fine Affair it would be if We could flit across the Atlantic as they say the Angels do from Planet to Planet. I would dart to Penn's Hill and bring you over on my Wings."[39]

She began to question whether her capacity to love was a blessing or a curse, given the relentless sorrow it produced when the outlet was an ocean away. She even attributed her own miserable condition—John did not strike her as similarly affected—to the biblical curse imposed on all women. "Desire and Sorrow were denounced upon our Sex," she speculated, "as a punishment for the transgression of Eve. I have sometimes thought that we are formed to experience more exquisite sensations than is the Lot of your Sex. More tender and susceptible by Nature of . . . happiness or misery, we Suffer and enjoy in a higher degree." Given the current downward spiral on her own emotional scale, she had discovered a new appreciation of "the philosopher who thanked the Gods that he was created a Man rather than a Woman."[40]

"WHEN HE IS WOUNDED, I BLEED"

If Abigail's problems were primarily emotional, John's were chiefly diplomatic. In effect, he had been appointed minister plenipotentiary to negotiate an end of the war with Great Britain more than a year before the British ministry was prepared to give serious consideration to such negotiations. During the spring and summer of 1780, in fact, British strategy called for a major campaign in the Carolinas and Georgia designed to deliver a blow that would demonstrate the futility of continued American resistance. Until the British came to recognize the futility of their own war policy, John could only wait.

Patience never came naturally to John, so in the summer of 1780 he began to question what he regarded as Franklin's overly solicitous posture toward the French government, thereby inserting himself into a conversation between Franklin and the French foreign minister, the comte de Vergennes. Both Franklin and Vergennes regarded this intrusion as unwelcome and potentially harmful to the Franco-American alliance, a landmark achievement that they, quite correctly, viewed as their joint triumph.

Vergennes took an immediate dislike toward this American interloper, who seemed to possess all the diplomatic grace of a cannonball and to regard stubbornness as a major virtue. "His obstinacy," Vergennes noted caustically, "will cause to foment a thousand unfortunate incidents." Eventually, on July 29, 1780, he announced the end of any and all communication with John Adams. From now on, he would deal only with Franklin when it came to American affairs. He also fired off an angry letter to La Luzerne, the French minister to the United States, urging him to use all his influence to have Adams recalled.[41]

What had John done to provoke such exasperation? His major offense was to insist that the United States be treated as an equal partner in the Franco-American alliance, a point that Franklin preferred to finesse. Lurking behind that insistence was the conviction that French and American interests, though temporarily aligned, were not enduringly identical. As he put it in his diary, French policy was to "keep us weak. Make us feel our obligations. Impress our minds with a sense of gratitude." Once the war with Great Britain was won—an outcome that John acknowledged to be quite dependent on French assistance—French and American goals were likely to diverge. France would probably seek to recover some portion of its lost empire in North America, for example, and hold American interests hostage to its larger European agenda in the global conflict with Great Britain. The time might very well come, in short, when America's gratitude toward the French became a major obstacle in negotiating favorable terms with the British.

However obstinate and ungrateful such convictions seemed to Vergennes and Franklin at the time, they were rooted in a highly realistic assessment of America's long-term interests that proved prescient as events unfolded pretty much as John predicted. He was, as Vergennes described him, temperamentally unsuited for the diplomatic refinements of the French court, irritatingly irreverent toward French appraisals of the size of the naval force required to subdue British prowess off the American coast, apparently deaf to all of Franklin's advice in favor of silence and deference. But on every strategic score, history proved him right.

History had not yet happened by the late summer of 1780, and back in Philadelphia, the delegates at the Continental Congress could know only that their minister plenipotentiary had become a political liability in Paris. The most damaging testimony came from Franklin, who chose to align himself with Vergennes: "Mr. Adams has given offence to the Court here . . . He thinks, as he tells me himself, that America has been too free in Expressions of Gratitude towards France . . . I apprehend, that he mistakes his Ground, and that this Court is to be treated with Decency and Delicacy." This was the diplomatic equivalent of a stab in the back, and the first formulation of Franklin's most famous evisceration, rendered three years later: "He means well for his Country, is always an honest man, often a Wise one, but sometimes and in some things, absolutely out of his Senses."[42]

Abigail was well positioned to learn of the campaign being waged against her husband, since several of the participants in the debate within the congress were regular correspondents, especially the ever-ingratiating Lovell. An old family friend, Elbridge Gerry, reported that there was a faction determined to see John humiliated, one that "would I fear go to greater lengths than Judas did to betray his Lord." The pro-Franklin faction in the congress, in fact, enjoyed a singular advantage. Given American dependence on French financial and military assistance, any request from Paris carried the force of a command.[43]

While Abigail recognized this political reality, she tended to view the campaign to remove John as a personal vendetta led by Franklin and his supporters. When she read Franklin's stiletto of a letter, she dismissed him as a "False, insinuating, dissembling wretch" who could best serve the American cause by dropping dead at the first opportunity. And, as she explained to Lovell, she experienced the assault on John's character as a personal attack: "Yet it wounds me, sir. When he is wounded, I bleed."[44]

Eventually, after a year of debate, the congress reached a compromise solution that left neither side wholly satisfied. John's commission as minister plenipotentiary was revoked, an implicit censure that he subsequently described as the greatest embarrassment of his public life. But he was then given another commission, this time as member of a five-man delegation to represent American interests in Europe, each minister representing a different region of the country—Adams for New England, Franklin for Pennsylvania, John Jay for New York, Thomas Jefferson for Virginia, and Henry Laurens for the Deep South. This meant that, despite the best efforts by Vergennes and Franklin to have him recalled, efforts that included bribing several members of the Continental Congress, John would remain in Europe.

It also meant that he was not coming home anytime soon, an outcome that Abigail found difficult to digest. Publicly, she expressed satisfaction that her man had been vindicated by the new diplomatic appointment. Privately, however, she harbored an unspoken hope that his enemies in Paris and Philadelphia would succeed, thereby delivering him back to her. The best of all scenarios from her perspective was his reappointment, then his voluntary decision to resign, perhaps orchestrated as a final slap in the face of those critics who had called his character into question. "Is it not in your power," she pleaded to him, "to withdraw yourself from a situation in which you are certain, no honour can be obtained to yourself or Country?" Given the abundantly clear hostility of Vergennes and Franklin, plus his status as persona non grata in the French court, what could he hope to achieve by remaining in Paris?[45]

In fact, John's mind was moving in the same direction, but on a different track. By the time Abigail made her plea, he had already moved his entire official family, to include John Quincy and Charles, to Amsterdam, far removed from the perpetual shadow of Franklin and the barely suppressed loathing of Vergennes. Acting on his own initiative, without any official authorization from the congress, and—best of all—against the expressed disapproval of Vergennes, he had decided to put himself squarely in the middle of the commercial and financial capital of Europe. There he would seek Dutch recognition of American independence and a loan from the notoriously tightfisted Amsterdam bankers that would, if granted, establish American credit throughout Europe. It was a bold, stunningly singular move that caught everyone by surprise, comparable to his decision to defend the British troops after the Boston Massacre. But for seasoned students of the Adams psyche—Abigail topped that list—it made perfect sense, for it allowed John to establish himself as a wholly independent agent, free to release his enormous energies in a cause that was simultaneously worthy, defiant, and entirely his own.

By the time Abigail's letters requesting his return arrived, he was already in midflight in the other direction, tossing off pamphlets designed to persuade the Dutch government that American independence was just a matter of time, Dutch bankers that investing in America now would pay huge dividends later, and Dutch citizens that New England was an American replica of the Netherlands. He worked twenty-hour days and invented shuttle diplomacy by traveling to Leiden, The Hague, and then back again to Amsterdam, making himself a one-man American embassy. He was more fully engaged than at any other time in his political career, save perhaps those hectic months in 1775–76.

About the last thing he wanted to hear, or could hear, was that his wife wanted him to come home. Most of her letters, which found their way to Amsterdam in six to eight months, went unanswered. "Methinks I might have been favoured in the course of eighteen months past with a letter," she complained. He eventually responded, explaining that every hour of every day was spent "amidst Courts, Camps, and Crowds," that he had been very sick, at one point on the verge of death—it was probably malaria—and fully invested in a cause that left him completely exhausted: "A Child was never more weary of a Whistle, than I am of Embassies."[46]

That was true enough, but a parallel truth, whether deeper or not we cannot know, was that John had allowed himself to become totally consumed by his Dutch crusade because it offered the promise of public recognition, and his lust for fame had temporarily nudged his love for Abigail into the distant background. For her part, Abigail did her best to suffer in silence, but her prolonged misery as a de facto widow occasionally seeped out: "O there are hours, days and weeks when I would not point to you all my feelings—for I would not make you more unhappy," she lamented. "I begin to think there is a moral evil in this separation . . . Can it be a voluntary separation? I feel that it is not."[47]

Both geographically and psychologically, they were in different places, farther apart than they had been at any time in the history of their marriage. As it turned out, he was doing brilliant diplomatic work with the Dutch that few, if any, American statesmen had the energy and ability to match. But Abigail was no longer capable of accepting John's public achievements as adequate compensation for her abiding loneliness. From her perspective, he was simply gone.

PARENTING

John's diplomatic mission split the Adams family down the middle. The older boys, John Quincy and Charles, were with John in Paris, then Amsterdam, then Leiden. Nabby and Tommy remained in Braintree with Abigail. The division of labor created by this separation forced both adults to become single parents, though letters to each other permitted some consultation and, not so incidentally, left a record of their parenting practices that otherwise would have remained invisible.

It is tempting to claim that neither Abigail nor John could possibly know that they were launching a dynasty—arguably the most prominent family line in American history—but the evidence demonstrates beyond much doubt that they intended to do precisely that. John was not only obsessed with posterity's judgment, but also determined that his name would live on in the achievements of his children and then their descendants. Although John Quincy was his major project on this score, all the Adams children were raised to believe that they had come into the world at a truly critical moment in

American history and into a family poised to play a major role in shaping that history. These huge advantages generated equally huge obligations on them all to fulfill their destiny: "These are times in which a Genius would wish to live," Abigail apprised John Quincy. "It is not in the still calm of life, or the repose of pacific station, that great characters are formed . . . The Habits of a vigorous mind are formed in contending with difficulties . . . Great necessities call out great virtues."[48]

Greatness was the goal, and in order to qualify as greatness in the Adams scheme, success had to manifest itself in ways that transcended mere worldly wealth. In fact, during their residence in Amsterdam, John worried that his boys might be corrupted by the Dutch obsession with making money, which he described as "an object that I hope none of my children will aim at." The watchword was not wealth but virtue, and the only success that really counted came in the public arena for men and the domestic arena for women. The role model for Nabby was Abigail, the highly literate but deeply dutiful wife and mother. The role model for the boys was John, one of the leading statesmen in an auspiciously talented generation. Nothing less would do.[49]

While all the boys were expected to master Latin and Greek, read widely in the classics, and eventually graduate from Harvard—all did—John

Quincy was always the major project. "You come into life with advantages which will disgrace you if your success is mediocre," John warned the young prodigy. "And if you do not rise to the head of your Profession, but of your country, it will be owing to your own Lasiness, Slovenliness, and Obstinacy." Abigail's injunctions were less fierce, but equally lofty. "Glory my son in a Country which has given birth to Characters . . . which may vie with the wisdom and valour of antiquity," she urged, adding that destiny had marked him "as an immediate descendent of one of those characters" for a life of "disinterested patriotism and that Noble Love of your country." While every American boy is encouraged to dream that he might one day grow up to become president of the United States, John Quincy spent his entire childhood hearing that anything less than the highest office in the land would be regarded as failure.[50]

Since the severity of that message sounds almost inhumane to modern ears, it merits mention that John's educational advice to his eldest son frequently had a softer side. While Latin and Greek were obviously the gateway to all learning, at one point John suggested that John Quincy put Thucydides and Cicero aside and nourish other parts of his mind with English literature, especially poetry, for the sheer fun of it. "You will never be alone," he rather famously observed, "with a poet in your pocket."[51]

Then there was the episode of the ice skates. John Quincy had asked his father for a pair as a Christmas present in 1780, claiming that he could then skate to school on the frozen canals of Leiden. Initially, John denied the request, apparently fearing that his son would waste his time skating away hours that should be devoted to study. Then he began to change his mind. (One could almost see paternal love slowly melting all the disciplined admonitions.) It now occurred to John that ice-skating might help John Quincy learn balance and rhythm, for it was "**not** simple Velocity or Ability that constitutes the Perfection of it, but Grace." Since John himself had so often been accused of being graceless, the ice skates would allow John Quincy to remedy a chronic deficiency in the Adams family. The more he thought about it, the more John regarded ice skates as essential for John Quincy's education. They should purchase a slightly oversize pair of boots, so that he could grow into them rather than outgrow them, another nod to hardheaded austerity that allowed John to feel responsible, not just indulgent, as a father. The son got his skates and the father retained his standards.[52]

Three years younger than John Quincy, Charles prompted different parental responses that also defied the harsher code. "I am sometimes afraid my dear boy," wrote Abigail, "that you will be spoilt by being a favorite. Praise is a dangerous Sweet unless properly tempered." John put it more poetically. Charles was the kind of "amiable insinuating Creature" whom everybody found beguiling, the designated charmer in the Adams family. Abigail reported that all the children in their Braintree neighborhood were asking when Charley would come home and play with them. Even John admitted that "I love him too much."[53]

Charles went to all the same schools as John Quincy, first in Paris, then in Amsterdam and Leiden, but John never focused his fire on Charles as he did on John Quincy, in part because Charles was three years younger, in part because he had a way about him that melted all parental lectures into pools of pure affection. Knowing as we do that Charles would live a short and tragic life that ended in alcoholism, it is tempting to speculate that the seeds of that sad fate were sown during an indulgent childhood. But hindsight wisdom of that sort is notoriously self-fulfilling. What does seem clear is that Abigail and John mixed quite demanding doses of discipline with routinized expressions of parental affection in their child rearing, and that John Quincy received more of the former and Charles more of the latter.

Both of these overlapping attitudes were put on

display in the summer of 1781. Although John Quincy was only fourteen, John decided that he should accompany Francis Dana to St. Petersburg, where he would serve as secretary to America's first minister to Russia, acquire another language, and launch his diplomatic career. Charles, on the other hand, had requested that he be allowed to return to family and friends in Braintree. John reluctantly complied, despite worries about sending an eleven-year-old boy across the Atlantic in the custody of strangers.

Charles departed on the **South Carolina** in August, but the ship was forced ashore in Spain after a series of mishaps that tested the mettle of all passengers, who described Charles as the pluckiest boy they had ever met. He transferred to a privateer, the **Cicero,** which sailed south to the Caribbean before heading north toward New England. The voyage took five months, a virtual eternity for both parents. John was so worried that he wrote that he would "never again have the Weakness to bring a child to Europe." Abigail worried even more, because reports in the Boston press indicated that the **South Carolina**, the ship she assumed Charles was on, had gone down at sea with the loss of all hands. When the **Cicero** landed on the Massachusetts shore in January 1782 and Charles showed up, unannounced and unexpected, Abigail almost broke down, saying that Charles had proved sufficiently resourceful to have come back from the dead.[54]

Abigail now had two young boys and one teenage girl to raise, but increasingly it was Nabby who became the chief focus of her attention. Late in 1782 a young lawyer by the name of Royall Tyler began showing up at the Adams house with obvious interest in Nabby, who was eminently eligible at seventeen. Tyler's appearance triggered all of Abigail's maternal instincts, since a daughter's choice of a husband carried all the lifetime consequences of a son's choice for a career. She did the equivalent of a background check on Tyler, interrogating her sister and brother-in-law, with whom Tyler was boarding, and during his visits to the house monopolized the conversations with him, undoubtedly to the annoyance of Nabby and the discomfort of Tyler, who must have felt that he was undergoing a domestic version of a cross-examination.

In a long letter to John, after bemoaning the fact that he was not there to participate in the process, she conveyed her conclusions. Tyler had sowed some wild oats while a student at Harvard, where he earned the reputation of being a ladies' man. After graduation he "dissipated two or three years of his life and too much of his fortune" writing poetry and even some plays, none of which ever saw the light of day. But he had recovered from these youthful dalliances to become a serious student of the law—John would be impressed with his legal learning—and was now generally regarded as a solid citizen and an up-and-coming lawyer in the Boston area. "I fancy I see in him," she explained, "Sentiments, opinions, and actions which endeared to me the best of friends." In other words, Tyler struck her as the second coming of John. Best of all, he was obviously smitten with Nabby.

Whether Nabby was smitten with him is difficult to know. What was clear beyond any doubt is that Abigail had decided that Tyler was the man that Nabby was waiting for, whether she knew it or not. As Abigail explained to John, their daughter was "a fine Majestick Girl who has as much dignity as a princess." On the other hand, she was "not beautiful" and "no air of levity ever accompanies her words or actions." It was, of course, much too early to panic about Nabby's prospects, but young men of Tyler's character and credentials were not common in Braintree. Abigail needed to know, as soon as possible, if John agreed with her maternal instincts on this score.[55]

John definitely did not. "I confess I don't like the subject at all," he explained, with considerable frustration that a matter of such significance for the family had proceeded so far without his knowledge, much less his consent. "My child is a Model," he pronounced, "and is not to be the Prize . . . of any, even reformed, Rake." (The inconvenient truth was that Nabby had grown up in John's absence, and he had not seen much of her since she was a little girl.) What most upset him, however, was Abigail's obvious orchestration of this entire episode. "You seem to have favoured this affair much too far," he warned, "and I wish it off." Though it came from afar, John's message had the distinct sound of a command, and Abigail took it as such. She wrote back immediately to say that the Tyler connection was "wholly done with."[56]

Apparently Tyler never got the word, or if he did, refused to accept its finality; several months later, in January 1784, he wrote John to request his permission to court Nabby. By then it was highly likely that Nabby would be leaving for Europe with her mother, though even that daunting fact did not deter Tyler, who claimed that he was willing to wait. John responded politely, expressing "much Esteem and Respect" for the obviously lovesick young man. He probably realized that time and distance would eventually make the matter moot, as it did. But he wanted Tyler to know, just in case, that his fatherly approval would always support "the Final Judgment and Inclination of my Daughter."[57]

Abigail's assessment of Tyler, by the way, proved prescient. He went on to a distinguished career as a lawyer and became America's first prominent playwright, a devoted husband and father, and eventually head of the Vermont judiciary. Nabby had, as

Abigail feared, missed a marvelous opportunity. And her own judgment about a mate a few years later proved considerably less shrewd than her mother's.[58]

TWO TREATIES

"Your humble servant has lately grown much into Fashion in this Country," John apprised Abigail in March of 1782, adding that "I shall recollect Amsterdam, Leyden and The Hague with more emotion than Philadelphia or Paris." He was pounding his chest with pride because, all of a sudden, Dutch diplomats and bankers, who had previously ignored his appeals for recognition of American independence and for a loan from the Bank of Amsterdam, were now courting him. The upbeat mood inspired a flurry of letters to Abigail—this after an inexplicable and, as Abigail saw it, unconscionable silence for nearly a year. He was going out to dine with dukes and duchesses, he wrote, but would much prefer to dine "upon rustocrat potatoes with Portia—Oh! Oh! hi ho hum!" Some sluice that had been closed for a year suddenly opened up again: "I have bought an House at the Hague," he bantered. "Will you come and see me?"[59]

Both the buoyant mood and the more receptive posture of the Dutch government were products of a dramatic shift in the strategic situation after the surrender of General Charles Cornwallis's army at Yorktown. "Some Folks will think your Husband a Negotiator, but it is not he, it is General Washington at Yorktown who did the substance of the Work," he acknowledged to Abigail; "the form only belongs to me." The Dutch were now prepared to listen because the argument that John had been making for over a year, namely, that American independence was inevitable, now appeared to be coming true. Both Dutch recognition of a sovereign American nation and a substantial loan that would restore American credit in the financial capitals of Europe, once so improbable, were now just a matter of resolving the diplomatic details.[60]

What's more, it had been a solo performance. Without any formal authority from the Continental Congress, John had assumed the initiative for a Dutch treaty, conducted all the negotiations by himself, and defied efforts by Vergennes to question his authority by orchestrating the campaign being waged in both Paris and Philadelphia to label him a diplomatic liability. For these highly personal reasons, John was excessively effusive in describing the Dutch treaty "as the happiest Event, and the greatest Action of my Life, past or future."[61]

Abigail was the principal beneficiary of his buoyant mood. She received more letters in one month than she had for the preceding two years.

The delays and losses at sea that had disrupted their correspondence before disappeared with the end of the war, so that they were able to recover some semblance of a conversation.[62] They concurred that the separation had gone on too long and could not continue, and the only question was whether she and Nabby should risk the Atlantic voyage to join John or he should come home. The answer to that question depended on the diplomatic duties, if any, the congress would require of him in the wake of his Dutch triumph. The issue was resolved in October 1782, when word arrived that the British were at last prepared to negotiate a peace. "I am now going to Paris," John wrote hurriedly from The Hague, "to another Furnace of Afflictions."[63]

The chief sources of affliction were Franklin and Vergennes, not the British negotiating teams, which arrived in Paris predisposed to acknowledge that their empire in North America was now lost. John could never forget or forgive Franklin's behind-the-scenes efforts to undermine his character with the Continental Congress, which he described as an "attempt at my assassination," but he vowed to swallow his pride: "As far as fate shall compel me to sit with him in public affairs, I shall treat him with decency and perfect impartibility." His problem with Vergennes also plucked at emotional chords that were still tormenting the Adams soul, but there was a serious substantive problem as well. The congress had made a point of instructing the American delegation to do nothing without the approval of the French government, which in practice meant Vergennes. John arrived in Paris convinced that such instructions were fatally misguided and that his highest diplomatic duty was to ignore them, which put him on a collision course with his superiors back in Philadelphia, as well as with both Franklin and Vergennes.[64]

Fortunately for John, the third member of the American negotiating team, John Jay, agreed with him. Neither as intellectually supple nor as psychologically inscrutable as Franklin, and more complacent and diffident than the ever-combustible Adams, Jay nevertheless was adept at grasping the strategic realities. In this case, he realized Adams was right in recognizing that American and French interests were not synonymous. The French, for example, would almost certainly make American interests hostage to their own imperial aspirations in Europe and the Caribbean.

Adams's urge to break ranks with the French was complicated by his personal loathing of Vergennes, whereas Jay's uncluttered vision was simply a case of a seasoned diplomat seeing America's abiding interests clearly. Franklin remained wedded to a sentimental French attachment rooted in the recognition that only French assistance had made American victory in the war possible. Adams and Jay were fully prepared to abandon the French and sign a separate peace with Great Britain.[65]

This was the crucial strategic decision, and even Franklin, albeit grudgingly, came to recognize its wisdom. Adams, on the other hand, found the act of violating the explicit instructions of the congress to be liberating: "It is glory to have broken such infamous orders," he wrote in his diary. "Infamous I say, for so will it appear to all posterity." Once freed of French entanglements, the negotiations proceeded remarkably swiftly and smoothly. Franklin, in fact, had already extracted major concessions in preliminary conversations with Richard Oswald, an elderly one-eyed British aristocrat who had made his fortune in the slave trade and harbored no illusions about the impossible task he had before him. Even before Adams arrived in Paris, the British had agreed to recognize American sovereignty, relinquish all claims to the land from the Atlantic to the Mississippi and from the Canadian border to Spanish Florida, and recognize American navigation rights on the Mississippi. These were huge concessions, but unless the British were prepared to resume the war—which they were not—their negotiators lacked the leverage to contest them.[66]

Only three outstanding issues remained, and they were resolved in daily sessions throughout November. First, the British insisted that prewar debts owed to British creditors, chiefly Virginia planters, be honored. Franklin and Jay resisted the claim, but Adams argued that the law was on the British side. His view prevailed, though how this provision would be enforced remained conveniently obscure. Second, the British sought to obtain compensation for loyalists whose property had been confiscated during the war. Adams joined Franklin and Jay in opposing this proposal, and the issue was eventually finessed by delegating the decision to the different states, where it was sure to languish forever. Third, the Americans sought to ensure the historic right of New England fishermen to catch cod off the Grand Banks of Newfoundland. For obvious reasons, Adams cared most about this question, stubbornly refused to accept any language that might compromise New England's interest, and successfully made it his signature issue.[67]

What was called the Provisional Treaty was signed on November 30, 1782. It was provisional because its terms applied only to America and Great Britain. Franklin received the thankless task of apprising Vergennes that the Americans had signed a separate peace, which he performed with his customary grace, even mustering up the nerve to request an additional French loan of six million livres.

Within the space of six months John had managed to play a leading role in two unmitigated diplomatic triumphs. Though he relished the singularity of his success in negotiating the Dutch treaty, the Treaty of Paris was by far the greater achievement. Indeed, the Treaty of Paris was destined to become the most consequential and lopsided victory in the history of American statecraft, achieving independence and control over the eastern third of the North American continent without making any major concessions to British designs.

Bad weather on the Atlantic delayed the treaty's arrival in Boston until April 1783. Abigail expressed pride in knowing that her husband had contributed to crafting a treaty that "sheaths the Hostile Sword and gives a pleasing presage that our spears may become pruning tools." A letter from John was already on the way, granting her unspoken but fondest wish. He had submitted his resignation to the congress, "and as soon as I shall receive their acceptance of it, I will embark for America."[68]

DEMONS AND DESTINATIONS

The problem with John's formulations—that he would come home as soon as the congress accepted his resignation—was that the congress refused to act. Rumors circulated in Philadelphia and Paris that he was under consideration for another European post, perhaps even to serve as America's first ambassador to the Court of St. James's in London.

But no official word of any sort arrived, leaving John to lament his equivocal status. "I had rather be employed in carting Street Dust and Marsh Mud," he complained to Abigail. She was equally equivocal, not knowing whether John was coming to her or whether she should make plans to go to him. The worst scenario was that they would pass each other on the Atlantic.[69]

The prospect of an ambassadorial assignment in London, so John claimed, did not interest him. "I shall be Slandered and plagued there, more than in France," he predicted. The British public was currently reeling from the realization that they had lost their American empire—copies of the Treaty of Paris were being burned in the streets—so the first American ambassador was certain to become a scapegoat. "In England," he wrote Abigail, "I should live the Life of a Man in a Barrell spiked with Nails." He shared a dream—actually a nightmare—with her, in which he envisioned himself running an endless gauntlet while the British press was "lashing him with scorpions all the Way." He claimed to find it inexplicable, given the obvious pitfalls that any American minister to Great Britain would face, that "in the Eyes of many [it is] the Apple of Paradise." All he wanted was for the congress to relieve him of his duties so he could take himself "out of the scramble."[70]

Abigail, who should have known better, was

predisposed to take these protestations at face value: "Few persons who so well Love domestic Life, as my Friend," she wrote, "have been called for so long a period to relinquish the enjoyment of it. Yet like the needle to the Pole, you invariably turn toward it, as the only point where you have fixed your happiness."[71]

This was naive. To be sure, John was utterly sincere about his desire for blissful retirement to Abigail's arms in Braintree. But the dominant "needle to the Pole," as she described his motivations, almost always pointed toward the next challenge in the public arena. Indeed, the very passion of his protestations about the London post was a clear sign that John's ambitions were vibrating so violently that he felt obliged to deny their very existence.

Throughout the spring of 1783, in addition to demonstrating a powerful penchant for denial, he started to swing between extreme expressions of his diplomatic achievements and equally extreme, indeed quasi-paranoid, statements about an invisible army of enemies plotting to do him in. On the former score, he wrote Abigail that his diplomatic successes in the Netherlands and Paris were unprecedented, claiming to have rendered "Such Services as were never rendered by any other minister in Europe, the most critical, important and decisive services." In the journal he submitted to the Continental Congress to document his diplomatic doings, he included a gratuitous compliment by Vergennes to the effect that John Adams had become the George Washington of European statecraft. When read aloud in the congress, this embarrassing piece of puffery produced gales of laughter, most especially from those delegates already predisposed to believe that Franklin's conclusion was correct, namely, that his diplomatic colleague on occasion seemed slightly out of his mind.[72]

Swollen thoughts about his own significance then led to exaggerated fears that unseen enemies were plotting to belittle his achievements. "Millions of Contrivances," he complained to Abigail, "by some invisible spirit" had made him the target of "Arrows shot in darkness designed to render an honest man's Life uncomfortable." And the more he thought about it, the more he concluded that his "french and franklinite" enemies were behind the scheme to make him minister to England, where he would encounter perpetual persecution in what was, in effect, a diplomatic graveyard.[73]

Though Abigail was the most astute student of John's psyche on the planet, and the only person capable of exorcising his demons when they rose up with such frightening force, she was an ocean away, dealing with demons of her own. One was her fear of the Atlantic crossing that, try as she might, she could not conquer. Another was the apprehension that she would embarrass her husband and herself by cutting an awkward figure in Paris or London society. "I have not a wish to join you in a scene of life so different from that in which I have been educated," she exclaimed. "I have so little of the Ape about me, that I have refused every publick invitation to figure in the Gay World, and sequestered myself in this Humble cottage." While they both agreed that their separation had to end, which meant that either she had to go to him or he had to come to her, Abigail's preference was clear: "I have considered your invitation to me, the arguments for and against it, with all the deliberations I am mistress of," she told him, "and upon the whole, your return here, is the object my Heart pants for."[74]

She had already made a more pointed argument. His recent letter had revealed a man worn down by his duties, fatigued to an extent that gave her cause for worry about his physical and mental health. He himself had recognized, she noted, that "the enveyed embassy to a certain Island, is surrounded with so many thorns, that the Beauty and fragrance of the Rose, would be but a small compensation for the wounds which might be felt in the gathering and wearing of it." Why lust after an appointment so obviously destined for disappointment? After all, lingering on the European stage could only dilute the glory he had already achieved. "The Golden Fleese is won," she observed, so his legacy would be best served by putting a decisive end to his diplomatic career and coming home.[75]

This was excellent advice, but John could not hear it. What Abigail described as the "Golden Fleese" was for him more like the Holy Grail, which by definition kept receding beyond his grasp. His own insatiable ambitions were masked behind an equally bottomless sense of duty, which obliged him to remain poised to answer whatever call—be it in Paris or London—that the congress made. He persuaded himself that he really had no choice in the matter, which in turn meant that Abigail had no choice but to abandon her preference: "Come to Europe with Nabby as soon as possible," he urged. "I am in earnest. I cannot be happy or tolerable without you." Abigail responded with somewhat reluctant acceptance: "My present determination is to tarry at home this winter," she wrote in November 1783, "and if I cannot prevail upon you to return to me in the Spring—you well know that I may be drawn to you." She was simultaneously honoring her husband's wishes and keeping her options open.[76]

Once she realized that John's political agenda was nonnegotiable, that he would never resign as long as the possibility of a new diplomatic assignment in Europe existed, she decided to discover whether such an assignment was likely. She wrote to Elbridge Gerry, the old family friend currently serving in the Continental Congress, to find out if John was under consideration for the London appointment. Gerry informed her that the London job was still problematic for John, but that it was virtually certain that he would be appointed, along with Franklin and Jefferson, as minister plenipotentiary in Europe for three years. Despite opposition from certain southern delegates, there was little chance that he would be recalled.[77]

This information made her decision, if not easy, at least foreordained. In January 1784, she made arrangements to send Charles and Tommy to live with her sister in Haverhill. "I shall immediately set about putting all our affairs in such a train," she apprised John, "as that I may be able to leave them in the spring." She still felt terrified about the voyage, and still believed that John's decision to linger in Europe was misguided, but her duty as a wife now needed to be aligned with his duty as a diplomat. She vowed to banish all "Idle Specters" and embrace the fact that "the desires and requests of my Friend are a Law to me." At forty years of age, she had never before ventured beyond the Boston area.[78]

Last-minute complications regarding care of the farm, along with shifting weather patterns on the Atlantic, delayed the departure until the summer. (Interestingly, she left the household in the hands of Phoebe Abdee, a former slave, who had become a dependable member of the household staff.) On June 20, 1784, Abigail and Nabby at last boarded the **Active,** bound for London. For the first time in her life, Abigail kept a diary. "Our ship dirty, our selves sick," it began, and she then proceeded to document her conviction that the conditions on board any oceangoing vessel were incompatible with a woman's integrity, chiefly because of the prevalence of dirt and the absence of privacy. A cow she had brought along for milk was injured during a storm and "was accordingly consigned to a watery grave." But despite her protestations—"the ship itself is a partial prison"—the voyage proved blessedly uneventful and uncommonly short. She and Nabby disembarked on July 21. John Quincy, just back from St. Petersburg, joined them in London a week later. It required another week for John to arrive from The Hague. He claimed to feel "twenty years younger than I was yesterday." She described him being "as happy as a lord!" After a separation that had put the partnership to the severest test it would ever face, they were, at long last, together again.[79]

CHAPTER FOUR

1784-89

"Every man of this nation [France] is
an actor, and every woman an actress."

ABIGAIL ACTUALLY SAW John in a painting before she
saw him in the flesh. While waiting for him to join
her in London from The Hague, she visited the stu-
dio of John Singleton Copley, after Benjamin West
the reigning American artist in England. Copley
had depicted John at the apparent zenith of his
diplomatic career, holding a scroll—presumably the
Treaty of Paris—while standing before a table covered with maps of the newly acquired American
empire east of the Mississippi. A globe stood off to
the side, suggesting that the emergence of an independent America had international implications. It
was a picture that glorified the stunning American
arrival into the world of nations, and it made John
Adams the preferred face of that glory.

Abigail's only recorded comment—namely, that
it struck her as "a good likeness"—was less innocu-

ous than it sounded, since John had warned her that his crushing workload and prolonged illness in Holland had extracted such a physical toll that she might not recognize him. Now that seemed unlikely. But the portrait was not just a physical rendering of her long-absent husband; it was also a visual endorsement of his epochal triumph. Copley seemed to confirm that all of John's fondest dreams and deepest ambitions had been fulfilled at last. In that sense, Abigail was looking at a painting that declared all of her own personal sacrifices through more than four years of loneliness and isolation had paid a public dividend, both for her country and for her fame-seeking husband. No one was going to paint her in equivalently brilliant colors, but in the privacy of her soul she could feel that her domestic version of patriotism had proved justified.[1]

The justification, however, had come at a price. Because of John's diplomatic duties, they had been together less than four months over the past six years. During that time, John's periodic failures as a correspondent struck Abigail as a violation of their covenant as a couple. And his refusal to leave his European post, despite her pleadings to do so, constituted a clear statement that his ambitions were more potent urges than his obligations as a husband. John could counter that if Abigail had insisted that he return to her, he would have done so. In truth, she had come pretty close to doing just that, but he was too distracted by his duties to hear her. And she was too proud to couch her requests in the form of demands that exposed her personal desperation.

From Abigail's perspective, then, damage had been done to their previously impregnable bond. Her major reason for joining him abroad was to repair that damage by recovering their lost rhythms in the form of those mutual touches, glances, and banterings only possible when together. All the evidence suggests that John was completely oblivious to Abigail's emotional agenda. He was so confident of her bottomless strength and devotion that it never even occurred to him that she harbored vulnerabilities that needed his attention. He presumed that they would simply pick up where they had left off.

In the end, that is precisely what happened. Perhaps the best way to put it is that Abigail and John spent the next four years, first in Paris and then more enduringly in London, being together in a constant and unrelenting way that seemed almost designed to compensate for the previous separation. It helped that a diplomat's wife was expected to accompany her husband on all ceremonial and social occasions, so they were effectively regarded as a political team, which gave Abigail a public role she did not have when John was laboring in the Continental Congress. Her unofficial status as an advisor and confidante was now the norm rather than the exception, so she was actually expected to stay abreast of ongoing diplomatic issues and controversies. She did not need to conceal her intelligence.

For several overlapping reasons, virtually all the outstanding foreign policy problems that John hoped to resolve soon showed themselves to be inherently intractable. Franklin, whose sense of timing was a version of perfect pitch, announced that there was nothing more for him to do in Paris, then sailed home in 1785, in plenty of time to become available as a delegate to the Constitutional Convention and make some more history. John, on the other hand, found himself trapped in the European sideshow, attending endless ceremonies at court and lavish but pointless dinner parties, all with Abigail at his side, while the truly significant debates that would shape the future of the American republic were occurring across the Atlantic.

To say that nothing of diplomatic substance happened during their four years abroad would be misleading. John did negotiate a commercial treaty with Prussia. And he used his excellent contacts with Dutch bankers to arrange several more loans that allowed the American government to consolidate its European debts and thereby affect at least the appearance of fiscal responsibility. But the main events were less visible and more intimate. Abigail and John were together virtually every hour of the day and night: dining together, socializing together, watching Nabby and John Quincy mature together, reading together, touring Paris, London, and the English countryside together, sleeping together. Never before in their twenty-year marriage had they enjoyed such prolonged and routinized proximity. And they would never again experience such abiding closeness until their retirement years at Quincy.

This chapter in their story as a couple, then, is rich with irony. For as they made their way through the ornate etiquette and swirling splendor of Europe's most cosmopolitan capitals, lived in luxurious mansions with small armies of servants, and bowed and curtsied to kings and queens, their major diplomatic achievement was the recovery of their own emotional connection. They learned to love each other at an even deeper level than before and locked that love in place, and nothing they experienced for the rest of their lives ever threatened their mutual trust.

THE EDUCATION OF ABIGAIL

The original plan was for Abigail and Nabby to join John and John Quincy at The Hague, then travel together to Paris. But John changed his mind, sending John Quincy ahead to London with a note to

Abigail, telling her to "stay where you are and amuse yourself by seeing what you can, until you see me." Abigail claimed that when she first saw John Quincy, who was now seventeen, she would not have recognized him, except for his eyes. Otherwise, her boy had become a man. The reunion with John was surely an emotional occasion, which she related to Mary Cranch, her sister, as being beyond description: "You know my dear sister that poets and painters wisely draw a veil over those scenes which surpass the pen or the pencil of the other." John Quincy was dispatched to purchase a carriage to take them to the English coast, along with a copy of Samuel Johnson's **Lives of the Poets**, so they could take turns reading to each other during the trip.[2]

Their destination was Auteuil, a village located on the banks of the Seine four miles west of Paris and one mile south of Franklin's quarters at Passy. John had rented an enormous villa, a three-story limestone of forty or fifty rooms—no one was quite sure—that also featured a huge ballroom able to accommodate five hundred guests as well as a small theater "gone to decay." Abigail's favorite adornment was the garden: five acres of orange trees, grapevines, flowers in constant bloom, a fishpond, and a somewhat dilapidated summerhouse. The villa came equipped with eight servants, each of whom, she quickly discovered, "had certain etiquette, and one will by no means intrude upon the department of the other." The cook, for example, would not wash dishes, and the hairdresser would not sweep.[3]

For Abigail, who had spent her entire married life in a six-room cottage, it was nothing short of overwhelming. She was, to be sure, an extremely well-read woman who had thereby traveled much in Braintree, but she had never experienced conspicuous luxury on such a majestic scale. Her first instinct was to filter the ostentation through the austere lens of a New England housewife, which produced a combination of bewilderment and disgust.

Efforts to improve efficiency by requesting the servants to perform multiple chores failed completely. She quickly gave up trying to perform certain chores herself, since the servants found it insulting. As a result, since her daily regime back in Braintree had required a good deal of physical exertion, her more indolent habits produced a sudden increase in weight. "I suffer through a want of exercise," she explained to her sister, "and grow too fat." It took several months for her to become accustomed to having her hair dressed every day and to applying rouge to her cheeks for a stroll in the garden with Nabby.[4]

Such splendor, she was at pains to insist, came at a moral cost: "If you ask me what is the Business of life here," she explained to Mercy Otis Warren, "I answer Pleasure . . . It is a matter of great speculation to me, when these People labour." However indispensable French economic and military assistance had been to the American cause—and she was fully prepared to acknowledge that fact—France more than England struck her as the epitome of European aristocratic decadence.[5]

And the epitome of French decadence was Madame Helvétius, the sixty-five-year-old widow of the distinguished French philosopher, whom Abigail encountered at a dinner party hosted by Franklin soon after her encampment at Auteuil. Even within the flamboyant code of the French aristocracy, Madame Helvétius was considered eccentric. Abigail watched with incredulity as she asked the guests, "How do I look?"; then kissed Franklin on both cheeks, then the forehead; then kissed her lapdog, who proceeded to wet the floor, which she cleaned up with the bottom of her dress. If Madame Helvétius's goal was to appear outrageous, which it was, she hit her mark with Abigail: "I hope however to find amongst the French Ladies manners more consistent with my ideas of decency," she wrote to her niece, "or I shall be a mere recluse."[6]

John's diplomatic duties made any attempt at solitary confinement impossible. The wife of an American minister was expected to make calls on the wives of all the other ministers to the French court, an exercise in diplomatic etiquette that Abigail performed only grudgingly. "I have not been very fond of so awkward a situation as going to visit ladies," she complained, "merely to make my dumb compliments, and receive theirs in return."[7]

She was accustomed to making small talk and sharing gossip with women friends back in Braintree, but the stilted official conversations with the ministerial wives were not really conversations at all, more like theatrical performances in which one was supposed to speak the lines from a script drafted by some mindless courtier. Abigail acknowledged that French women had developed a disarming proficiency in this exceedingly languid and arched style, had in fact become "mistresses of the art of insinuation and persuasion" in which words were less important than dramatic facial expressions and sweeping physical gestures, just the sort of operatic style that Madame Helvétius had perfected to the point of parody. Abigail was not very good at this kind of hauteur, which struck her as inherently false and hollow. "So that it may with truth be said," she observed to a cousin back home, "every man of this nation is an actor, and every woman an actress."[8]

One role that John's position forced her to play was hostess: "It is necessary in this country for a Gentleman in a publick character to entertain Company once a week," she explained to her sister, "tho it would take 2 years of an American ministers Sallery to furnish the equipage of plate which you will find upon the tables of all the Foreign ministers here." Most of the other European ministers to the

French court were titled aristocrats with inherited wealth, which permitted lavish standards for entertaining that Abigail could not begin to match on the budget afforded by John's salary. She hoped that the quality of conversation would compensate for more modest accoutrements—the Spanish minister had eighty servants to her eight—and that inviting guests like the naval hero John Paul Jones might impress her guests more than the number of courses or the elegance of the silverware. (Abigail herself found Jones surprisingly ordinary: "I expected to have seen a Rough Stout warlike Roman. Instead of that, I should think of wraping him up in cotton and putting him in my pocket, than sending him to contend with Cannon Ball.") But no matter how modest the fare at her dinner parties, she always worried afterward that she had wasted money that should have been saved for her sons' college education.[9]

Paris invoked in her the same double-edged reaction that John had offered at his first exposure. On the one hand, the art, architecture, and pervasive mood of refinement justified its reputation as the cultural capital of Europe. On the other, such luxuries were inevitably linked with indolent habits and political corruption. This was the Adams version of civilization and its discontents, and while it had a discernibly moralistic and judgmental dimension, with deep roots in the religious traditions of

New England, it reflected Abigail and John's understanding of the way consolidated wealth simultaneously made great achievements in the arts possible and undermined the disciplined habits that had generated the wealth in the first place. "Riches always create luxury," as she put it, "and luxury always leads to Idleness, Indolence and effeminacy, which stifles every noble purpose and whithers the blossom of genius."[10]

Unlike John, Abigail tended to focus on how the moral corruption of Paris affected women. For example, she was shocked to learn that there were fifty-two thousand registered prostitutes in Paris, which required its women of the night to sign up on the public rolls. "Blush O, my sex," she exclaimed to her sister when she reported the numbers. Her powerful maternal instincts were challenged when she learned that the largest foundling hospital in the city accepted six thousand abandoned infants annually and that one-third of them died. "I have been credibly informed," she wrote her sister, "that one half of the children annually born in this immense City of Paris, are **enfans troives** [i.e., abandoned]." She claimed that the only French woman she knew who took her duties as a wife and mother seriously was the marquise de Lafayette, who was considered strange because she was simultaneously "a French lady and fond of her Husband!!!"[11]

The one area of Parisian culture that most confounded her was the theater, especially the opera. The entire Adams family—Abigail, John, Nabby, and John Quincy—attended an early performance of **The Marriage of Figaro** by Beaumarchais, which challenged the pretensions of the French aristocracy by exposing its presumed superiority as a mere accident of birth and by making Figaro, a valet, more admirable than his noble master. Abigail applauded the message, but acknowledged that, as a medium, the French theater celebrated the aristocratic values that Figaro criticized. She was especially shocked by the blatant sexuality of the dances: "Girls clothed in the thinnest Silk . . . Springing two feet from the floor poising themselves in the air . . . and as perfectly showing their Garters and drawers, as tho no petticoat had been worn." Nevertheless, she kept going to the performances, often with Nabby alongside, obviously enchanted by theatrical productions that would have been banned in Boston.

Gradually, she found herself lowering her guard and succumbing to the seductive magic of the stage: "I have found my taste reconciling itself to habits, customs and fashions, which at first disgusted me," she confessed to her sister. "Shall I speak a Truth and say that repeatedly seeing these Dances has worn off that disgust which I first felt, and that I see them now with pleasure?" She was not sure whether she should feel guilty about her moral backsliding or proud of her newfound appreciation of a different world. If her New England conscience needed reassurance, she could—and did—tell herself that regular attendance at the theater markedly improved her French.[12]

Abigail's infatuation with the Parisian theater proved the exception to the rule, which was to measure the excesses and extravagances of French culture against her own austere standards and find them sinfully lacking. "My Heart and Soul," she assured her uncle, "is more American than ever." She apprised her sister that no matter how exciting her social life might sound, it was like eating a box of chocolates, an indulged habit that soon wore thin: "I take no pleasure in a life of ceremony and parade," she explained. "I had rather dine in my little room in Braintree with my family and a set of chosen old Friends, than all the Counts and Countesses." If not quite a judgment rendered in the Puritan-in-Babylon mode, it was a clear statement of preference by a self-confident New England woman for the simpler virtues that her entire life had come to embody.[13]

If the core of those simpler virtues was family, and for Abigail it surely was, day-to-day life at Auteuil afforded a surprisingly ample opportunity to recover the old domestic rhythms despite the diplomatic and social obligations. Most elementally, Abigail and John were at long last living under the same roof. The accommodations were much more capacious than the Quincy cottage, permitting Abigail to enjoy a full room of her own, not just a closet, overlooking the gorgeous gardens. The two older children, Nabby and John Quincy, were right down the hall, periodically popping in to interrupt her letter writing with a question about the evening's agenda or the availability of a book.

The family made a point of eating breakfast together every morning; then John Quincy would retreat to his room to study Horace and Tacitus, which John would quiz him on that evening. Nabby and Abigail would often take walks together in the garden, exchanging gossip about the apparently embedded inefficiency of the servants, upcoming plays at the Parisian theaters, or the latest outrage of Madame Helvétius. In one letter Abigail described the scene: she at a table next to the fire, John at the other end of the table reading Plato, Nabby sewing, and John Quincy dropping in to ask John's assistance on an algebra problem.[14]

There they were, surrounded by servants, ensconced amid aristocratic splendor, all, save John Quincy, still trying to master a foreign language, but interacting in the old and ordinary ways as the Adams family. For John, it was a slice of serenity. For Abigail, it was heaven.

THE JEFFERSONIAN CONNECTION

The most frequent guest at Auteuil, so frequent that at times he seemed a permanent resident, was Thomas Jefferson, now a widower after the recent death of his wife. He had been chosen to replace Franklin as American minister to France but had fallen ill upon arrival, a victim of the damp French weather that forced him to undergo what he called "seasoning." John had applauded his appointment, recalling their political partnership in the Continental Congress in the heady days of 1776, and let everyone know that he still regarded Jefferson as "an excellent hand" and "the same wise and prudent Man and Steady Patriot."[15]

Abigail extended him an open invitation to regard their sumptuous villa as his second home, an offer that Jefferson found as irresistible as it was generous. Familiarity, in this instance, bred just the opposite of contempt, for once folded into the domestic routine of the Adams family, Jefferson became, as Abigail described him, "the only person with whom my companion could associate with perfect freedom and unreserve." Many years later, recalling Jefferson's ongoing conversations with John Quincy at Auteuil, John reminded Jefferson that "he was as much your son as mine."[16]

The Adams-Jefferson partnership was destined to become one of the most consequential, tumultuous, and poignant relationships in American political history, with an ending that no novelist would dare to make up. And for at least two reasons, the French chapter in their fifty-year story of cooperation and competition proved particularly significant. First, Adams and Jefferson bonded as friends and not just as diplomatic colleagues, which ever after gave their political relationship an intimate edge that cut through their deep differences over no less a question than the true meaning of the American Revolution. Second, the first indication of those profound differences, which were both ideological and temperamental in origin, became visible at this time, as they worked together to coordinate a coherent American foreign policy toward Europe.

Their major mission as American ministers was to negotiate treaties of amity and commerce with as many European nations as possible. Jefferson's mind worked from the theoretical downward to the practical, starting with his own vision of the preferred policy, which was often quite visionary, then trying to make it fit the actual historical conditions. With regard to international trade, for example, he described his beau ideal as the permanent elimination of all tariffs and embargoes, in effect the creation of a global marketplace committed to free trade, unencumbered by national restrictions of any sort. He proposed that all commercial negotiations with European powers, most especially Great Britain, proceed from these utopian assumptions, which he was convinced were destined to shape the international economy of the future. It was Jefferson's anticipation of globalization.[17]

John's thoughts flowed in precisely the opposite direction. He began with the assumption that nations viewed the international marketplace through the prism of their own sovereign interests. Great Britain, for example, already enjoyed the lion's share of American exports, so it had no incentive to drop import duties or make concessions to American merchants or shippers: "We must not, my Friend, be the Bubbles of our own Liberal Sentiments," he lectured Jefferson. "If we cannot obtain reciprocal Liberality, we must adopt reciprocal Prohibitions." Jefferson's romantic prescriptions were surely beautiful, but their implementation must await arrival of the Second Coming, when all men became angels at last.[18]

In the meantime, as American negotiators they must impose their own restrictions and protections, lest European powers "take an ungenerous Advantage of our Simplicity and philosophical Liberality." Moreover, as the British negotiators kept reminding them, the American government as currently constituted under the Articles of Confederation refused to recognize federal authority over foreign trade, which was retained by the sovereign states. This fatal flaw rendered all their efforts at negotiating treaties, to include Jefferson's grand scheme, essentially futile. Best, then, to launch their diplomatic effort together, hope for a miracle, but realize from the start that they were on a fool's errand.[19]

The same kind of intellectual collision also occurred when they attempted to solve the problem posed by the Barbary pirates. Muslim corsairs sailing out of Tripoli, Tunis, and Algiers were plundering European and American vessels in the western Mediterranean and eastern Atlantic, seizing the cargoes as prizes, sending the passengers and crew into slavery, then demanding exorbitant ransom for their release. It was a clear case of state-sponsored terrorism, though when Adams and Jefferson met with the ambassador of Tripoli to demand an explanation for such outrages, they reported that he had a ready answer: "The Ambassador apprised us that it was founded on the Laws of the Prophet [misspelled as "Profit" in the original], that it was written in their Koran, that all nations who should not have acknowledged their authority were sinners, that it was their right and duty to make war upon them wherever they could be found, and to make slaves of all they could take as prisoners."[20]

Jefferson's response to this glorified version of blackmail once again began on the high moral ground and then reasoned downward from his own elevated ideals. The Barbary pirates were nothing less than international criminals, so to negotiate with them on their terms only made America complicitous in their barbarism. Instead, Jefferson proposed an alliance of the United States and all European states victimized by these pirates and the creation of a joint naval force in the Mediterranean to destroy their corsairs, ravage their ports, and put an end, once and for all, to their savagery. He was suggesting an early version of NATO.[21]

John concurred that this was the honorable course of action, but then confronted Jefferson with three inconvenient facts. First, the European powers, so jealous of each other, would never agree to such an alliance. Second, the cost of such an enterprise, which he calculated at $500,000, would be larger than the requested ransom and more than the American government would ever approve. And third, Jefferson's plan presupposed the presence of a potent American naval presence in the Mediterranean, but the awkward truth was that no American navy existed.[22]

John was at pains to assure Jefferson that the day might come when the American government was capable of mounting a successful campaign against the North African terrorists, but that day lay somewhere in the distant future. In the meantime, "we ought not to fight them at all unless we determine to fight them forever." The only realistic option, then, as unpalatable as it was unavoidable, was to pay the ransom. "You make the result differently from what I do," Jefferson responded, adding that "it is of no consequence, as I have nothing to say in the decision," meaning that, as the senior American minister in Europe, John's judgment was sovereign.

Oddly, the sordid business of paying a bribe ended on a comical note. In negotiating the size of the ransom payments with the ambassador of Tripoli, John managed to talk him down by blowing larger smoke rings from a huge Turkish pipe, which prompted the ambassador to exclaim, "Monsieur, vous êtes un Turc."

In their early diplomatic collaborations it became abundantly clear that the Jefferson-Adams team embodied the classic contrast between idealistic and realistic approaches to American foreign policy. The two former colleagues in Philadelphia, who had agreed about the inevitability of American independence, discovered in Paris that they disagreed fundamentally about the direction an independent America should take. It was also clear that their differences were somewhat obscured because Jefferson routinely deferred to John's seniority and experience. If there was a Jefferson-Adams team, Jefferson at this time saw himself as the junior partner.[23]

His relationship with Abigail was also deferential, though in a more playful and flirtatious manner. Abigail nursed Jefferson through the flulike symptoms that afflicted him during the winter and early spring of 1785, when he spent most afternoons with the Adams family at Auteuil, tutoring John Quincy in mathematics and swapping stories with Abigail about everything from the bizarre etiquette of the French court to Nabby's new French hairdo. Abigail was also the conversational link between policy discussions, such as the interest rate charged by the Dutch bankers, and domestic topics, such as the current price of linen. She was the first woman that Jefferson came to know well who combined the traditional virtues of a wife and mother with the sharp mind and tongue of a fully empowered accomplice in her husband's career. The gender categories that Jefferson carried around in his head envisioned men and women occupying wholly separate spheres. Abigail's androgynous personality confounded his categories.

Their conversations at Auteuil were obviously unrecorded, but the letters they exchanged after the Adams family moved to London do allow us to recover some themes: for example, Jefferson's efforts to engage Abigail's several sides, and Abigail's willingness to confront Jefferson in a way that he had never before experienced from a woman.[24]

They shared a running joke about the misguided arrogance of the British press, which reported, for example, that Franklin, upon his return to America, had been stoned to death by irate citizens, who blamed him for severing the connection with the British Empire, which they now deeply regretted. Jefferson noted "a blind story here of someone attempting to assassinate your king [George III]." He hoped it was untrue, joking that "no man upon earth has my prayers for his continuance in life more sincerely than him. He is truly the American Messias." Abigail explained that all stories originating in the British press were lies, "if it were not too rough a term for a lady to use, I would say false as Hell, but I would submit one not less expressive and say false as English."[25]

Many of their letters fluctuated between fashionable frivolities and serious exchanges about European politics and American foreign policy, again all dashed off in a conspicuously playful style. Jefferson explained that he had decided not to send her a small statuette of Venus for her dining table, since "I thought it out of taste to have two at the table at the same time." For her part, Abigail apologized for asking him to survey the Parisian shops for black lace and evening shoes, which was "a little like putting Hercules to the distaff."[26]

On the more substantive side, Abigail felt an obligation to keep Jefferson abreast of reports from America reproduced in the Boston press concerning the impact the British military garrison on the Great Lakes had on the fur trade, the failure of the Confederation Congress to fashion a responsible fiscal policy, and the decision by Massachusetts to close its ports to British imports. Jefferson presumed that John and his secretary were too busy to convey such information, "so they left it to you [Abigail] to give me the news." Noting her command of the issues, he claimed that "I would rather receive it from you than them." It is difficult to imagine Jefferson saying this about any other woman he had ever known.[27]

When news reached London and Paris of a popular insurrection in western Massachusetts, later dubbed Shays's Rebellion after one of its leaders, a spirited debate ensued about whether it represented a serious threat to the embryonic American government. Jefferson concluded that the threat was exaggerated and shared the reasons for that conclusion with Abigail: "The spirit of resistance to government is so valuable on certain occasions," he observed, "that I wish it to be always kept alive . . . I like a little rebellion now and then. It is like a storm in the atmosphere." Abigail thought such liberal sentiments were only possible from someone safely ensconced in Paris, far from the trauma. She lectured Jefferson on the very real danger such popular uprisings posed for political stability, an essential condition that Jefferson seemed to take for granted. "Ignorant, wrestles desperados, without conscience or principles," she warned, "have led a deluded multitude to follow their standard." They should be punished rather than pardoned, an outcome that Jefferson would be well-advised to embrace.[28]

Finally, Abigail drew upon her own experience as a mother to question Jefferson's demeanor as a father. When they were together at Auteuil, she had questioned Jefferson's judgment in sending his eldest daughter, Martha, nicknamed Patsy, to a Catholic convent in Paris, which struck Abigail as an abdication of his parental responsibilities. Then, partly as a result of her prodding, Jefferson decided to bring his younger daughter, Maria, called Polly, over to France from Virginia, and Abigail agreed to meet her at the London docks. Polly, who was nine years old, was accompanied by a fourteen-year-old mulatto slave named Sally Hemings, described by Abigail as "quite a child" but soon destined to strike Jefferson as a good deal more than that.

Abigail almost immediately began to bombard Jefferson with pointed accusations of parental negligence. Apparently quite the charmer, Polly won Abigail's heart right away. "I never saw so intelligent a countenance in a child before," she wrote Jefferson, "and the pleasure she has given me is an ample compensation for any little services I have been able to render her." But it quickly became clear that Polly had no knowledge of her father, not even what he looked like: "I showed her your picture. She says she cannot know it, but how could she when she could not know you."[29]

It got worse. Jefferson wrote to explain that diplomatic duties made it impossible for him to leave Paris, so he was sending his chief household servant, Petit, to fetch Polly. Abigail minced no words: "Tho she says she does not know you," Abigail apprised Jefferson, Polly "depended upon you coming for her. She told me this morning that as she had left all her friends in Virginia to come over the ocean to see you, she did think that you would have taken pains to have come here for her, and not send a man [Petit] whom she cannot understand. I express her own words."[30]

She could not resist one parting shot. Jefferson's decision to place Patsy in a convent had always mystified and disappointed her. Now that Polly was also joining her father, "I hope that she will not lose her fine spirits within the walls of a convent too, to which I own I have many, perhaps false prejudices." Even stronger than her prejudices against Catholicism were convictions Abigail harbored about the obligations of parenthood. She made sure to let Jefferson know that he did not meet her standard.[31]

Looking back, with all the advantages of hindsight, one can see clearly that bonds of mutual affection were forged between Jefferson and the Adams family during their time together in Europe. But one can also see with equivalent clarity that the seeds of an eventual conflict based on deep-rooted ideological and temperamental differences were present from the start. For now, however, the shared intimacies blotted out the latent differences. In May 1785, when the Adamses departed for London, Jefferson reported that he was "in the dumps" and that "my afternoons hang heavily on me." John wrote from the road to Calais, saying not to fret, because the Jefferson mind was traveling with them in the form of his recently published **Notes on the State of Virginia,** which he and Abigail were reading out loud to each other in the carriage.[32]

MAROONED IN LONDON

Both John and Abigail realized that they were entering enemy territory. The British press had greeted the news of John's appointment as American ambassador much like the Vatican would have greeted the appointment of Martin Luther, for the very man who had played a leading role in instigating the American rebellion, then again in negotiating the loss of the British Empire in North America, now must be extended the civilities of the British court and society. From the very start, Abigail noticed that her husband's presence "bites them like a serpent and stings them like an ader." The large numbers of loyalists in exile, who could only explain their misfortune as the result of a diabolical plot by a few unscrupulous American agitators, regarded John as one of the radical ringleaders. One loyalist editorial proposed that, instead of being introduced to royalty at court, he should be sent to the gallows and hanged for treason.[33]

After attending a ball in his honor at the French ambassador's residence, John recorded his impressions in his diary: "These People cannot look me in the Face. There is a conscious Guilt and Shame in their Countenances, when they look at me. They feel they have behaved ill, and that I am sensible of it." This was a quite charitable interpretation. Most Britons were having considerable difficulty digesting the calamitous loss they had recently suffered, and hatred rather than guilt was the common reaction toward the most palpable reminder of their humiliation. Throughout their three-year stay in London, this abiding hostility remained the prevailing if unspoken opinion at all the official functions that Abigail and John attended. The sense of isolation this generated, or perhaps the sense of siege they felt from the British press, only drove them closer together. There was no one else to rely upon.[34]

The one exception to this pattern, though hardly someone to count on, was none other than George III himself. As John reported to John Jay, the interview to present his credentials before the British king, whom he had once described as a tyrant unfit to govern a free people, went remarkably well. According to John's account of the interview, after he had made his introductions, George III showed himself to be a gracious sovereign: "The circumstances of this interview are so extraordinary," George III observed, "the language you have now used is so extremely proper . . . that I must say that I not only receive with pleasure the assurance of friendly dispositions of the United States, but that I am very glad that the choice has fallen upon you to be their minister." This stroking of John's psyche had the desired effect, for ever after, even when George III's apparent madness made him the butt of jokes in America, John defended his integrity.[35]

Abigail, for her part, remained more skeptical. After she had waited for over four hours at court to be introduced to the king and queen, George III asked her if she had taken a walk that day—the standard question he had just asked all guests. "I could have told him," Abigail wrote her sister, "that I had been all the morning preparing for him." The chief advantage of overcrowded court ceremonies that featured the king, she observed, "is that you may go away when you please without disturbing anybody."[36]

London struck Abigail as less visually impressive than Paris, but more livable. (It helped that everyone spoke English.) Their quarters at Grosvenor Square were less palatial than the Auteuil villa, though they once again employed multiple servants, who seemed more disposed to share domestic duties than their French counterparts. The London ladies she was required to call upon wore less rouge than the Parisians, and cultivated a more subdued, less theatrical, style. There was no London version of Madame Helvétius.

But the urge to shock was replaced, so Abigail thought, by the desire to bore, which was institutionalized, she observed, in "Supremely stupid card games at all official events and parties," and in the marathon waiting lines that kept all guests at court standing around for several hours until the royal family reached them and spoke a few meaningless words. In the end, despite their differences, Abigail found the aristocratic societies of Paris and London variations on the same degenerate theme: "All is lost in ceremony and Parade, in venality and corruption, in Gamery and debauchery, amongst those who stile themselves . . . the fashionable World."[37]

Although there is no record of their private conversations, Abigail and John clearly worked out their responses to life in London together, both as a married couple isolated within an openly anti-American environment and as a diplomatic team determined to speak about matters of policy with one voice. Indeed, they often used almost identical language to describe their reactions to distinctive features of English life, almost always finding them inferior to the American version.

For example, Abigail wrote her sister about the ornate and highly manicured English gardens, which represented a cultivated and tightly organized kind of man-made beauty. But she found the wilder and more wide-open American landscape more appealing because it was more natural. Meanwhile, John confided to his diary that the fashionably arranged English parks and fields were symptomatic of an older European world that made a virtue of confinement or limited space: "But Nature has done greater things and furnished noble Materials there [i.e., America]," where "the Rivers, Mountains, Valleys are all laid out upon a larger scale."[38]

The same anti-English echo resounded from their different sides of the gender divide. Abigail thought that American women were more attractive than English women, once all the makeup and hairdressings were removed from the equation. The most beautiful woman in all of London, she declared, was Anne Bingham, the famously beguiling wife of the immensely wealthy William Bingham of Philadelphia. "I have not seen a lady in England who can bear a comparison with Mrs. Bingham . . . who taken altogether is the finest woman I ever saw."[39]

John preferred more masculine comparisons. English farmers kept bragging about the superiority of their techniques for fertilizing the soil. But John insisted that American farmers in Pennsylvania produced larger crop yields per acre and, a bit of special pleading, that the quality of manure he spread over his fields at Braintree surpassed anything used on English farms. During a visit from Jefferson in the spring of 1786, when they spent a week together touring the English countryside, John was unimpressed by an English artisan who claimed to have devised a new way to bend wood for making wheels. He was sure that farmers in New Jersey had perfected an even better technique, and Jefferson, chiming right in, speculated that they had gotten their idea from a passage in the **Iliad,** "because ours are the only farmers who can read Homer."[40]

Such partisan pleading for American landscapes, American women, American farmers, even American manure, could sound almost laughingly provincial, and at least on one occasion, Abigail felt compelled to parody her own excesses: "Do you know," she wrote her sister, "that European birds have not half the melody of ours, nor is their fruit half so sweet, or their flowers half so fragrant, or their Manners half so pure, or their people half so Virtuous? But keep this to yourself." Isolated as they were among an English population that resented their presence, and routinely subjected to ridicule in the British press, Abigail and John took refuge in each other and in the stories they shared about the intrinsic superiority of the American values that were being so casually and caustically vilified around them.[41]

The British ministry was less openly hostile than the British press but, in its own officially polite fashion, remained implacably opposed to substantive negotiations of any sort with the American ambassador. John discovered there was really no diplomacy to conduct soon after his arrival in London, when he met with Lord Carmarthen, the young foreign minister who also happened to be a neighbor at Grosvenor Square. On the matter of British troops garrisoned on the Great Lakes, a clear violation of the Treaty of Paris, Carmarthen informed John that they would remain until the Americans lived up to their treaty obligations by paying off the prewar debts that southern planters, mostly Virginians, owed to British creditors. On the matter of British trade policy, Carmarthen acknowledged that American exports would always be welcomed at British ports, as long as they came in British bottoms and paid the required duties. British exports to America, however, were another matter, and the loss of such trade, which had flourished in the prewar years, was the price Americans must be prepared to pay for their glorious independence.[42]

As for the only other outstanding issue, compensation to southern slave owners for the slaves liberated by the British army, then carried away by the British fleet from New York at the end of the war—well, that was never going to happen. John did his diplomatic duty in raising this awkward issue but never pushed it. Off the record, he also thought that the indebted southern planters, Jefferson among them, were violating the Treaty of Paris and should be forced to pay.

Based on her letters to friends and relatives back in America, it is clear that Abigail was fully informed about the diplomatic impasse John was facing, and familiar with the details as well as the grand shape of the gridlocked negotiations. She estimated, for example, that the continued presence of British troops on America's northwestern frontier would cost the economy $50,000 a year from losses in the fur trade. During John's early career opposing British policy in Boston and Philadelphia, it was clear that Abigail fully supported his decisions and the ultimate goal of American independence, but it was not clear how involved she was in the formation of his political goals or the tactics used to achieve them. In London there could be no doubt that she was a full-fledged partner, abreast of all the diplomatic issues, a colleague as well as a wife.[43]

In fact, on one elemental issue affecting American foreign policy, Abigail was more outspoken than John. While the stand-pat intransigence of the British ministry was a major problem, and John understandably focused on it because it was the immediate source of his frustration, Abigail tended to emphasize American complicity in creating the

diplomatic deadlock by failing to provide the Confederation Congress with a clear mandate to oversee
foreign trade and make foreign policy: "In vain will
they call for commercial treaties," she lamented, "in
vain will they call for respect in Europe; in vain will
they hope for Peace with the Barbary states," until
the state governments ceded powers to the federal
congress, "which would allow them to act in concert
and give vigor and strength to their proceedings."[44]

In the absence of agreed-upon federal jurisdic-
tion over foreign policy, America could not speak
with a single voice in Europe. Instead, there were
thirteen separate sovereignties, a cacophony rather
than a chorus, all in the hands, as she put it, of
"beardless Boys" in the state governments, who
were just as ignorant of international affairs as that
infamous member of Parliament "when he talked of
the Island of Virginia." This was a dominant theme
in Abigail's correspondence, much more than in
John's, and it placed the lion's share of responsibility
for the futility of John's diplomatic mission—or
perhaps their diplomatic mission—squarely on the
shoulders of their own countrymen.[45]

INTIMACIES

During Abigail and John's time abroad, the most significant fact about their relationship was that they

were together almost all the time. This meant that they talked, touched, bantered, argued, commiserated, and bonded more routinely than they had ever done before in their married life. We can only imagine their conversation upon returning from an especially boring court function, sharing impressions of the most supercilious guests or the most obnoxious courtiers. And we can only infer, based on Abigail's richly detailed letters to relatives back home, that they spent many hours discussing the intractability of their diplomatic agenda in London, the shifting factions within the British ministry, the interest rates charged by Dutch bankers, and the interlocking virtues and vices of Europe's aristocratic culture.

We can imagine, and we can infer, but we can never know for sure, because none of their intimate conversation was recorded. In that sense, the most crucial piece in the Adams family puzzle during this extended time together is lost forever or, perhaps more correctly, never made its way into the historical record in the first place. Intimacy is by definition an inherently private affair, shielded from public view back then, even more sequestered from our well-intended snooping over two centuries later. The best we can do is to catch a few glimpses, based on faint traces left in letters that are usually about something else, grainy snapshots of moments in their overlapping interactions as lovers, friends, partners, and parents.

In December 1786, for example, Abigail and Nabby made a trip to Bath so that Abigail could "take the waters" to alleviate what she described as "Bellious disorders" and "a slow intermitting fever," which might have been early symptoms of her chronic battle with rheumatism in her later years. It was one of the few occasions when John and Abigail were apart, and Abigail wrote him for reassurance that he was able to manage without her: "Don't be solicitous about Me," John replied. "I shall do very well—if I am cold in the night, and an additional quantity of Bed Cloaths will not answer the purpose of warming me, I will take a virgin to bed with me—Ay a Virgin—What? Oh Awful!" After this attempt at mock shock, John went on to explain that **virgin** was the name Londoners gave to a hot-water bottle.[46]

This little episode demonstrates with near certainty that Abigail and John routinely slept together in the same bed. It also suggests that they were comfortable with the subject of sex, or at the very least that John was. (Abigail was allowed to smile upon receiving such a letter, but not to send anything so explicit herself.) It also seems plausible, if not quite provable, that at ages forty-two and fifty-one, respectively, they continued to enjoy a physical connection.

Race, it would seem, was a more uncomfortable subject than sex. There were some passages in Jefferson's **Notes on the State of Virginia** that might have prompted a reaction, passages describing Africans as a biologically inferior species, forever condemned to inferiority as long as they retained their blackness. John chose not to notice these passages, preferring to focus on Jefferson's critical remarks on slavery, which he said are "worth Diamonds."[47]

It is clear that Abigail and John, who never owned a slave, regarded slavery as incompatible with the values of the American Revolution, and therefore an awkward anomaly that British critics of American independence liked to throw in their faces. Abigail expressed her sense of embarrassment at a London dinner when seated next to William Blake, a wealthy South Carolina planter: "I am loth to mention that he owns 1500 Negroes," she observed, "as I cannot avoid considering it disgraceful to Humanity." (Though it made no moral difference, according to the 1790 census Blake owned 695 slaves.) Slavery, then, was one of those countless issues about which Abigail and John thought identically and almost seamlessly. Both took considerable pride when the Massachusetts Supreme Court ruled slavery illegal on the grounds that it violated the language John had written in the Massachusetts Constitution.[48]

Yet, consider this stunningly candid confession, offered by Abigail after viewing a performance of **Othello** at a London theater: "Othello was represented blacker than any African. Whether it rises from prejudices or Education or from a real natural antipathy I cannot determine, but my whole soul shuddered whenever I saw the sooty More touch the fair Desdemona . . . That most incomparable Speech of Othello's lost half its force and Beauty to me, because I could not separate the Colour from the Man." As Abigail implied, her racial reaction was instinctive, not an idea that emerged from her mind so much as a feeling that surged, as she put it, from her soul. It was obviously not a feeling she liked, but, just as obviously, not something she could control. Her honesty in acknowledging its potency was quite rare. The fact that these racial prejudices were present inside her, however, was the norm rather than the exception. It suggests that however liberated she was on the gender front, and however comfortable she and John were with their sexuality, race imposed hurdles she could not clear.[49]

Their parental roles were complicated by an elemental reality. Though they were together as a couple, they were not together as a family. All the boys, in fact, were back in New England, in various stages of preparation for Harvard. Charles and Thomas were boarding with their aunt at Haverhill. John Quincy had sailed home at the same time as his parents had departed Paris for London. Always the dutiful young man, he spent most of the voyage caring for seven hunting dogs that the marquis de Lafayette was sending to George Washington, who was now in retirement at Mount Vernon.

If the number and length of Abigail and John's letters are a fair measure, John Quincy remained their favorite son, a project almost as much as a person. After he passed the admissions exam to Harvard, doing brilliantly, as expected, Abigail reminded him, given all the educational advantages he had enjoyed, "how unpardonable it would have been in you, to have become a Blockhead." Charles received a few letters from both parents, usually warning him that his inveterate charm, while endearing, was no substitute for diligent work habits. Poor Thomas, who received but one letter in four years and sent none of his own that have survived, had become almost invisible.[50]

John's letters to John Quincy were full of diplomatic news, as if he were a junior colleague as much as a son. Once he began his courses at Harvard, John urged him to take full advantage of the educational opportunities: "You are breathing now in the Atmosphere of Science and Literature," he observed, "the floating particles of which will mix with your whole Mass of Blood and Juices." John Quincy's senior oration was a variation of the Adams family mantra on virtue and public service, almost calculated to make his father swoon: "It seems to me, making allowance for a fathers' Partiality, to be full of manly Sense and Spirit," John wrote. "By the sentiments and Principles of that oration, I hope you will live and die, and if you do, I don't care a farthing how many are preferred to you." The paternal pride was palpable.[51]

Despite the dramatic difference in attention paid their three sons, it was clear that Abigail and John presumed they had a responsibility to see them all through childhood and adolescence under their demanding parental gaze—most demanding for John Quincy—and then make sure that they all received a college education, an expectation then uncommon, except among elite New England families. Abigail worried that the expensive lifestyle John's position required had prevented them from saving enough money to cover the looming educational expenses. "We will return poor," she informed John Quincy, "but if we can get you all through college, the World is all before you, and providence your guide." In other words, there would be no Adams trust fund. Once launched into the world after Harvard, they were on their own.[52]

For two elemental reasons, Nabby was a different matter: first, she was a young woman, which meant that educational expectations did not include college; second, she was living with her parents in London, which in practice meant that she spent a good deal of time in the company of her mother. Abigail was, without question, one of the most intelligent and independent women of her time, but she harbored a realistic recognition that the liberation of women from the sexist assumptions of the day—a liberation she correctly considered to be a latent implication of the American Revolution—lay somewhere in the distant future. As she saw it, her maternal obligation was to prepare her daughter to function in the world that was rather than the world that ought to be. When all was said and done, this meant that Nabby needed to become a literate lady who married well.[53]

For a time, Nabby's suitor in Braintree, Royall Tyler, remained steadfast, promising to wait for her and formally propose upon her return from Europe. He and Nabby had exchanged miniatures (locket-size portraits) upon her departure and had promised to correspond regularly. Tyler's prospects ascended when Abigail learned upon meeting John in London that he would bless any decision that Nabby made with her whole heart.

But Tyler failed the distance test. His letters became increasingly infrequent, and the local gossip reported by Abigail's sisters suggested, albeit in highly elliptical language, that he was seeing other women on the side. This was enough to convince Abigail that her high estimate of Tyler's character had been misguided. In August 1785, Nabby returned Tyler's miniature and letters, effectively breaking off the engagement. Abigail's comment had a terminal tone:

"A woman may forgive the man she loves an indiscretion, but never a neglect."[54]

A new suitor was already waiting in the wings. In person and on paper, he appeared nothing short of perfect. William Stephens Smith was a dashingly handsome young man appointed by the Continental Congress to serve as John's private secretary in London. Abigail described him as "a Gentleman in every thought, word and action, domestic in his attachments, quick as lightening in his feelings, but softened in an instant." His résumé was equally impressive. A graduate of the College of New Jersey, now Princeton, he had served as an officer in the Continental Army with distinction throughout the war, including a stint on Washington's staff. He was almost too good to be true. And best of all, he was obviously infatuated with Nabby.[55]

At first, Abigail played her accustomed managerial role. She drafted letters to family and friends in New England, singing the praises of this young man whom no one back home had ever met. And she most probably convinced Smith to give Nabby some space to recover fully from the Tyler affair, which he then did by arranging a somewhat sudden trip to Europe to witness military maneuvers of the Prussian Army. But upon his return, Abigail lost control of the courtship. "What shall I do with my young soldier," she complained. "I wish he would not be in such a hurry." Apparently, Nabby and

Smith took matters into their own hands and insisted on an accelerated schedule aligned with their own hearts. On June 12, 1786, John gave his only daughter away in a small ceremony at their home on Grosvenor Square. The night before the wedding Abigail confided that she had dreamed of Royall Tyler, and felt emotions toward him that defied description.[56]

Finally, on another front, it bears notice that John experienced no emotional excesses of the sort that caused him such trouble with Vergennes and the French court, or damaged his reputation back in the Continental Congress with vain statements about his beleaguered sense of self-importance. Given the frustrations he was feeling at the intransigence of the British ministry, one might have expected at least a few Vesuvian moments that defied diplomatic decorum and enhanced his image as a man who was sometimes slightly out of control.

But no such incidents occurred in either Paris or London after Abigail joined him. While it is possible that John suffered from a thyroid imbalance, which provides a physical explanation for his severe mood swings, Abigail's presence reduced the stress that triggered the emotional reactions. She was his most effective medicine. With her constantly at his side, the explosive energies were drained off before they could build up. Their sense of mutual trust made it more difficult for him to feel isolated and alone, and she could tell him, like no one else, when he was on the verge of making a fool of himself.

CONSTITUTIONS

"Tis true I enjoy good Health," Abigail informed her sister, "but am larger than both my sisters compounded! Mr. Adams keeps pace with me, and if one horse had to carry us, I pity the poor Beast." This was her way of warning her relatives that when they eventually saw her after her European sojourn, she was going to be much heavier. She was at pains to assure them, however, that any change in her physical constitution—mostly a function of multiple servants who performed all the household tasks, plus required attendance at lavish dinners—should not be regarded as evidence of her conversion to aristocratic habits. "I shall quit Europe with more pleasure than I came to it," she insisted, "uncontaminated I hope with its Manners and vices." The longer she remained in London, the greater was her desire to return to "my little cottage . . . which has more charms for me than the drawing rooms of St. James, where studied civility, and disguised coldness, cover malignant Hearts."[57]

Abigail's frequent references to her humble Braintree abode, while heartfelt, masked the fact that John had already requested Cotton Tufts, Abigail's uncle, to begin searching for a larger house, an implicit acknowledgment that a mere cottage, no matter how symbolically resonant, could no longer satisfy their more expansive household require-ments, which had grown like Abigail's girth. Even-tually, Tufts arranged for the purchase of the Vassall-Borland house in Braintree, a quite modest country estate by the standards of any French or British aristocrat, but by American standards a handsome home. (Ironically, Royall Tyler was a pre-vious owner.) Later dubbed Peacefield, it became the domestic centerpiece for the Adams family over four generations. Once the purchase was com-pleted, John claimed that knowing it was there, awaiting his return, allowed him to envision the remainder of his life with newfound clarity: "My view is to lay fast of the Town of Braintree," he wrote Tufts, "and embrace it, with both my Arms and all my might. There to live and there to die— there to lay my Bones."[58]

In August 1786 both John and Abigail traveled to the Netherlands, where John completed the nego-tiations for a commercial treaty with Prussia. Abigail described the Dutch countryside as a monotonous series of "meadows, Trees, Canals, then more Canals, Trees, and meadows" so boring that she found herself almost hoping to be waylaid by a roadside robber in order to break the spell. Once back in London, John barricaded himself in his study and refused to see official visitors or maintain his diplomatic correspondence. He entered one of those all-consuming zones where, as Abigail described him, "he was as much engaged upon the Subject of Government as Plato was when he wrote his Laws and Republic."[59]

He had decided to write a major treatise on the proper shape of constitutions. Given the paralysis on the diplomatic front, it seemed a more productive way to spend his time. And given the reports from Jay back home, which described a mounting recognition that the Articles of Confederation were proving inadequate as the basis for American union, it seemed more important to make a contribution to that looming political debate than to continue his futile conversations with the British ministry.[60] Moreover, his own frustrations in Paris and London with an American government unable to speak with one voice on foreign policy predisposed John to accept Jay's view that reform of the Articles was long overdue. In 1776, he had stepped forward to offer his **Thoughts on Government** at a crucial political moment. Now he intended to do the same thing at the next stage of the American experiment with republicanism.[61]

The result was a massive three-volume treatise entitled **A Defence of the Constitutions of Government of the United States of America.** The title conveyed the main argument, which was a defense of the tripartite arrangement—executive, legislative, judiciary—John had proposed in **Thoughts on Government** and then implemented in the Massachusetts Constitution. In that sense, **Defence** was an elaborate recapitulation of his case for three separate branches of government, balanced and counterpoised to check one another, that had become the model for most of the state constitutions. (Pennsylvania and Georgia were the only exceptions.) It was also a lengthy legal brief against the simpler framework of a single-house legislature favored by the French philosophes and currently embodied in the Articles of Confederation; it was an argument for making the state constitutions the model for a revised federal constitution. There was nothing particularly original in this proposal. Jay informed him that most advocates for reform of the Articles were already thinking along the same lines.[62]

The ostentatious display of learning in **Defence**—lengthy citations from Machiavelli, Plato, Aristotle, Milton, Hume, Thucydides, Hobbes, and Cicero, to name just a few—exposed John's need to brandish his credentials as a constitutional authority. One London reviewer described the whole work as a pathetic case of posturing, which he likened to a college essay "written by a youth with a view to obtain some academic prize." In John's case, the prize he sought was recognition of his standing as one of America's premier political thinkers. But the conspicuous erudition of **Defence,** plus its swollen size—it ran on for nearly a thousand pages—only seemed to reinforce John's reputation for vanity.[63]

For those with the stamina to plow through **Defence,** it was clear that John had inadvertently provided evidence that seemed almost calculated to have a negative impact on his own reputation. His discussion of executive power, for example, reiterated his conviction, first articulated in his draft of the Massachusetts Constitution, that the executive should be empowered to veto a decision by the legislature, a right of veto that could not be overturned by a two-thirds majority. The delegates at the Massachusetts Convention had found this excessive, indeed smacking of monarchy, and had revised his draft so as to restore the legislature's authority to override. Undeterred, John went back to his original formulation in **Defence,** claiming that unfettered executive power was essential to ensure balance by offsetting the more dangerous ambitions of political elites sure to dominate the legislature. He argued that the American aversion to a strong executive, while a plausible response to George III's travesties in the prerevolutionary years, had become anachronistic in the postrevolutionary era, when all the state constitutions required that governors be selected by some form of direct or indirect election.

Abigail, who was reading drafts at the end of each day, tried to warn John that his warm embrace of executive power, no matter how repub-licanized by the American electorate, effectively invited misunderstanding back home. "I tell him," she informed John Quincy, "that they will think in America that he is setting up a king." Her instincts on this score proved impeccable, but John was not listening. The only voices he heard came from inside his own head. For **Defence** had become his all-consuming obsession, the pages pouring out in torrents that defied Abigail's editorial suggestions much in the way that a catharsis defied correction.

Another theme, also sure to alienate American readers, was his insistence that in all societies, to include the United States, "an aristocracy has risen up in a course of time, consisting of a few rich and honorable families, who have united with each other against both the people and the first magis-trate." Whether this was a hereditary aristocracy, as in Europe, or a natural aristocracy or meritoc-racy, as in America, was less important than the fact that wealth and talent were never evenly dis-tributed, that elites were an abiding presence in all societies, and one of the main tasks of government was to manage them so as to make use of their tal-ent while preventing their outright domination. His somewhat simplistic solution was the Senate, which would serve as a podium from which to project their power and a prison that confined their ambitions.[64]

None of this translated very well into the American context, where an all-powerful executive sounded suspiciously like a king, and where the rhetoric of republican equality left no room for an embedded aristocracy, whether hereditary or natural. Abigail was torn between her duties as a wife and as a political partner. As a wife she encouraged John's emotional investment in **Defence,** which lent some sense of purpose to their London exile and kept her husband so preoccupied that he did not even look up from his papers when she served him tea. As a political partner, however, she feared that **Defence** would turn out to be a lengthy political death warrant.

She reconciled these roles by reverting to her "little cottage" refrain, which visualized a life of bucolic splendor in retirement upon their return to America. The damage John was doing, in effect, was irrelevant, because he had no intention of resuming his public career after leaving London. This was a convenient illusion, but Abigail embraced it with all her might. She asked her uncle to spread the word that John was no threat to other aspiring political candidates in Massachusetts, because "he has always dealt too openly and candidly with his Countrymen to be popular." This was simultaneously a shrewd analysis and a classic case of wishful thinking.[65]

GOOD-BYE TO ALL THAT

In December 1787 news arrived from Philadelphia that John's resignation, which he had submitted a year earlier, was finally approved. Abigail was over-joyed. She immediately began writing friends and relatives back home to expect her the following spring. Jefferson received the news with mixed feel-ings: "I learn with real pain the resolution you have taken of quitting Europe," he apprised John. "Your presence on this side of the Atlantic gave me a con-fidence that if any difficulties should arise within my department, I should always have one to advise with on whose counsels I could rely. I now feel wid-owed."[66]

As it turned out, fate in the form of the Dutch bankers brought Jefferson and John together for a final joint venture, which proved to be the last time they would work together on public business in perfect harmony. In March 1788 John had decided, without official authorization from the congress, to make a quick trip to The Hague to negotiate an extension of the American loan and a new timetable for the interest payments. Jefferson decided to join him in order to familiarize himself with the finan-cial details, since he would become the responsible American minister upon John's departure. As he prepared to dash up from Paris, Jefferson alerted John to his plans: "I hope to shake your hand within 24 hours after you receive this."[67]

The Dutch bankers, notoriously hard bargainers, had demanded a substantial increase in interest payments because the American government wanted to delay its obligations for two years, when a new federal government would presumably be up and running. John, instead, persuaded them to float several bonds to cover the gap. Jefferson acknowledged that he was a complete innocent on all matters of high finance—indeed, throughout his life he found it impossible to balance his books or to comprehend the impact of compound interest on his debts. John's deft handling of such details struck him as a kind of magic.

John worried about Jefferson's competence once he was senior minister in Europe, warning him to be on guard "against the immeasurable avarice of Amsterdam." He knew he was leaving America's financial fate in inexperienced hands: "I pity you, in your situation, dunned and teased as you will be, all your philosophy will be wanting to support you. But be not discouraged . . . Depend upon it, the Amsterdammers love Money too well to execute their threats."[68]

Back in London, Abigail relayed the American news reported in the British press. Seven states had ratified the new Constitution, Massachusetts by a narrow margin of 19 votes out of 340 cast: "Thus my dear Friend," she observed, "I think we shall return to our country at a very important period and with more pleasing prospects opening before her." This did not quite sound like someone poised for her husband's retirement.[69]

John and Jefferson managed one last exchange of opinion on the shape of the new Constitution, which proved to be a preview of coming attractions. They agreed that the document should have included a Bill of Rights, and that drafting one should be the first business of the new government. Beyond that, however, their reactions were polar opposites. Jefferson thought that the Articles of Confederation required revision, not wholesale replacement: "I think that all the good of the new constitution might have been concealed in three or four articles to be added to the good, old, and venerable fabrick," he explained to John, "which should have been preserved even as a religious relique." John thought that the Constitution should have gone further in asserting federal sovereignty over the states, which was also seriously compromised by the vague powers allocated to the executive. Jefferson, on the other hand, feared the office of the presidency was too powerful, permitting routinized reelection for life in the manner of an American king. John's response was unequivocal: "So much the better it seems to me."[70]

Abigail and John had to wait at Cowes for nearly a week before their ship, the **Lucretia,** could clear the harbor. "I have never before experienced to such a degree what the French term ennui," Abigail confided to her diary, eager as she was to get the inevitable seasick phase of the voyage over and to set foot at last on New England soil. Looking back on England's shores as the winds carried them out to sea in early April 1788, she offered a clear conclusion about her time in Europe: "I do not think four years I have past abroad the pleasantest part of my life. Tis Domestic happiness and Rural felicity in the Bosom of my Native Land that charms for me. Yet I do not regret that I made this excursion since it has only attached me more to America." And, she might have added, to her "dearest friend."[71]

CHAPTER FIVE

1789–96

"[The vice presidency is] the most insignificant office that ever the Invention of Man contrived or his Imagination conceived."

THE CANNONS ON Castle Island boomed in celebration as the **Lucretia** approached Boston Harbor, welcoming two American stalwarts back home. John and Abigail had spent three years as pariahs in London, where they were an unwelcome reminder of American independence. But the crowd at the Boston dock loved them for the same reason that Londoners loathed them, as prominent embodiments of that improbably successful achievement called the American Revolution.[1]

Governor John Hancock's ornate carriage was dispatched to pick them up, then sped them through the streets as church bells sounded all around. The ocean voyage had transformed them from outcasts into celebrities. In case John had somehow forgotten, the jubilant reception reminded him that, alongside George Washington and Benjamin Franklin, he stood at the very peak of the American version of Mount Olympus.

The downside of this triumphal return came when they arrived at their new home in Braintree, which they had purchased sight unseen. Abigail's first impression was disappointment. "In height and breadth," she reported to Nabby, "it feels like a wren's house." They had grown accustomed to the spacious, high-ceilinged rooms of their residences in Paris and London, which made the rooms of their new home feel like cubicles. Abigail warned Nabby that the ceilings were so low that she would not be able to wear her feathered hats when visiting, and her husband would have to stoop if he wore his heeled boots.[2]

In July 1788, as Abigail and John were moving into their new home, New Hampshire became the ninth state to ratify the Constitution, thereby ensuring that a newly empowered federal government would be elected in November. A new chapter in the evolution of the American Revolution was beginning, a chapter in which an aspiring American nation-state replaced a loose-knit confederation of individual states. The question facing Abigail and John was whether or not to participate in this next round in the American experiment.

Both of them had made a point of signaling a preference for retirement to the bucolic splendors of Braintree. While utterly sincere, such Ciceronian testimonials had become formulaic refrains among the top echelon of the revolutionary generation, less statements of their true intentions than ritualistic posturings. In this venerable tradition, anyone exhibiting a conspicuous craving for political office was presumed unqualified to serve.

Nabby reported from her new home in New York, already identified as the first capital of the aspiring nation, that no one took such protestations seriously. There was as yet no organized party structure, no agreed-upon process for selecting candidates, so the "smoke-filled rooms" of the day were the taverns and coffeehouses where informal conversations weeded out prospective nominees. Nabby apprised her father that—no surprise—George Washington was the foregone conclusion for the top spot, and that "You will be elected to the second place on the continent," meaning the vice presidency. Moreover, as she observed to John Quincy, if the informal appraisals proved correct, there was no way that their father would refuse the summons to serve. "The Happiness of our family," she shrewdly noted, "seems ever to have been so interwoven with the Politics of our Country as to be in a great degree dependent upon them."[3]

If subsequent generations of the family had ever

devised a plaque to be placed over the Adams plot, these words might very well have been chosen as the most appropriate testimonial. As the first national election approached, however, John was psychologically incapable of acknowledging that his own personal fulfillment depended upon being chosen for a prominent post in the new federal government. Though he was perhaps the most astute student of the role that ambition played among his political peers, he rather lamely insisted that any summons to serve would entail a huge personal sacrifice for both him and Abigail. "My mind has balanced all circumstances," he told Abigail while awaiting the election results, "and all are reducible to . . . Vanity and Comfort." If he was not chosen, so he claimed, they would live out their lives in relative serenity at Braintree. If he was elected, they would dutifully answer the call, once more placing the public interest above their private happiness.[4]

He twitched back and forth between anxiety and denial: "I am willing to serve the public on manly conditions," he wrote Nabby, "but not on childish ones." Only the vice presidency would do. It was not the power of the office that attracted him—indeed, as he was soon to discover, the vice presidency was almost designed as a political cul-de-sac—but the status it carried as the second-ranking office in the government. The election, as he saw it, was a referendum on revolutionary credentials, and Washington was the only person whom John was prepared to recognize as his superior on that score. Abigail concurred that anything less than the vice presidency was "beneath him."[5]

Conveniently, he did not need to campaign or even declare his candidacy. The political etiquette of the time regarded outright campaigning for office akin to an act of prostitution, and therefore clear evidence that one was unworthy. Moreover, the electoral process for president described in the new Constitution did not yet distinguish between candidates for the first or second spot. The winner, if he received a majority of electoral votes, became president, while the runner-up became vice president.

Both Abigail and John assumed a somewhat studied posture of nonchalance as they awaited the results of the election. Abigail decided that politics ought not take precedence over her new obligations as a grandmother, so she traveled down to New York to assist Nabby with the birth of her second child, another boy, who was named John Adams Smith, despite John's objection ("I wish the child every Blessing from other Motives besides its name"). She reported that a visit with the Jay family in the city yielded the opinion that John was virtually certain to be elected vice president, despite opposition from factions in Virginia and New York that objected not so much to him but to any consolidated federal government whatsoever.[6]

Though she presumed that the nights were cold back in Braintree, she wished to hear no more jokes about "virgins": "I would recommend to you the Green Baize Gown, and if that will not answer, you recollect the Bear Skin." In keeping with his custom of silence whenever the voters were deciding his fate, John hunkered down while the snowdrifts piled up at Braintree: "The new government has my best wishes and most fervent prayers," he wrote to Jefferson, who was still ensconced in Paris. "But whether I shall have anything more to do with it, besides praying for it, depends on the future suffrage of freemen."[7]

That was not technically correct. John's fate depended on electors chosen by each state, mostly by the respective state legislators, who themselves were determined by the "suffrage of freemen." When these electoral votes were counted in February 1789, Washington had won unanimously, receiving 69 votes. Eleven other candidates received some measure of support, but, with 34 electoral votes, John was the clear runner-up. It was not quite the resounding chorus of confidence that John had hoped for, but as Abigail reminded him, it showed that only Washington ranked higher in the minds of the American citizenry.

The Boston newspapers tended to reinforce this interpretation of the election, describing John's victory as a recognition of his distinguished service in the Continental Congress and then in Paris and London. No one mentioned the fact that the vice presidency was largely a ceremonial office, ill-suited to his outspoken and passionate temperament, or, as he put it a few years later, "the most insignificant office that ever the Invention of Man contrived or his Imagination conceived."[8]

Reservations about the limited powers of his new post never crossed John's mind at that exuberant moment. Both he and Abigail were wholly focused on the status conferred by being recognized as second only to Washington, and therefore the second-ranking family in the United States. John was also thrilled with the long-term implications of his election, for it constituted an early referendum on the primacy of his place within the revolutionary generation, and therefore boded well for his prospects in the most important election of all, namely, the judgment of posterity.

Abigail chimed in with her sense of satisfaction that the location of the new capital in New York would allow her to spend more time with Nabby and the grandchildren. And John beamed with pride when the fishermen of Marblehead offered to provide the vice president's household with a steady supply of cod, in recognition of his earlier insistence in the Treaty of Paris on their fishing rights off the Grand Banks. Even if his duties were largely ceremonial, this final assignment—which is how John regarded the vice presidency—was the perfect capstone to his political career. There at the start to launch the movement for American independence. There to negotiate the end of the war and the new borders of a continental republic. And now there to help establish the first national government. What more could anyone ask?[9]

ETIQUETTE AND EMULATION

"We are most delightfully situated," Abigail explained to her sister. "The prospect around us is Beautiful in the highest degree, it is a mixture of sublime & Beautiful." She was describing the new Adams residence at Richmond Hill, a thirty-acre estate overlooking the Hudson, located about a mile north of the city in what is now the west side of Greenwich Village. While it was not quite up to the magisterial standards of their mansion at Auteuil, it was the most elegant American home that John and Abigail had ever occupied. Soon after Abigail's arrival in June 1789, it immediately became social headquarters for the second-ranking official in the new American government and his famously impressive wife. "Our House has been a

Levee ever since I arrived," Abigail observed. "Had visits from 25 ladies, all [the wives of] senators and all foreign ministers."10

No couple in the country was more experienced at managing the social obligations of political office than Abigail and John. Their diplomatic duties in Paris and London had provided an unmatched education in courtly etiquette at the highest levels of refinement. John recognized that Abigail was his greatest asset on the all-important social front, and he expressed his impatience when she delayed her departure from Braintree to make arrangements for their farm. "You must sell Horses, Oxen, Sheep, Cowes, anything at any Rate rather than not come on—if no one will take the Place, leave it to the Birds of the air and Beasts of the Field." He needed her by his side.11

Since a nation-size republic was a novelty—no such creature had ever existed before—and since the courtly etiquette of European monarchies seemed to defy the very core of republican values, no one was quite sure what the social side of a republican government was supposed to look like. One solution was a weekly open house called the levee, where the president and vice president, along with their respective wives, greeted elected officials, foreign dignitaries, and distinguished guests in a format that attempted to strike the proper middle note between courtly formality and republican simplicity.

Abigail described the scene, which was thoroughly choreographed. She always stood to the right of Martha Washington, who received curtsies from the women guests and bows from the gentlemen: "The president then comes up and speaks to the lady, which he does with a grace, dignity, and ease that leaves Royal George far behind him." The guests were passed on to Abigail and John with the requisite curtsies and bows; then the assembled throng made small talk for about fifteen minutes while consuming small portions of ice cream and lemonade—substantive conversations about matters of policy were strictly forbidden—then more curtsies and bows when Washington exited the room. It was a somewhat awkward contradiction in terms, a republican court, and the major venue in which Abigail and John were on display as ranking members of—another contradiction—republican royalty.[12]

Abigail was the point person for the Adams family at the levees as well as the weekly dinners she hosted at Richmond Hill. And in a reprise of her diplomatic role in Paris, she visited the wives of fifteen to twenty government officials or foreign ministers each week. John's role, chiefly ceremonial, was to preside over the Senate, usually for six hours every day.

According to the language of the Constitution, the vice president was allowed to vote only in order to break a tie and was required to remain silent during debates. In his maiden speech before the Senate, John acknowledged that the latter requirement would not be easy for him: "I have been more accustomed to take a share in the debates, than to preside in their deliberations," he confessed, which was an implicit reference to his prominent role in the Continental Congress. Nevertheless, he promised to do his best, and if he forgot the limitations periodically, he hoped his colleagues would forgive his lapses. To John Quincy he confided that the office of vice president required "a kind of Duty, which, if I do not flatter myself too much, is not quite adapted to my Character." For the passionate and combative veteran of several truly historic debates that shaped the direction of the American Revolution, silence was not a natural act.[13]

A minor matter of official etiquette prompted the first violation of his oath of office and made him the centerpiece of the first political controversy to afflict the new government. The issue at stake was an apparently harmless question: By what title should the president be addressed? The real protagonist in the debate was Senator William Maclay, who hailed from the western frontier of Pennsylvania, where republican values assumed a decidedly egalitarian character and all forms of pomp and ceremony carried with them the distinct odor of monarchy. Maclay insisted that the proper title for

President Washington should be "Mr. President," and that all efforts to affix greater grandeur to the office conjured up the decadent legacies of British royalty, which he thought the American Revolution had long ago consigned to the oblivion they deserved.

John interrupted Maclay on several occasions, delivering quasi lectures to the Senate on the importance of visible trappings of authority for an infant republic that desperately needed to project symbols of national unity. And besides, since everyone agreed that President Washington was genuinely majestic, why not recognize that fact by referring to him as "His Majesty"? If that sounded too reminiscent of European monarchy, then perhaps "His Highness" would be preferable.

Maclay went on a tirade, protesting the interruptions from someone purportedly required to remain silent during debates, then suggesting that the vice president had apparently been infected by the disease called "nobilmania" during his long sojourn in Europe. Other senators agreed, reprimanding John for his violation of procedure and joking that perhaps he himself would prefer to be referred to as "the Duke of Braintree" or, better yet, as "His Rotundity."

Maclay's diary, hardly a neutral source, is the fullest account of the exchange, so that most subsequent historical accounts of the episode reflect his hostile opinion of John, whom he described as an "avowed monarchist" and "a monkey just put into breeches." But even after one adjusts for Maclay's biased version, the consensus within the Senate was that John had made a fool of himself. Jefferson, recently arrived from Paris, when apprised of John's insistence on high-sounding titles, observed that it struck him "as the most superlatively ridiculous thing I have ever heard." The Senate voted for the simple title "Mr. President," thus repudiating John's advice, and from that time forward he refrained from injecting himself into debates.[14]

Instead of feeling chastised, John felt that he had been misunderstood. And the way to correct the misunderstanding was to demonstrate to all concerned that the hovering ghost of monarchy that haunted all American conversations about government needed to be exorcised if the infant republic was to enjoy any prospect of success. Every afternoon, after presiding over the Senate debates, he returned to Richmond Hill and poured his thoughts onto paper. In typical Adams fashion, the stream of words became a flood, eventually taking the form of thirty-one essays printed in the **Gazette of the United States** over the next year and subsequently published as a separate volume entitled **Discourses on Davila.** Looking back many years later, John pronounced **Davila** his most profound attempt to identify the primal forces shaping all human effort at government.

Much of **Davila,** in fact, was a repetition or extension of arguments already made in **Defence.** To wit, any balanced constitution required a singular figure empowered to embody the will of the nation, much in the way that every human body required a head. This "monarchical principle" was a universal tenet, true for all societies throughout history, though the understandable loathing toward the British monarch during the American war for independence had rendered otherwise intelligent American thinkers blind to this fact. (Abigail made the same point in the more specific context of Washington's presidency: "It is my firm opinion that no man could rule over this great people & consolidate them into one mighty Empire but He who Set over us.") In most European states—John was thinking primarily of France—it was probably necessary for the monarchy to remain hereditary for the foreseeable future in order to permit a more gradual transition to full-blown republican principles.[15]

By conflating the American presidency with "the monarchical principle," however, John almost invited misunderstanding, because the very term "monarchy" had become an epithet that provoked near-universal condemnation within the American political context. It was one thing to acknowledge that Washington was indispensable, quite another to talk so openly and approvingly of "the monarchical principle." In that sense, **Davila** only confirmed the murmurings that John had lost the true republican faith during his long residence in Europe. (The truth was that he had harbored the conviction that a strong executive presence was essential for many years, and had embedded the principle in his draft of the Massachusetts Constitution.) But **Davila** only fed the rumors that he was a closet monarchist who favored making the presidency a hereditary office that, if he ever was elected to it, he intended to pass along to John Quincy.[16]

There was one section of **Davila,** however, that had nothing directly to do with the main theme about monarchy, and indeed seems an impulsive aside that popped into John's head as he was writing. It began with the story of a pauper who was starving but chose to starve rather than eat his dog's food. When asked why he opted for his dog instead of himself, he responded: "Who will love me then? With these words," John observed, "there is a key to the human heart—and to the rise and fall of empires."[17]

He then proceeded to make the argument that passions or emotions, not ideas, were the driving force in history, and the most potent passion of all was, as he put it, "the need to be considered, esteemed, praised, beloved and admired by his fellows." The pursuit of wealth was a secondary drive, not an end in itself but only a means to a greater end, "because riches attract the attention, consideration, and congratulations of mankind." (A hundred years later, Thorstein Veblen would give the economic version of this notion a name: **conspicuous consumption.**) The primal political urge, often unconscious and beyond rational control, he called "emulation," which was the compulsion to rise above your rivals and become the focus of public veneration. And the ultimate version of emulation was lasting fame beyond one's own lifetime by winning the affection and admiration of posterity: "For what folly it is," he observed. "What is it to us what shall be said of us after we are dead? Or in Asia, Africa, or Europe while we live? There is no greater or imaginable illusion. Yet the impulse is irresistible."[18]

There can be little doubt that John's diagnosis of the role that human ambitions played in the political arena was primarily rooted in his intimate familiarity with his own internal urges. Although the references in **Davila** were all drawn from European history—whole sections were lifted from English, French, and Italian texts without attribution—the seminal text was his own soul. There John acknowledged his endless quest for recognition in the public arena, which in its ultimate manifestation became an unquenchable desire to live forever in the memory of future generations.

PERIPHERAL VISIONS

At the ceremonial level, when he was with Abigail at the presidential levees or at a dinner party at Richmond Hill, John was regarded as a central player in the new government. When he was presiding over the Senate, however, he was a mere cipher. Significant legislation came before him during Washington's first term, to include the chief provisions of a national fiscal policy, the location of the new capital city, and a treaty designed as a model for policy toward the Native Americans. But he had nothing to do with the crafting of this legislation, and no influence over its ultimate fate. He frequently complained to Abigail about his abiding irrelevance, and she did her best to reassure him that his ceremonial role as president of the Senate made a difference: "Altho it is so limited as to prevent you from being so useful as you have been accustomed to, yet these former exertions and services give a weight of Character, which like the Heavenly orbs silently diffuse a benign influence."[19]

The truth was that John's status as an established icon of the American Revolution was beginning to seem like an increasingly distant piece of nostalgia, glorious in its day, to be sure, but part of an earlier chapter in the story that had now moved beyond the struggle for American independence to the quest for American nationhood. A new generation of political leaders was emerging, men like Alexander Hamilton and James Madison, who were almost young enough to be John's sons. (In 1790 John was fifty-five, Hamilton was thirty-five, and Madison was thirty-nine.) He could not help but think of them as latecomers to the cause that he had championed in its most fragile and formative phase. As he confided to Abigail, it was sheer torture to sit in the Senate and listen to speakers who struck him as "young, inconsiderate, and inexperienced," mere babes in the woods, while he sat sullenly and silently. It was difficult to think of the indefatigable "Atlas of independence" in the Continental Congress as extraneous and irrelevant, but that is what the vice presidency had made him.[20]

He felt more comfortable with veteran revolutionaries of his own age, men who had run the gauntlet with him when the odds seemed stacked against success. When Washington arrived in Boston to start his tour of the New England states in November 1789, for example, John and Samuel Adams met with him, and reporters, to John's immense satisfaction, described the trio as "the three genuine Pivots of the Revolution." John concurred with the historical significance of the meeting, writing Abigail that an artist should have been commissioned to capture the scene for posterity, painted "with the greatest care, and preserved in the best Place." If an artist had been commissioned to paint a group portrait of the major players in the Washington administration, however, John would not have been included in the picture.[21]

His absence from such a putative picture was also reflected in the written record. Whatever the reasons—his wounded pride, his reluctance to write anything about his own personal opinions that might damage the legislative agenda of the administration—John had precious little to say about the political issues passing before him. He had been assigned a minor role that, in truth, he did not know how to play, despite Abigail's somewhat forced reassurances of his significance. Quite uncharacteristically, apart from complaining about his abiding irrelevance, he said virtually nothing in his personal correspondence about his thoughts on the highly controversial legislation passing before him, except that he felt duty-bound to support whatever the executive branch proposed.

The same was not true of Abigail. Her letters to family and friends back in Massachusetts provide a running commentary on the increasingly shrill political arguments. It is safe to assume that she and John talked on a daily basis about the current issues at stake. And, at this stage of their partnership, it is also safe to assume a seamless symmetry between them that made conflicting convictions virtually impossible. If the Adams family had an opinion about the legislative agenda of the infant republic, the best source turned out to be Abigail.

She recognized from the start that the most controversial and critical provision in Hamilton's financial plan, presented to Congress in January 1790 as **A Report on Public Credit,** was the federal assumption of state debts—taking $25 million in state debt, most of it a function of wartime expenditures by the thirteen states, and putting it into one pile. This made excellent economic sense, since by consolidating the state debts, the United States was sending a signal to the international markets that the new nation fully intended to pay its bills.

But politically, assumption was extremely controversial, for it meant that the federal government had also assumed control over the national economy, thereby asserting federal supremacy over the states, even though many of the states, Virginia most strenuously, believed they had fought the American Revolution to protest just such domination by distant authorities in London and Whitehall. "The members of the different states think so widely from each other," Abigail observed, "that it is difficult to accommodate their interests . . . What one member esteems the pillar, the Bulwork of the Constitution, an other considers as the Ruin of his State." She was calling attention to the fact that the Assumption Bill presumed the existence of an established national ethos that, in fact, did not exist because allegiances remained confined within state or, at best, regional borders. She supported assumption, as did John, but she recognized that the debate over its implications was so fierce because it provided a clear resolution of the question of federal versus state sovereignty that the Constitution itself had deliberately left ambiguous.[22]

As it turned out, Abigail's enthusiastic support for assumption was not wholly disinterested. She had invested in war bonds issued by Massachusetts during the war, probably for patriotic reasons. The value of these bonds, and the interest they paid, increased considerably once the federal government assumed the Massachusetts state debt, because interest payments were thereby assured. Her profits were hardly huge, but the passage of the Assumption Bill in the summer of 1790 earned her a tidy sum. It is not clear whether John ever knew about this unspoken conflict of interest. It is clear that Abigail's sense of her own independence included control over financial investments that she regarded as hers and hers alone.[23]

The debate over the Residence Act did not raise the constitutional questions posed by assumption, but the studied ambiguity of the Constitution virtually assured partisan bickering that came to resemble a political circus. Congress was required to identify a permanent "seat of government" without any guidance on the specific location. All the regional voting blocs—New England, the Middle Atlantic, the South—could imagine schemes placing the national capital within their borders, and none seemed capable of imagining it anywhere else. Abigail found the debates, some of which she witnessed from the Senate gallery, extremely offensive because of the blatantly partisan atmosphere and the wholly argumentative context of the legislative process. "The more I see of Mankind," she lamented, "the more sick I am of publick Life, and the less worthy do they appear to me." She thought it was a mistake to open the Senate gallery to the public, since ordinary citizens would now see that making laws was like making sausage: not a pretty sight, and not a scene likely to inspire confidence in the new government. So much for John's idealistic vision of the Senate as the arena for America's virtuous elite.[24]

Nor did Abigail like the eventual selection of Philadelphia as the temporary capital while the designated permanent site on the Potomac, negotiated in a behind-the-scenes bargain, was being built. "You will see by the publick papers that we are destined for Philadelphia," she wrote to John Quincy, "a Grievious affair to me I assure you, but so it is ordained." She loved the lavish estate and grounds at Richmond Hill, with its majestic view of the Hudson, and saw no reason why the government should not remain in New York until the Potomac location was ready. She would have to leave Nabby and the grandchildren for a hot and humid place that was infamous as a breeding ground for mosquitoes and infectious diseases. And why would a government seeking to create an impression of permanence decide to move around so often, what she described as "continual roling"? Finally, it was a question of aesthetics and "the Schuylkill is not more like the Hudson, than I to Hercules."[25]

What we might call Abigail's perspective from the periphery enjoyed a crescendo moment near the end of the first congressional session in August 1790. A delegation of twenty-seven Native Americans, all chiefs of the Creek Nation, arrived in New York to negotiate and sign a treaty designed to end hostilities on the southern frontier. Washington and Secretary of War Henry Knox also intended the treaty to serve as a model for American policy toward all the Native American tribes located east of the Mississippi. For the first time, the tribes would be legally recognized as sovereign nations, with rights to land that could not be violated without their consent. And once boundaries were agreed to by treaty, the federal government was committed to protecting the Native American residents from encroachment by white settlers, using military force if necessary. Washington envisioned a series of Native American enclaves east of the Mississippi that would be bypassed by the surging wave of settlements. It was his attempt at a just resolution of the Native American dilemma.[26]

It so happened that the entire Creek delegation was lodged at an inn adjoining Richmond Hill. For nearly a month, Abigail was fascinated with what she described as "my Neighbours the Creek Savages, who visit us daily." It was quite a scene: "They are very fond of visiting us as we entertain them kindly and they behave with much civility . . . Last night they had a great Bond fire, dancing around it like so many spirits, hoping, singing, yelling and expressing their pleasure and Satisfaction in true Savage State. They are the first Savages I ever saw."

The soaring optimism of that moment—the possibility of a just accommodation with the indigenous population of the American continent—was destined to be dashed very shortly, when Washington discovered that the federal government lacked the resources to honor its pledge of protection. But Abigail participated in the short-lived celebratory mood, attending the signing ceremony in Federal Hall, where the Creek chiefs formed themselves into a chorus and sang a song that, as an interpreter explained, was about perpetual peace. That evening she invited a Creek chief to dine at Richmond Hill, and he proceeded to make her an honorary member of the Creek Nation: "He took me by the Hand, bowed his Head, and bent his knee, calling me

Mammea, Mammea," presumably her Creek name. All the chiefs, she observed, "are very fine looking Men, placid countenances & fine shape," almost perfect physical models in the manner of Greek statues. There were very few high points in the tragic story of Indian-white relations in the United States, but Abigail was able to participate in one of them.[27]

Although John witnessed the same events as Abigail, he did not leave a written record of his reactions, in part because of his vows to embrace the required role of silence as vice president, in part because he was channeling his intellectual energies into the **Davila** essays. These provoked the only occasion when he, or at least his name, emerged from the invisible background, and he went from being essentially harmless to politically dangerous. The incident was provoked, albeit inadvertently, by his old friend and former colleague Thomas Jefferson.

Washington had persuaded a reluctant Jefferson to serve as the first secretary of state. Jefferson was late to arrive in New York, delayed until May 1790 because he needed to oversee the marriage of his eldest daughter at Monticello. He had previously written a glowing tribute to John on his appointment as vice president, and it is virtually certain—though the historical record is blank on this score—that he resumed his social interactions with Abigail and John that summer. The old intimacies of Paris were recovered.[28]

A few months later, however, Jefferson was asked to provide an endorsement of Thomas Paine's new book, **The Rights of Man,** which was a soaring argument for viewing the recent French Revolution as a European version of the American Revolution. Misguidedly thinking that his endorsement would be anonymous, Jefferson praised Paine's book, which accurately expressed his own somewhat romantic political conviction about ongoing developments in France. He described it as an antidote "against the political heresies which have sprung up among us." The reference was widely and correctly seen as a swipe against John's defense of "the monarchical principle" in the **Davila** essays, and was quickly picked up by all the major newspapers.

Deeply offended, John confronted his old friend for what he regarded as a gratuitous slap and blatant distortion of his views. Jefferson's remark, he later observed, "was generally considered as an open personal attack upon me, by insinuating the false interpretation of my Writings as favouring the introduction of hereditary Monarchy and Aristocracy into this Country." His clear intent, so he explained, was to insist that a strong executive was essential in the new American government, and that in France the retention of some version of constitutional monarchy was probably wise in order to ease the transition to more full-blooded republican principles.[29]

Jefferson had already responded apologetically, but also somewhat elusively. Whatever political differences existed between them mattered less to him than their personal friendship: "And I can declare with truth in the presence of the almighty that nothing was further from my intention or expectation than to have had either my name or your name brought before the public on this occasion." This was surely sincere, for Jefferson had not expected his name to be cited in an endorsement of Paine's book. Then he added—and this was not sincere— that he was "not referring to any writing that I might suppose to be yours."[30]

Whether John actually believed Jefferson is unclear, but he chose to accept the apology because he wished to avoid a rupture in a friendship that, as he put it, "has subsisted for fifteen years between us without the slightest interruption . . . and is still dear to my heart." A series of eleven essays under the pseudonym "Publica" soon appeared in the Boston newspapers, quite deftly criticizing Paine's linkage of the American and French revolutions, questioning Jefferson's political judgment in embracing the connections, and defending the opposing views of **Davila**. Most pundits assumed that Publica was John, arguing on his own behalf. But it was really John Quincy, in his first—albeit anonymous— appearance on the national stage, defending his father.[31]

It was only a minor incident with no immediate policy implications, a small crack in the friendship, swiftly repaired with the aid of Jefferson's well-intentioned duplicity and John's eager gullibility. But it turned out to be a premonition of the looming chasm in both the Adams-Jefferson friendship and, more significantly, the political division between warring camps within the infant American republic. This little flurry was a preview of the debate between two revolutionary veterans over nothing less than the true meaning of the American Revolution, the first skirmish in the battle between self-styled Federalists and Republicans over the proper shape of a republic that also aspired to be a nation.

MIDLIFE

In November 1790, when John and Abigail moved to the temporary capital at Philadelphia, he was fifty-five and she was forty-six. The euphemistic term **middle-aged** had yet to be coined, but they both felt that they were closer to the end than the beginning. At one point Abigail seemed to suggest that the running biological clock had, albeit gradually, transformed the very character of their relationship: "Years subdue the ardour of passion," she observed, "but in lieu thereof a Friendship and affection deep Rooted persists which defies the Ravages of Time, and will survive whilst the vital Flame persists."[32]

To the extent that Abigail's observation suggested that the sexual dimension of their marriage was finished, both of them furnished evidence that the "vital Flame" remained at least partially physical. For example, when John ended a letter with "I am impatiently yours," Abigail confessed that the phrase prompted her "to be a little Rhoguish and ask a Question." Or when she referred to his advancing age in one letter, he reprimanded her in a suggestively jesting way: "But how dare you hint or Lisp a Word about Sixty Years of Age. If I were Here, I would soon convince you that I am not above Forty." One can never be sure about such long-ago intimacies, but the bulk of the evidence indicates that John and Abigail remained lovers in the physical sense of the term well into middle age.[33]

Although she was nine years younger than John, the inevitable ravages of time struck Abigail sooner and more dramatically. The first symptoms of rheumatoid arthritis appeared during her London years, but the chronic and degenerative disease advanced to new levels of intensity in the 1790s. "I have been so weakened & debilitated as to be unable to walk alone," she reported in 1791, "and my Nerves so affected as to oblige me to seclude myself from all company except my most intimate companions." Her rheumatic symptoms, chiefly swelling of the joints, ebbed and flowed in waves of pain and paralysis, often exacerbated by cold weather and the rigors of travel. During one especially acute attack she was confined to her bed for six weeks. Even writing letters became difficult, because she could not hold a pen.[34]

By 1792, the end of John's first term as vice president, the extra weight she had put on in Paris and London was gone. "I have scarcely any flesh left in comparison of what I was," she reported, probably a function of not being able to eat for prolonged periods. The trip from Braintree to Philadelphia became an excruciating ordeal, limited to only a few hours of travel each day. This was the major reason for her decision to remain at Braintree for John's entire second term. (Actually, Braintree's north precinct was incorporated into the town of Quincy in February 1792, so her letters to John ever after reflected the new postmark.) During her last season in Philadelphia she found her social obligations "an Egyptian task" because of her chronic condition, and she was forced to decline about half the invitations for health reasons. Better to remain at home, she decided, than become a burden.[35]

John's health problems at midlife were less debilitating. His hair continued to fall out, but that was nothing new, and the practice of wearing wigs on all official occasions, though a dying tradition, conveniently covered his naked skull. His teeth went the way of his hair—for whatever reason he never replaced them with a false set—but his speech had not yet become slurred as a consequence. He periodically experienced a feverish condition accompanied by violent chills, what he called an "ague," malaria-like symptoms that were probably latent remnants of his illness in Amsterdam ten years earlier. But he always recovered quickly and fully.

His most troubling ailments were failing eyesight and persistent tremors in his hands that affected his ability to read and write. When several long letters from John Quincy received only brief responses, he offered his physical degeneration as an excuse: "It is painful to the Vanity of an Old Man to acknowledge the decays of Nature," he explained, "but I have lost the habit of Writing . . . from weak Eyes and from a trembling hand to such a degree that a Pen is as terrible to me, as a Sword to a Coward, or as a rod to a child."[36]

The tremors, however, came and went, and when in remission allowed him to toss off ten pages without pause. The bloodshot eyes he attributed to a lifetime of reading without proper light, but he stubbornly refused to change his reading habits, declaring in full bravado mode his determination "to sacrifice my Eyes like Milton [i.e., go blind] rather than give up the Amusement without which I should despair." When Abigail urged him to cut back on his nightly reading, he refused to comply. "The more one reads," he protested, "the more one sees."[37]

In part because he was older, John took these annoying biological reminders of his aging more seriously. He began to fear that he was approaching some chronological line beyond which lay only a downhill slide into senility and death: "How soon will my Sands be run out of the Glass?" he asked Abigail, adding that once you crossed an invisible line "the Days and Hours have additional Wings which then waive and beat with increasingly rapidity."[38]

He was especially worried about what he called "dying at the top," meaning a loss of mental coherence because of dementia or senility. Samuel Adams, then governor of Massachusetts, was apparently suffering from the early stages of dementia, and John cringed when he witnessed "the debilitating Power of Age" during a speech in which the old man made a fool of himself. He had the same reaction when one of his old acquaintances in the Senate lost his train of thought and stumbled his way into complete confusion before his colleagues. The scene, John reported, "moved the tender feeling of any heart for a Friend advanced in years, not many however beyond my own." Most disconcerting was the alarming realization that neither man was aware of how pitiful he had become, a fate that John vowed to avoid at all costs.[39]

Abigail was the designated truth teller if such a senior moment arrived, but she herself was having foreboding thoughts about her own final chapters. They were prompted by caring for John's mother, who was in her mid-eighties and undergoing all the painful tribulations of physical decline, including constant coughing, sleepless nights, an emaciated body, and a listless mind: "My constant attendance upon her has very much lessened my desire of long life," Abigail confessed to John. "Her fear lest she should recover and become useless, her appearing to have lived out every enjoyment, shows that life is at best a poor play, and the best that can come of it is a miserable Benediction." Abigail's chronic battle with rheumatism made her especially sensitive about becoming a hopeless invalid like her mother-in-law, a premonition that paralleled John's fear of becoming a mindless embarrassment on the public stage. Abigail tended to sustain a stoic stance about the morbid uncertainties of aging, while John veered toward more melodramatic predictions of imminent decline: "My forces of Mind and Body are nearly spent," he warned. "Few Years remain for me, if any." At the time, in 1795, he had thirty-one years to go.[40]

Midlife also required them to renegotiate the relationship with their children, all of whom were now adults out of the nest and no longer mere receptacles into which they could pour their parental wisdom with impunity. Both Abigail and John were accustomed to being hands-on parents, presuming and assuming an authority over their children that verged on the absolute. Now that had to change.

Nabby, after all, was a mother of her own. Abigail relished her new role as grandmother, and when Nabby became pregnant for the third time, she volunteered to take the two young boys for several weeks. She quickly discovered that Nabby's parenting style was more permissive than her own, since John Adams Smith, a mere toddler, presumed he had the run of the house. "One great mistake in the education of youth," she apprised Nabby, "is gratifying every wish of their hearts." All young children, she thought, "should know how to suffer want." Eventually, however, she acknowledged that her own views "are so old fashioned that . . . they are illsuited to modern style and fashion." Her disciplinary standards continued to melt away as she watched her grandson persuade John to pull him around the room in a chair, "which is generally done for half an hour, to the derangement of my carpet and the amusement of his grandpa."[41]

Both Abigail and John developed a growing concern for the career choices that Nabby's husband was making. William Stephens Smith had presumed that he would be offered a prominent post in the new government. He even had the temerity to propose himself for the ambassadorial vacancy in

London based on his previous experience as John's secretary there. This was considered a quite flagrant act of arrogance by all concerned and was summarily rejected; Smith reacted huffily, vowing to prove his critics wrong by making a private fortune in the lucrative but highly speculative market in western lands. Initially, he enjoyed a measure of success, though John did not approve of his new career or his inflated sense of importance: "He boasts too much of having made his fortune."[42]

After Smith spent two weeks with him in Philadelphia, John confided to Abigail that their daughter's husband "is tormented by his Ambitions, but has taken unsagacious measures to remove his Pains. I know not what he is in Pursuit of." They both felt that their daughter and grandchildren were dependent on a man whose future depended on winning a high-stakes game of speculation in western lands. But they kept their concern to themselves. Nabby's fate was no longer within their control.[43]

At least to a slight extent, John Quincy's was. As the designated protégé, he was the recipient of the same kind of educational injunctions from his father at twenty-five as he was at five: make yourself a master of the classics, to include Cicero, Livy, Polybius, and Sallust; moreover, you must "read them all in Latin—Nor would I by any means consent that you forget your Greek." In truth, however, John Quincy was now a young man with an emotional and professional agenda of his own. He had become infatuated with a sixteen-year-old girl named Mary Frazier while setting up his law practice in Newburyport—an entanglement that exposed how his emotional immaturity rested uncomfortably alongside his intellectual precociousness. The love affair—his first—ended when he moved to Boston in search of clients. But they failed to show up. John Quincy was humiliated when he had to inform his father that he could not support himself.[44]

John rose to the occasion. His son was, he told everyone who would listen, "as great a Scholar as this Country has produced at his Age." He was not one of those "flashing Insects [who] glitter and glow for a moment and then disappear." A bit later he claimed that his son "has more Prudence at 27, than his father at 58." The boy simply needed some help over this temporary hump before soaring to the heights that were his destiny.[45]

John offered to provide an annual stipend of $100, plus free use of one of his Boston properties as an office and home, until John Quincy could support himself. This was a violation of all his earlier pronouncements against providing financial support beyond college for his children. But once decided, John extended the same level of assistance to Charles and Thomas, presumably as a statement of equity. John Quincy was mortified at the fact of his abiding dependence but was in no position to refuse his father's offer. John preferred to regard it as a safe and shrewd investment in an extraordinarily talented young man whom he had personally groomed for greatness.[46]

This investment earned dividends in 1794, when John Quincy was nominated by Washington to serve as American minister to The Hague. The vote in the Senate, which John oversaw, was unanimous, despite John Quincy's tender age, and despite the inevitable whisperings about nepotism. (But who else could claim fluency in Dutch, French, and Russian?) Washington, who had demonstrated over his long career a true genius at spotting talent, assured John that the choice was based entirely on merit and was likely to be merely the first step in John Quincy's brilliant career. "I shall be much mistaken," wrote Washington, "if, in as short a Period as can well be expected, he is not found at the head of the Diplomatic Corps." Like so many of Washington's judgments, this proved prescient.[47]

With John Quincy now launched as an erstwhile American statesman—his brother Thomas was appointed as his secretary, so both of John's boys would be treading the same paths in The Hague that he had walked a decade earlier—John acknowledged that the torch had been passed to the next generation. John Quincy's official correspon-

dence from his listening post in the middle of
Europe, currently aflame with the political and military conflagration generated by the French Revolution, was immediately recognized for the brilliance
of its panoramic scope and mastery of detail. At the
height of his own powers, John observed, he could
never have duplicated his son's sagacity. "Go on, my
son, in your glorious Career," he wrote, "and may
the Blessings of God crown you with success." He
was an extremely proud parent, who fully recognized that his boy had become his own man.[48]

The same was not true of Charles, the spoiled
son in the Adams family, whom John decided to
make his special project. Because the etiquette of
the era forbade direct discussion of private domestic
problems, the family correspondence makes only
elliptical references to the rumors that Charles was
drinking heavily. He had apparently fallen in with a
rowdy crew at Harvard, been disciplined by the college for running naked while drunk through Harvard Yard, and persisted in his bad habits and bad
associations after graduation. John Quincy claimed
that he had warned his brother that his behavior, if
ever discovered by their father, would produce massive explosions: "I wrote him a very serious letter
three weeks ago," he confided to his uncle, "upon
the subject in such a manner as must, I think, lead
him to be more cautious." Abigail took the view
that Charles had sowed some wild oats at Harvard,

but would recover once removed from the influence of his college companions.[49]

Nevertheless, the decision that Charles should read law in New York reflected the recognition that he required parental supervision, which could best occur if he lived with Abigail and John at Richmond Hill. By all accounts, Charles was a model law student. "I sometimes think his application too intense," Abigail observed, "but better so, than too remis." After his parents moved to Philadelphia, Charles opened his law office just off Wall Street and, unlike John Quincy, was flooded with clients based on his growing reputation as one of the brightest and most personable young lawyers in the city.[50]

John decided to initiate what became a voluminous correspondence with Charles in 1792, not so much because he still harbored fears of his son's addiction to alcohol, but mostly because he wanted to carve out a more mature adult-to-adult relationship based on their mutual interests in politics and the law. He sold his own horses in order to purchase the most up-to-date law books for Charles.

During a four-month period in the spring of 1794, John wrote thirty long letters to Charles, asking his legal opinion on America's treaty obligations to France; bombarding him with lengthy discourses on the misleading doctrine of equality as promulgated by the French philosophes; urging him to broaden his base of knowledge by reading Confucius, Socrates, Plutarch, Seneca, and Epictetus; asking his advice about the convoluted politics of New York; and answering his questions about the existence of any thoroughly democratic societies in world history ("Yes, my son, there are many Such Societies in the Forests of America, called Indian Tribes").[51]

He invited Charles to visit him for a week in Philadelphia (offering to pay all expenses), join him to observe the Senate, attend a levee, mingle with the prominent players, let a proud father show him off. Charles did visit, and after he left John described his favorite scene: father and son sitting together after attending a dinner, smoking cigars, sharing their reactions to the political gossip, bantering as friends into the night.[52]

Once back in New York, Charles received a letter from John in the parental mode: "You appeared to me, when you were here," wrote John, "to be too plethorick," meaning bloated. "There are innumerable Disorders which originate in Fulness, especially in a sedentary and studious life. You must rouse yourself from your Lethargy and take your Walk every Day." Only with the advantage of hindsight, knowing as we do that Charles would die of complications from alcoholism five years later, is it possible to recognize that his bloated condition was most probably not the result of inadequate exercise.

He had become an alcoholic who was extremely adroit at concealing his addiction from his father and, for that matter, from everyone else, except his wife.[53]

PARTISAN POLITICS

When John returned to his post in the Senate in December 1792, the first order of business was to oversee the official counting of the electoral votes for president and vice president. Washington's reelection was assured, and the tally revealed that, once again, he was a unanimous choice with 132 electoral votes. John's reelection was less foreordained, creating the awkward prospect of certifying his own rejection by the electorate. Despite opposition from New York and several southern states, which rallied behind Governor George Clinton of New York, John was comfortably reelected with 77 votes to 50 for Clinton. "It does not appear," he wrote Abigail, "that I am born to so good Fortune as to be a mere Farmer in my old Age."[54]

The letter was necessary because Abigail had decided to remain at Quincy. Despite his pleadings, she refused to accompany him to Philadelphia, using her rheumatic condition and her aversion to that city's heat and humidity as excuses. John complained that her decision produced a nefarious pattern, "to be separated both when we were too young and now when we are too old." It also broke the prevailing pattern of the preceding eight years, when she was by his side as a full partner in the interstices of politics and life. The only compensation was her letters: "They give me more entertainment than all the speeches I hear," John observed. "There is more good Thoughts, fine strokes and Mother Wit in them than I hear in a whole Week."[55]

This time the roles were reversed; it was John who complained of being lonely and miserable: "I pore upon my Family at Quincy, my Children in Europe, and my Children and Grandchildren in New York till I am Melancholy and wish myself a private Man." He adopted a refrain about his altered sense of time: "It is a common observation of old People, that as they advance in Life, time appears to run off faster." But during his solitary days in Philadelphia, without Abigail to quicken his pulse, time seemed to slow down. Abigail, on the other hand, found the distance less daunting this time around, and noted that the existence of dependable postal service created the possibility of an ongoing conversation. She thought it almost eerie that they found themselves, despite the distance, having the same thoughts at the same time: "It may be called the telegraph of the Mind," she noted admiringly.[56]

Whether it was telegraphic or telepathic, Abigail and John had nearly identical reactions to the sudden surge of fiercely partisan politics that came to dominate John's second term. Both of them located the source of the emerging opposition in the southern states, most especially in Virginia, which viewed the entire fiscal program of Hamilton as an engine designed to transfer power from the agrarian to the commercial sector, which effectively meant from South to North. Jefferson and Madison were the highly capable leaders of the Virginia-writ-large view that the federal government had no authority to legislate for the states and that Hamilton's fiscal program, especially the National Bank, was therefore unconstitutional. Abigail was particularly outspoken in describing this purportedly principled position as a mere mask to conceal the sectional interests of the slave-holding south. "I firmly believe," she wrote to her sister, "that if I live ten years longer, I shall see a division of the Southern and Northern states." They both regarded the selection of a Potomac location for the national capital as a victory for Virginia, which was obsessed with ensuring that the federal governent speak with a southern accent.[57]

The political agenda shifted dramatically in the spring of 1793, when the French Revolution exploded into spasms of violence that sent shock waves throughout Europe. In both **Defence** and

Davila John had predicted that any attempt to impose the utopian schemes of the French philosophes would produce anarchy, though he claimed to take no satisfaction in being proved correct: "It is melancholy that everything in France . . . should conspire so perfectly to demonstrate over again all my Books . . . Yet they do not good." The only thing to do when the guillotine was moving so methodically was to steer clear and allow the bloodletting to run its murderous course. "Dragons Teeth have been sown in France," he observed, "and come up Monsters."[58]

Washington had reached the same conclusion, and in April 1793 issued the Neutrality Proclamation, declaring the United States a disinterested spectator to Europe's ongoing calamities and, most especially, a neutral in the looming war between France and Great Britain. Though the proclamation represented a repudiation of the nation's obligations in the Franco-American Treaty of 1778, John could claim that he had long ago abandoned those obligations by negotiating a separate peace with Great Britain in 1783.

While Abigail and John both agreed with the president on the policy of American neutrality, for at least three reasons that policy was much easier to proclaim than enforce. First, the vast majority of American citizens loved the French and loathed the British, for the obvious reason that French assistance had rendered possible the American victory over the British leviathan. Second, diplomatic detachment was difficult to reconcile with commercial entanglements, for the American economy was heavily dependent on trade with both France and Great Britain. (This was an intractable problem that would surface again in 1812 and 1917, in both instances drawing the United States into war.) Third, the burgeoning political opposition, now styling itself the Republican Party to differentiate itself from the Federalists, was more than willing to play politics with the issue, seizing upon the enormous popularity of the French cause throughout the land.

The new French minister, Edmond Genet, after coaching from Jefferson, stirred the pot by urging American citizens to defy the neutrality policy of the elected government and demonstrate their loyalty to the French cause of liberty, equality, and fraternity. Charles reported from New York that the city was delirious over Genet: "every man who now ventures to disapprove of a single measure of the French is, according to modern language, an Aristocrat." The popular sentiment for a pro-French foreign policy, which almost surely meant war with Great Britain, reached a crescendo during the last months of 1793, with popular demonstrations in all the major cities and advocates on each side blazing away at each other in the newspapers. While he could plausibly claim to be the most experienced student of foreign policy in the government, John played no role in the debates or the deliberations of the executive branch. "My own Situation is of such compleat Insignificance," he lamented to Abigail, "that I have scarcely the Power to do good or Evil." As Republican editorials targeted Washington and Hamilton for their betrayal of the French connection, John jokingly observed that he was so irrelevant that no one bothered to vilify him: "Poor me," he confided to Abigail, "I am left out of the Question."[59]

This was also the moment when the cracks that had already begun to appear in the friendship between Jefferson and the Adams family became a chasm. It was an open secret that Jefferson, while serving as secretary of state in the Washington administration, was orchestrating the Republican opposition to the very government he officially served. John apprised Abigail that she would not recognize the man they had welcomed into their family in Paris: "I am really astonished at the blind spirit of Party which has seized on the whole soul of this Jefferson," he reported. "There is not a Jacobin in France more devoted to Faction."[60]

Though he claimed to be acting on principle—opposing the excessive exercise of federal authority and embracing the glorious cause of the French Revolution—in John's opinion Jefferson's true motives were blatantly self-serving. Like so many of the Virginia planters, he was heavily in debt to British creditors, and therefore predisposed toward an anti-British foreign policy that would delay repayment into the indefinite future: "I wish someone would pay his Debt of seven thousand pounds to Britain," John confided to Abigail, "and then I believe his Passions would subside, his Reason return, and the whole Man and his whole State [Virginia] become good Friends of the Union and its Govt."[61]

As one of the most seasoned students of the Jefferson psyche, John reached the conclusion that his former friend was extremely adept at playing hide-and-seek within himself: "Ambition is the subtlest Beast of the Intellectual and Moral Field. It is wonderfully adroit in concealing itself from its owner." In Jefferson's case, John believed that he could not candidly confront his own ambition to succeed Washington as the next president.

When Jefferson announced that he was stepping down as secretary of state, leaving public life for the bucolic serenity of Monticello, John predicted that his retirement would prove temporary: "Jefferson thinks he shall by this step get a Reputation as a humble, modest, meek Man, wholly without ambition or vanity. He may even have deceived himself into this Belief. But if a Prospect opens, the World will see and he will feel, that he is as ambitious as Oliver Cromwell." A year later, Jefferson claimed to be completely consumed by his new crop rotation scheme at Monticello and wholly oblivious to the mounting efforts of Republican operatives in several states to launch his candidacy for the presidency.[62]

It is difficult to avoid the conclusion that John's insights into the ambitions simmering away in Jefferson's soul proved so prescient because they mirrored the presidential ambitions he himself was harboring. If so—and it would seem highly unlikely that the thought never crossed his mind—he suppressed any mention of it in his correspondence. Quite the contrary: his letters to Abigail conveyed the impression of an aging patriarch, eager to complete this last assignment of his public life and then join Abigail in retirement at Quincy. Moreover, the scene he was then witnessing from his perch in the Senate was so full of partisan bickering and nasty political infighting that no sane observer, he suggested, would have been able to think of the presidency as anything but a thankless task fit only for masochists and martyrs.

The chief occasion for this circuslike spectacle was the debate over the Jay Treaty, the controversial centerpiece of Washington's second term, much as Hamilton's financial program had been in the first. In both instances, the debate was so fierce because of the embedded resistance to any explicit projection of executive power, which immediately conjured up the dreaded "consolidation" by some far-away federal government and the equally threatening emergence of a "monarchical presence" within the republican temple. John regarded these fears as groundless, and the Republican effort to exacerbate and exploit them as a diabolical plot to topple the Federalist government by partisans of the Virginia-writ-large persuasion.

Here is the essential background. By 1794 the prospects of war with Great Britain were approaching a crisis. It was one thing to proclaim American neutrality in the war between France and Great Britain, quite another to maintain a neutral posture when British troops remained stationed on the northwestern frontier, inciting and supplying Indian raids on American settlers in the Ohio Valley, and British frigates were scooping up American merchant ships in the Caribbean with impunity in order to block all grain shipments to France.

Washington dispatched Chief Justice John Jay to London, where he was charged to negotiate a realistic bargain that would remove the British troops and redefine commercial relations with Great Britain in terms that avoided war. Adams had no say in this decision, though he concurred completely that avoiding war was America's highest diplomatic priority. Jay returned with a treaty that, on the positive side, required the removal of British troops on the frontier and also committed the British to arbitrate American claims of compensation for cargoes confiscated by the British navy. On the negative side, however, the treaty recognized British naval supremacy in deferential terms that gave American neutrality a decidedly British tilt, a tacit admission that trade with Great Britain was the lifeblood of the American economy. And it required American debtors, chiefly Virginian planters, to pay off their prewar debts to British creditors.[63]

In retrospect, the Jay Treaty was a shrewd bargain, for it not only avoided a potentially ruinous war but also aligned the United States with the dominant global power over the next century. At the time, however, it was overwhelmingly unpopular. Jay later claimed that he could have walked the entire eastern seaboard at night with his way lit by fires from his burning effigies. Adams thought that Jay had performed the ultimate act of political virtue, the trademark Adams act, by defying popular opinion to further the long-term public interest: "He will live to see the Federal City," Adams predicted, "and inhabit the proudest House," meaning that Jay's contributions would eventually lead to his election as president. Meanwhile, popular opinion raged against the treaty: "No event since the Commencement of the Government," Abigail observed, "has excited so much undue heat, so much bitter acrimony, so much base invective."[64]

In June 1795, with John watching in stony silence, the Senate approved the treaty on a straight party-line vote (20–10), thereby behaving in accord with John's description of the Senate as the custodian of America's enduring interests, regardless of popular disapproval. "It is well the Senate only have the discussion of it [the Jay Treaty]," Abigail noted, "for if it was to go to the House for Ratification, and was a Treaty from the Kingdom of Heaven, proclaiming Peace on Earth and Good Will to Men, there would not be wanting characters to defame and abuse it."[65]

Although Senate approval should have ended the matter, the Republican opposition under Madison's adroit leadership devised a strategy to sabotage the treaty by denying the funds for its implementation in the House, which had authority over all money bills. John believed he was watching the triumph of party politics in its most partisan form. "There is an Inveteracy and Obstinacy on this occasion as I scarcely ever saw," he lamented to Abigail. The Republican opposition was highly orchestrated, "all moving as one Man, not a dissenting Voice among them, appearing as if drawn by one Cord." And if he could have read the correspondence between Madison and Jefferson, John would have seen that the cord stretched back to Monticello, where Jefferson had roused himself from retirement to assume command of Republican strategy to kill the treaty.

The Republicans had a clear majority in the House, but as petitions poured in from merchants, Quakers, and frontier settlers, all of whom had come to the realization that failure to pass the treaty meant war with Great Britain, the majority began to melt away. "Mr. Madison looks worried to death," John reported to Abigail. "Pale, withered, haggard . . . They have brought themselves into great embarrassment." Funding for the Jay Treaty passed by a slim majority (51–48) on April 30, 1796.[66]

What John had witnessed in the debate over the Jay Treaty was the emergence of a highly partisan brand of party politics for which he was both intellectually and temperamentally unprepared. And because this episode would prove to be a preview of coming attractions, indeed the first appearance of what would become a two-party sys-tem that made the very idea of the disinterested statesman into an anachronism, he was also witnessing the arrival of a political culture almost designed to torment him until his dying days. His political irrelevance as vice president had allowed him to avoid the full force of the partisan game: "I have escaped in a whole skin," he wrote to John Quincy, "as Mr. Jay and the President have attracted almost the whole Attention, Genius, Inventions and Industry of the Libellers." But this was all about to change.[67]

HEIR APPARENT

In January 1796 Washington leaked the news that he intended to step down after his second term as president. Although he had been hinting at his intentions for nearly four years, Washington's stature as the only self-evident truth in American politics made it difficult to imagine an American government without him as the centerpiece. There had been, therefore, an unspoken assumption that he would continue to serve until his soul was carried to its heavenly reward, dying in office like an American king. Now the indispensable man let it be known that he was leaving.

John's initial response to this news was extremely revealing: "You know the Consequences of this, to me and to yourself," he wrote to Abigail. "Either we must enter upon Arduors more trying than any yet experienced, or retire to Quincy, farmers for Life." He obviously recognized that he was a viable candidate to succeed Washington, but he had not allowed himself to think about that prospect until the moment arrived. And now that it had, Abigail needed to be an equal partner in the decision. His initial instinct, or at least his first conscious reaction, was to lean toward retirement: "But I think upon the whole the Probability is strong that I shall beat the hasty Retreat," he wrote her, "and spend the rest of my days in a very humble Style with you." On the other hand, he wanted Abigail to know that the decision was not entirely theirs to make: "I am Heir Apparent, you know, and a Succession is soon to take place," he half joked. "I have a pious and philosophical Resignation to the Voice of the People in the Case, which is the Voice of God." In other words, he was waiting to gauge the prospects of his candidacy before making a final decision.[68]

Abigail's reaction was less ambivalent: "My Ambition leads me not to be first in Rome," she responded. "If personal considerations alone were to weigh, I would immediately say retire." Then she added a crucial caveat: "But in a Matter of such momentous Concern I dare not influence you. I must pray that you have Superior Direction." It was a repeat of the pattern established when John was in Europe and she urged him to come home. Her own preferences were clear, but she would support whatever decision he made. She did feel free to remind him that the partisan politics surrounding the Jay Treaty debates boded badly for the next president, who would also face the nearly impossible task of succeeding the greatest hero of the age: "I am sure it will be a most unpleasant Seat," she warned, "full of Thorns, Briers, thistles, murmuring, fault finding, calumny . . . and what not."[69]

John acknowledged that the political atmosphere had become quite toxic, and he could testify that it had taken its toll on Washington, who had aged a decade over the past two years. He also harbored doubts about his own health, at one point concluding that it made more sense to retire "before my Constitution failed, before my Memory failed, before my Judgment failed." And, yes, he had to admit that he was "weary of the Game." But then he added: "Yet I don't know how I could live out of it."[70]

Abigail surely realized that, when all the internal twitchings and vacillations were done, when all the arguments for and against were exhausted, her husband would find the summons to serve irresistible. But as he rocked back and forth among all his demons and doubts, she felt an obligation to let him know what he would be up against: "You know what is before you. The Whips and Scorpions, the Thorns without Roses, the dangers, anxieties and weight of Empire." Moreover, she had some doubts about herself: "I am anxious for the proper discharge of that share which will devolve upon me." Over the past four years she had grown accustomed to the serenities of her Quincy home, where she could speak her mind: "I should say that I have been so used to a freedom of sentiment," she observed, "that I know not how to place so many guards about me." John concurred that the social obligations of the office would be a burden for them both: "I hate Levees and Drawing Rooms. I hate to speak to 1000 People to whom I have nothing to say." But then came the caveat: "Yet all this I can do."[71]

Although the ultimate decision had probably been made by March, John's wrestling match with his own ambitions continued throughout the spring. Once again, as in the two previous presidential elections, the absence of a formal nomination process meant that he did not need to declare his candidacy. But in newspaper editorials, even toasts at dinner parties, his name topped most lists throughout New England as the obvious choice. He had, after all, received more votes in the two previous elections than anyone except Washington. And if the chief criterion was revolutionary credentials, one would be hard-pressed to find anybody else who could match his. Abigail assured him on this point: "There remains not a Man in America whose Publick Service [more] entitled him to the office."[72]

Prospective voters south of the Potomac did not quite see it that way, insisting that there was a certain Virginian currently in retirement at Monticello who possessed impeccable revolutionary credentials of his own, and whose views on the proper limitations that should be placed on federal power were more akin to their own. By the summer of 1796 it was clear to all concerned, except apparently to Jefferson himself, that the contest for the presidency would match the two former friends. Jefferson later claimed that he was wholly oblivious that he was a candidate, and that he was too busy harvesting his vetch crop to notice that the Republican opposition had rallied around his candidacy. Madison endorsed this rather incredible version of Jefferson's indifference, claiming that he made a point of not visiting his friend at Monticello that summer for fear that any mention of the presidential election might cause Jefferson to withdraw his name.

John could not claim that he was unaware of his own candidacy, in part because he lacked Jefferson's powers of self-deception, in part because he was receiving letters from Abigail and John Quincy about his prospects. Abigail made a survey of newspaper editorials on the eve of the election and reported that his endorsement of American neutrality and support for the Jay Treaty would cost him most of the electoral votes in the South. She predicted a clear sectional split in the final tally and a very close contest. If he did not win but came in second, she requested and received a solemn promise that he would refuse the vice presidency and join her in retirement in Quincy.[73]

For his part, John took refuge behind the classic code of silence. Anyone who uttered any statements on his own behalf, or even commented on the ongoing campaign being conducted by surrogates, thereby exposed his own vanity and was deemed unqualified to serve. On good days he boasted to Abigail that he would be fine regardless of the outcome: "I feel myself in a very happy temper of mind. Perfectly willing to be released from the Port of Danger, but determined, if call'd to it, to brave it." On bad days he confided his emotional confusion: "I laugh at myself twenty times a Day, for my feelings and meditations . . . It really seems to be as if I wished to be left out. Let me see. Do I know my own heart? I am not sure." Could he, with proper decorum, announce Jefferson's victory in the Senate, where the electoral votes were counted? Or would he be too mortified to do his duty? He did not know.[74]

After the election, but before the results were known, Abigail reported to John that she had had an interesting dream. She was riding in a coach when a barrage of twenty-four cannonballs came flying at her. She was terrified and fully expected to be blown to bits. But the cannonballs all exploded in midair before they reached her. She interpreted the dream as a kind of supernatural signal not to worry. Either way, they would be fine. And the dream probably meant that, despite all the anguish, John was going to win.[75]

He did. As Abigail had predicted, the vote was extremely close (71–68). As she also predicted, the split was mostly sectional, with John's margin of victory dependent on two electoral votes in western Virginia and North Carolina. The results were reasonably clear over a month before the votes were officially counted in the Senate in February 1797. "According to present Appearances," John apprised Abigail in late December, "Jefferson will be Daddy Vice," a fate that would require him to adjust his indulgent living habits to the meager salary of the office.[76]

Abigail wrote back to report that congratulatory compliments were pouring in from all their friends and relatives. The only sour note concerned the revelation, based on several reliable sources, that Alexander Hamilton, in a brazen act of skullduggery, had attempted to manipulate the electoral votes on behalf of Thomas Pinckney, a South Carolina Federalist, in the apparent hope of sneaking Pinckney in ahead of John. The plot failed, but it probably cut into John's margin of victory.

This was clinching evidence that Hamilton could not be trusted. "He is a Man ambitious as Julius Caesar," Abigail warned. "His thirst for Fame is insatiable. I have ever kept my eye on him." The clear implication was that John had rather nonchalantly taken Hamilton's support for granted and vastly underestimated his ambition to control the Federalist agenda after Washington's departure. Hamilton must now be regarded as a rival.[77]

Although she had made her own preferences for

retirement clear, now that the voters had spoken, Abigail was prepared to embrace the verdict and join John again as a partner in this final triumph of his public career. It was so cold in Quincy that it was freezing her ink and chilling the blood in her veins, she observed, but his election had quickened her heartbeat in defiance of the cold. They were in all eyes, including hers, a team, so in some sense she, too, had been called to serve. She promised to be at his side, "in the turbulent scenes in which he is about to engage."[78]

CHAPTER SIX

1796–1801

"I can do nothing without you."

Although both John and Abigail were well aware of the supercharged political atmosphere they were entering, the shrewdest assessment of the scatological climate came from no less than Thomas Jefferson: "The President [Washington] is fortunate to get off just as the bubble is bursting, leaving others to hold the bag . . . No man will bring out of that office the reputation which carries him into it." Editorials in the **Aurora,** the chief Republican newspaper, seemed designed to illustrate Jefferson's point, firing several salvos at the departing hero that verged on criminal slander. The Farewell Address was described as "the loathings of a sick mind," and Washington was urged to ask himself "whether you are an apostate or an imposter, whether you have abandoned good principles, or whether you ever had any." Given Washington's singular status, one could only imagine the gauntlet being prepared for his successor. Abigail conjured up the picture of "being fastned up Hand and foot and Tongue to be shot at as our Quincy lads do at the poor Geese and Turkies."[1]

She soon suggested a political path designed to flank this fate, which John immediately adopted as his own preferred course. It entailed opening up a discreet line of communication with Jefferson; offering him cabinet status and a major say in foreign policy; designating him or Madison as the new American envoy to France, where the most ominous threats were brewing; and in effect creating a bipartisan presidency. Despite the recent breach in their relationship, Abigail observed, "I do not think him [Jefferson] an insincere or corruptible man," adding that her own "Friendship for him has ever been unshaken," and that "all the discords may be atuned to harmony by the Hand of a skillfull Artist." Besides, a political alliance with Jefferson was vastly preferable to depending on the loyalty of the ultra-Federalists, who were infatuated with Hamilton, whose misguided attempt to manipulate the recent election had exposed his anti-Adams agenda. "Beware of that spare Cassius," Abigail warned. "I have read his Heart and his wicked Eyes many a time. The very devil is in them."[2]

John leaked word of his bipartisan intentions to Jefferson through Elbridge Gerry, a mutual friend. The initial response from Monticello, a letter to

Madison, dutifully confided to mutual friends in Philadelphia, seemed encouraging: "I can particularly have no feelings which would revolt at a secondary position to Mr. Adams," Jefferson observed, also noting that "I am his junior in life, was his junior in Congress, his junior in the diplomatic line, his junior lately in government."[3]

A second letter was equally gracious, recalling his long friendship with the entire Adams family and saluting John's generosity "at the prospect of administering the government in concurrence with me." Jefferson eventually wrote directly to John, agreeing that the partisan political atmosphere had become truly poisonous and hoping to recover the old spirit of '76, "when we were working together for our independence." Rumors were rampant on the streets of Philadelphia that the venerable Adams-Jefferson partnership was back. Abigail reported attending a dinner at Harvard, where the students proposed a toast: "Adams and Jefferson, or Checks and balances."[4]

The course of the Adams presidency, perhaps even the early path of American history, would have gone in a different direction if John's bipartisan proposal had worked. But it quickly became the victim of the party spirit it was intended to replace. When John floated the idea past several dedicated Federalists, they expressed disbelief, claiming that it amounted to dragging the Trojan horse into the Federalist fortress. Meanwhile, down at Monticello, Jefferson was having second thoughts, prompted by Madison's insistence that the Republican cause must take precedence over nostalgic bonds of brotherhood, no matter how heartfelt; a political alliance with Adams was rooted in a merely sentimental attachment, Madison observed, and not in the abiding interests of the Republican opposition that Jefferson must now prepare himself to lead.[5]

The prospects for an Adams-Jefferson partnership died in a poignant fact-to-face encounter that both men saw fit to record in their memoirs, a clear sign they recognized its political and personal significance. After dining with Washington on March 6, 1797, they walked together down Market Street to Fifth, two blocks from the very spot where Jefferson had drafted the Declaration of Independence that John had so forcefully defended in the Continental Congress almost twenty-one years earlier. John reiterated his offer to bring Jefferson into cabinet deliberations—he had apprised members of his cabinet that anyone who felt strongly opposed to Jefferson's presence should feel free to resign—and repeated his willingness to dispatch either Jefferson or Madison to Paris as American envoy. But Jefferson dismissed both proposals as impossible. They parted at Market and Fifth as former friends who were now poised to become bitter political enemies.[6]

Abigail received a somewhat cryptic letter from John a week later, saying that "Mr. Jefferson has been here . . . He is as he was." She immediately recognized the significance of the message: "There is one observation in your Letter which struck me as meaning more than is exprest. Jefferson is as he was! Can he still be a devotee to a cause and a people run mad? Can it be." John delivered his own answer to the question in a letter to John Quincy: "You can witness for me how loath I have been to give him [Jefferson] up. It is with much reluctance that I am obliged to look upon him as a man whose mind is warped by prejudice . . . as to be unfit for the office he holds." He did not know that, at that very moment, Jefferson was engaged in clandestine conversations with the French consul in Philadelphia, urging him to ignore any peace initiative from Adams, who did not speak for the true interests of the American people, despite his recent election. By most measures, such behavior verged on treason.[7]

Jefferson's rejection increased John's awareness of the bitterly partisan political world emerging in the wake of Washington's departure: "From the Situation, where I am now," he lamented to Abigail, "I see a Scene of Ambition beyond all my former suspicions or Imaginations . . . Jealousies and Rivalries have been my Theme . . . but they never Stared me in the face in such horrid forms as at present."[8]

The inaugural ceremony was awkward for John,

in part because Abigail, who was tending to his dying mother at Quincy, was not present to calm his nerves, in part because everyone in the audience was sobbing at the sight of Washington's final appearance on the public stage. At the end of the ceremony, so he reported to Abigail, Washington whispered to him, "Ay! I am fairly out and you fairly in! See which of us will be happiest." In the ensuing weeks, with Washington gone back to Mount Vernon and Jefferson gone over to the opposition, he suddenly felt lonely and isolated, and sent a cri de coeur to Quincy: "I never wanted you more in my life. The times are critical and dangerous and I must have you here to assist me . . . You must leave our farm to the mercy of the winds . . . I can do nothing without you."[9]

ELEMENTAL INGREDIENTS

John's sudden sense of desperation was based not on an overripe imagination, but on an accurate assessment of the foreign and domestic dilemmas facing him at the start of his presidency. The most pressing problem was France, which had reacted to the Jay Treaty by deploying its privateers in the Atlantic and Caribbean to prey on all American vessels carrying contraband cargo bound for British ports. By May 1797 they had seized more

than three hundred American ships, thereby placing the Franco-American relationship on the cusp
of war.

Nor was that all. The ever-shifting French government, misleadingly called the Directory, had
moved into an anti-American phase, expelling the
new American minister, Charles Cotesworth Pinckney, effectively breaking off diplomatic relations with
the United States. Rather incredibly, this was pretty
much what the previous American minister, James
Monroe, who was a devoted Jefferson protégé, had
recommended. (Monroe had described the Federalist
administration as a hopeless gaggle of pro-British
sympathizers wholly out of touch with the pro-
French sympathies of the American people, which
was the same line that Jefferson was taking with the
French consul in Philadelphia.) As a result, the
Directory had developed grandiose plans for declaring war against the American government, based on
the belief that the vast majority of American citizens
would rally to the French cause. The French foreign
minister, Charles-Maurice de Talleyrand-Périgord,
envisioned a resurgent French empire in North
America based in the Republican stronghold in the
southern states.[10]

All this was a preposterous illusion, of course,
but as the armies of the French Republic swept vic-
toriously across Europe, even the most extreme
forms of Gallic infatuation seemed credible. Writ-

ing to his father from The Hague, John Quincy caught the French mood of nearly delirious invincibility: the fate of the world was now, he wrote, "in the hands of a Corsican stripling [Napoleon], whose name two years ago might have been hidden under a dog's ear on the rolls of fame, but which at the moment disdains comparison with less than Caesar or Alexander."[11]

John's instinctive response to the French threat, rooted in the same realistic convictions about America's abiding interests that Washington had proposed in the Farewell Address, was that war must be avoided at almost any cost. And so in May 1797, soon after Abigail came down from Quincy—"I come to place my head upon your Bosom"—he decided to send a three-man delegation to Paris to negotiate a French version of the Jay Treaty. He coupled this diplomatic commitment with a buildup of the American navy, which would enable the United States to fight a defensive war on the high seas if negotiations broke down.[12]

It was extremely likely that they would. Within the larger context of the Anglo-French competition for primacy in Europe, the United States remained a piddling power of relative insignificance. And given the information they were receiving from the French consul in Philadelphia, fully briefed by Jefferson to dismiss any Federalist initiative as irrelevant, the Directory was poised to treat the American envoys with consummate indifference. At least at this early stage, the central problem facing the Adams presidency was inherently unsolvable.

John's predicament was rendered even more difficult by two political anomalies no president before or since has had to face. The first was the result of a flaw in the Constitution that made the runner-up in the presidential election the vice president. (This was corrected by the ratification of the Twelfth Amendment in 1804, which eliminated the awkward burden of a vice president who happened to be head of the opposition party.) As we have seen, as soon as Jefferson rejected the bipartisan overture from John, he quickly moved behind the scenes to undermine the administration he was purportedly serving. In a sense it was a repeat of the equally duplicitous role Jefferson had played as secretary of state under Washington. It must have taxed even Jefferson's psychological agility to appear at weekly levees alongside Abigail and John, then write coded letters to Madison orchestrating Republican strategy and pass juicy bits of anti-Adams information to Benjamin Franklin Bache, editor of the **Aurora**, but he somehow managed it with apparent serenity.

The second anomaly was the cabinet. One of John's biggest blunders was to retain Washington's chief advisors, a decision that he made without much thought and later attempted to explain as forced upon him by Federalists eager to convey the seamless transition from Washington to Adams. In effect, he somewhat lamely claimed that he lacked the authority to pick his own team.

What he did not realize, and it took him an inordinately long time to figure it out, was that three members of his cabinet—Timothy Pickering at State, Oliver Wolcott at Treasury, and James McHenry at War—were loyal disciples of Hamilton and regarded "the little lion of Federalism," and not John Adams, as their political chief. Hamilton described the arrangement in terms that left no doubt: there was "the President's administration," with John an elected figurehead, and then there was "the actual administration," with Hamilton exercising power as the acknowledged leader of the Federalist Party. Virtually every cabinet vote was run past Hamilton for his approval, and all major cabinet proposals originated with Hamilton. It is difficult to decide what was more bizarre, Hamilton's stunning arrogance at presuming his supremacy over a duly elected president, or John's blind indifference to what was going on around him.[13]

One final ingredient in the political chemistry, perhaps the most elemental of all, was John's distinctive personality. Despite his distinguished résumé, he had no executive experience, had never commanded troops like Washington or served as governor like Jefferson. He was not equipped, by either temperament or experience, to delegate authority to subordinates or to manage them through a difficult decision-making process. All his major public achievements—defending the British troops after the Boston Massacre, leading the Continental Congress toward independence, drafting the Massachusetts Constitution, insisting on a separate American peace treaty with Great Britain—were singular acts of leadership, usually performed in defiance of either conventional wisdom or popular opinion. He harbored a strong contrarian streak that, for example, made him uncomfortable with popularity, because it seemed to him a symptom of someone who would trim his sails rather than pursue the correct if unpopular course. He was an elitist who, unlike Jefferson, believed that majorities were wrong more often than right, and he periodically carried this conviction to the level of perversity, claiming that he was confident that a policy was correct because of its current unpopularity.

All these personal tendencies had hardened into permanent habits of mind and heart by the time John reached the presidency. (Abigail referred to him as an "old oak" who might be torn up by the roots but would never bend, whereas Jefferson was "the willow" who would shift with the wind.) At the policy level, he was completely clear about the direction in which American history needed to flow: neutrality abroad, unity at home, and peace at all costs. By sending an American delegation to Paris, he had planted his standard, which he was prepared to defend to the death, no matter how few American citizens rallied round it.[14]

The only advisors who had his ear were John Quincy, his designated one-man listening post in Europe, and Abigail, his one-woman cabinet. He urged John Quincy "to continue your Practice of writing freely to me, and cautiously to the Office of State," thereby suggesting that he intended to keep foreign policy under his own control. As for Abigail, when the **Aurora** fired a salvo that described the president as "old, querulous, Bald, blind, crippled, Toothless Adams," she joked that only she possessed the intimate information to verify the description, and that its very virulence indicated that he must be on the correct political course. Living with John all those years had turned her into a contrarian, too.[15]

ABIGAIL'S EVOLUTION

Abigail settled into her new duties—the term **First Lady** had not yet been coined—with all the ease one would expect of the veteran diplomat she had become. On a typical day she rose at five o'clock, tended to her correspondence until joining John for breakfast at eight, then received guests for two or three hours. She met John again for dinner at three, usually with a gathering of eight to ten guests, once a week hosting a much larger state banquet and twice a week hosting the more public levees. They spent two or three hours alone together most evenings, reading, talking, or writing letters at the same table.

They almost certainly discussed John's decision to nominate John Quincy as American minister to the Prussian Court in Berlin. Though both parents were aware that the nomination would smack of nepotism, they also had Washington's judgment to bolster their confidence. Washington had been extremely impressed with John Quincy's performance at The Hague and had urged John not to have any reservations about appointing his son to another post. "For without intending to compliment the father or mother," Washington wrote, "I give it as my decided opinion that Mr. Adams is the most valuable public character we have abroad, and there remains no doubt that he will prove himself to be the ablest of all our diplomatic corps." When John Quincy learned of the nomination, however, he recoiled at the thought of being appointed by his father and declined the offer.[16]

John was insistent: "Your Delicacy about holding a Commission from your Father, Seems to me, too refined . . . It is the worst founded opinion I ever knew you to conceive." John Quincy eventually relented, but he asked his mother to apprise the president "that no nomination of me to any public office whatsoever, may ever again proceed from the present first magistrate." His reasons were honor-driven, to be sure, but his reasoning was more sound than his father's. Granted, merit alone should always be the criterion, John Quincy observed, "but the President is the constitutional judge of merit . . . and as it respects **me**, I **know** that he is a favorably partial judge." What John Quincy did not know was that John had seriously considered appointing him to the highly controversial delegation to France, a decision that would have provoked a political firestorm.[17]

Predictably, Bache, at the **Aurora**, trained his guns on the appointment, charging that "our monarchical president" was positioning his son for "a succession to the throne" and claiming, in defiance of the evidence, that John Quincy's salary was much higher than the norm. This was all mixed with sarcastic references to "our three vote president," referring to John's narrow margin in the election, and dusted-off references to "His Rotundity."[18]

It was all too much for Abigail, who found it excruciating to sit still while her husband and son were being vilified. She began to refer to the Republican press, and eventually all critics of John's policies, as "Jacobins," a smear term that conjured up radical devotees of the guillotine during the French Revolution, declaring herself fed up with "the Billingsgate of all the Jacobin papers, the Lies, falsehoods, calamities and bitterness." Her growing sense of revulsion spread to all of Philadelphia, which she described as "a City that seems devoted to calamity," suggesting that the political atmosphere mirrored the contaminated air that produced yellow fever every summer.[19]

Throughout the fall and early winter of 1797, while the nation awaited word from the American envoys to France, Abigail became increasingly partisan in her characterizations of the Republican opposition. It was not just a collection of insufferable critics; it was a "frenchified faction that is spreading sedition." Their purported principles, she charged, were merely a convenient cover "to calumniate the President, his family, his admistration until they oblige him to resign, and then they will Reign Triumphant, **headed by the Man of the People**," presumably Jefferson. Though her information was not far off the mark, she was crossing a line by suggesting that critics of her husband's policies were guilty of treason and should be treated accordingly. "In times like the present," she warned, "all Neutral Ground should be abandoned, and those who are not for us, be considered against us."[20]

It did not help that diplomatic prospects looked bleak. John Quincy wrote her to counsel low expectations from the current French government: "We shall find her to be at last, what she has been to us from the first moments of her existence, a domineering, captious, faithless and tyrannical sister." John was equally pessimistic: "What are We to expect from the Negotiations? Europe seems to be one burning mountain, whose Bowells are full of Materials for Combustion." Abigail was reaching the conclusion that war with France was unavoidable; indeed, France was already waging an undeclared war against American commerce. In such a situation, then, it was sheer folly to regard critics of government policy as anything but the modern-day equivalent of Tories. On this score, she had become more of an ultra-Federalist than John.[21]

XYZ

John did not think of himself as a Federalist at all. His model as chief executive was the same as Washington's, the "patriot king" celebrated in Henry St. John Bolingbroke's writings on English history, the statesman who levitated above all partisan interests and attempted to act in the long-term public interest of the nation regardless of the popular enthusiasms of the moment. This was an elevated conception of the presidency that was becoming increasingly anachronistic in the ferocious and highly orchestrated party battles of the 1790s, in which anyone attempting to carve out a centrist position soon found himself in a political version of no-man's-land, raked by the crossfire from both sides.

That was precisely the position that John found himself in after deciding to make a last-ditch effort to avoid war with France. His policy was both realistic and prudent—give diplomacy a chance to avoid a crippling and costly war that the infant American republic could ill afford to wage, and at the same time create a more formidable American navy in case war became unavoidable. But at the time, the policy alienated the ultra-Federalists, who regarded the diplomatic initiative as blatant appeasement, as well as the Republican opposition, who saw the naval buildup as provocative and the peace initiative itself as a transparent sham designed to clear the ground for war with France. (In fact, this was Hamilton's position.) In such a situation, the center could not hold because it did not exist.

The bad news arrived on March 4, 1798, the first anniversary of John's inauguration. Talleyrand, the French foreign minister, had refused to receive the American delegation, and, even more devastating, his three anonymous operatives, designated X, Y, and Z, had demanded a bribe of $250,000 as the prerequisite for any further negotiations. President Adams was also required to make a public apology for critical remarks about the French government delivered to Congress the previous summer. Secretary of State Timothy Pickering insisted that the only possible response to such gratuitous insults was a declaration of war.

Though equally indignant about French demands, John rejected Pickering's advice. He ordered the American envoys to return home, but refused to share the correspondence that exposed the indignities suffered by them with Congress, because he realized that those revelations would provoke popular outrage that would virtually force him into a declaration of war. Interestingly, Abigail described this decision as "a very painful thing [because] the President could not play his strongest card." She misconstrued his decision because she herself, like Pickering, believed war with France was now unavoidable. John, however, was playing a different game, still clinging tenaciously to his core conviction that a premature war threatened to kill the infant American republic in the cradle. For one of the few times in their long partnership, Abigail and John were not on the same political page.[22]

What happened next was richly ironic. Thanks to their two-to-one majority in the House, the Republicans were able to pass a resolution demanding that the president share with Congress all the dispatches from the American envoys, convinced as they were that the correspondence would reveal that the negotiations had broken down because of skullduggery on the American side. (This conviction followed naturally from their operating assumption that the president's peace initiative had, from the start, been designed to fail.) And, double irony, Jefferson himself, as president of the Senate, was required to read the dispatches that described in excruciating detail the insulting behavior of the French government, bribes and all. Abigail, who was present in the gallery for this melodramatic scene, noted with enormous satisfaction that "the Jacobins in the Senate and House were struck dumb and opened not their mouths."[23]

Popular opinion shifted almost overnight. Abigail reported with great glee the newspaper accounts of a riot in Philadelphia's major theater when the orchestra attempted to play "French Songs and Airs." The audience shouted down the musicians, demanded that they play "the President's March," and when they refused, drove them off the stage.[24]

Rumors began to circulate that French émigrés, who constituted a substantial minority population in Philadelphia, were plotting to set fire to the city and massacre the inhabitants. While Abigail found such wild rumors credible, John dismissed them as incendiary threats based on forged documents designed to stir up anti-French hysteria. He was almost surely correct, though even he lent his tacit support to the fearmongering when an anti-French mob estimated at ten thousand gathered outside the presidential residence, purportedly to protect it from firebombers. Rather ridiculously, John appeared before the crowd in military uniform, complete with sword, and obviously relished one of the few opportunities in his life to embrace the status of popular hero. The crowd chanted the new battle cry, "Millions for defense, not a cent for tribute."[25]

If vanity made him vulnerable, and it clearly did, his deep distrust of mobs and wild swings in popular opinion virtually ensured that his dalliance with the cheers of the crowd would prove transitory. Moreover, he remained convinced that the shouts of the multitude were just as misguided now, when they were demanding war with France, as they had been not so long ago, when they were hypnotized by the ideological illusions of the French Revolution. He remained wedded to a centrist course of American neutrality, which was attuned, or so he believed, to the deeper rhythms of American history and ought not be influenced by the turbulent cacophonies of the moment.

Given the accusations of emotional instability that would be hurled at him in the ensuing months, it is instructive to recover his stubborn refusal to surrender his strategic vision to the impulsive cries for war in the spring and summer of 1798. His behavior is a textbook example of diplomatic patience, delaying a decision while waiting for the political templates to move. A letter from John Quincy buoyed his hopes on this score, for it provided intelligence about shifting factions within the Directory, an emerging recognition that French military resources were already spread too thin in Europe to contemplate another front in North America, and a new willingness to open negotiations with one of the American envoys, Elbridge Gerry, who had decided to remain in Paris in order to make himself available if and when French policy changed. Gerry was being pilloried in the Federalist press for this apparent act of insubordination, but he was one of John's closest friends, which was the only reason he was appointed to the American delegation in the first place, and now John Quincy was reporting that Gerry's insubordination had proved prescient. The French were having second thoughts.[26]

Meanwhile, Abigail's thoughts were moving in a different direction. Her comments on the French government became more strident and absolute (e.g., "the most dissolute and corrupt Nation now existing"). Unlike John, she held open no realistic hopes for a diplomatic resolution; indeed, she believed the nation was already engaged in an undeclared war with France, and therefore urged that Bache and his pro-French minions be identified as enemy agents: "As the French have boasted of having more influence on the United States than their own Government," she wrote her sister, "the Men who now espouse their cause against their own Country . . . ought to be carefully marked."[27]

More specifically, she favored federal legislation designed "to punish the stirrer up of sedition, the writer and printer of base and unfounded calumny." Foreigners were also a problem, especially French émigrés and recent Irish immigrants, who harbored French or anti-British sympathies and appeared to constitute foot soldiers for Republican candidates in several states. She predicted that the Republican leaders "will take ultimately a station in the public's estimation like that of the Tories in our Revolution."[28]

In short, Abigail was an enthusiastic advocate for the four pieces of legislation pushed through Congress by the ultra-Federalists in late June and early July 1798 and known collectively as the Alien and Sedition Acts. These infamous statutes were designed to deport or disenfranchise foreign-born residents who were disposed to support the Republican, pro-French agenda, and make it a crime to publish "any false, scandalous, and malicious writing or writings against the Government of the United States." John played a passive role as the legislation made its way through Congress, and lived long enough to acknowledge that the Alien and Sedition Acts constituted a permanent stain on his presidency.[29]

While he never blamed Abigail for his blunder, it is difficult to imagine that her strong support did not influence his decision. (Or perhaps a better way to put it is that it's difficult to imagine him signing the controversial legislation if she had opposed it.) Through their long partnership, her political judgment usually provided reinforcement for his excellent instincts, which were often unpopular at the time but proved correct as history unfolded. When she had offered a critical suggestion, it was almost always cautionary, designed to calm him down and rein in his more impulsive urges. In this instance, however, their customary roles were reversed. She had allowed herself to get caught up in the ultra-Federalist frenzy, to develop a highly melodramatic understanding of the political forces at play and lose any perspective on the hyperbolic assessments she was making. Instead of providing her usual gift of ballast, she helped to pull John over the edge and into a free fall from which his legacy never, in truth, completely recovered.

How could this happen? It helps to remember that the entire Adams presidency seems to have been enveloped within an electromagnetic cloud that caused otherwise sensible statesmen to temporarily lose their bearings. George Washington, for example, by almost all accounts the most sober and realistic political leader of the era, wholly endorsed the Alien and Sedition Acts. And on the other side of the ideological divide, Jefferson and Madison managed to convince themselves that the entire XYZ Affair had been orchestrated by President

Adams or his behind-the-scenes henchman, Hamilton. Speaking of Hamilton, his arrogant assumption that he was the de facto president had a delusional dimension, and his imperial ambitions as head of a putative standing army made Napoleon seem cautious by comparison. Abigail's mental aberration, then, was part of a larger pattern of widespread political paranoia.

Moreover, some of Abigail's fears were not wholly unfounded. Jefferson **was** providing confidential intelligence to French partisans and to Bache at the **Aurora**. The Directory **had** entertained a scheme—it was Talleyrand's brainchild—to incite a civil war designed to make the southern states part of a new French empire in America. Indeed, in some respects more conspiracies were afoot than she realized, since she was as ignorant as her husband of Hamilton's duplicities with the cabinet.

Context is also crucial. The national government was still too new to have developed clear criteria for what constituted treason, the press had yet to work out standards to distinguish responsible journalism from scandal sheets, and our modern conception of First Amendment guarantees of civil liberties and freedom of the press remained blurry hopes for the future. Abigail was doing her best to negotiate this hothouse environment and, like everybody else, making it up as she went along.

Finally, her judgment was a victim of her love for John. Ever the lioness protecting her lair, she was watching the pressures of the presidency and the incessant salvos from the Republican press age John beyond his years: "I never saw Mr. Adams look so pale," she reported to her sister, "and he falls away [loses weight?] but I dare not tell him so," adding in a motherly vein that "he smoaks more sigars then I wish he did." He was the love of her life, father of her children, accomplice in negotiating midlife, political mentor, intimate confidant, and best friend. She also so wanted him to succeed that she was thrilled rather than shocked at a Fourth of July toast: "Mr. Adams. May he, like **Samson**, slay thousands of Frenchmen with the **jawbone** of Jefferson."[30]

Her strong endorsement of the major misstep of John's public career is, then, both poignant and paradoxical: poignant because it was motivated by the purest and strongest human affection possible; paradoxical because the very intensity of her love blinded her to the damage she was doing to his political legacy.

THUNDERSTRUCK

John's signature on the Sedition Act—eventually the most regretted signature of his life—was barely dry when he drafted an urgent request to his retired predecessor at Mount Vernon. Congress had recently seen fit to order the creation of a ten-thousand-man Provisional Army. It was "provisional" because it was contingent upon the appearance of the French fleet off the American coast. The previous day John had ordered Secretary of War McHenry to visit Washington at Mount Vernon and ask him to head that army. The letter was designed to alert Washington to the looming request, which John was at pains to describe as a last resort: "If it had been in my power to nominate you to be President of the United States," he somewhat strangely claimed, "I should have done it with less hesitation and more pleasure."[31]

Even more curious than his purported willingness to step aside for Washington, John's endorsement of the Provisional Army to oppose a putative French invasion seems strange, because his central assumption until then had been that any war with France would be fought on the high seas. He was an advocate of what he called "wooden walls," an American fleet fully capable of contesting French naval power in the Atlantic and the Caribbean, where the undeclared war was already going on. He was also on record as opposing "standing armies," which in English and European history had served as the vehicles for tyrannical takeovers of republican governments—witness Caesar, Cromwell, and now Napoleon—a pattern that John Quincy had noted in his forecast of Napoleon's likely course. Moreover, even if all the diplomatic initiatives failed and war with France proved inevitable, the likelihood of a French invasion of the United States was remote in the extreme. As John put it to McHenry: "Where is it possible for her [France] to get ships to send thirty thousand men here? At present there is no more prospect of seeing a French army here than there is in Heaven." Why, then, was the greatest hero of the age being asked to recruit and then lead an army that John regarded as both dangerous and unnecessary?[32]

The short answer is that the ultra-Federalists in Congress had approved the creation of the Provisional Army in the same session that also produced the Alien and Sedition Acts. Both measures were justified as guarantees of American security in response to the looming war with France. John's posture toward both initiatives was some combination of indifference, passivity, and dazed acquiescence. To say that he had lost control of the Federalist agenda would be misleading, since he had made no effort to exercise control of it in the first place. But it was one thing to embrace an elevated, float-above-partisanship conception of the presidency, quite another to watch helplessly from the heights as both the foreign and domestic policy of the government marched forward in a direction he neither supported nor opposed.

The most concise version of a longer answer required only two words: Alexander Hamilton. In the immediate aftermath of the XYZ revelations, when popular opinion was shifting decisively against France, Hamilton charged into print as the anonymous author of a seven-part series entitled **The Stand,** in which he effectively set the Federalist agenda for the following year. The humiliating treatment of the American envoys constituted a de facto declaration of war, he argued, and from now on "the frenchified faction" of the Republican Party, to include Bache and his followers, needed to realize that apologies for the despicable French behavior would not be tolerated. Moreover, reliable reports that a massive French fleet was gathering at Brest meant that the Directory was preparing to mount an invasion of either England or America. (As it turned out, Napoleon sailed the fleet into the Mediterranean, bound for Egypt.) Any prudent American response, Hamilton argued, must assume that the nation was the next target of French imperialism, so a substantial American army—Hamilton suggested fifty thousand troops—should be raised to meet the threat. In effect, the legislation promoted and passed by Congress in June and July 1798—the Alien and Sedition Acts and the creation of the Provisional Army—were efforts to implement Hamilton's vision.[33]

Moreover, the decision to recruit Washington to command the army was also Hamilton's, passed along as an order to Pickering and McHenry, who complied like the loyal soldiers they were. McHenry was instructed to insist that Washington be given complete autonomy in selecting the officers to serve under his command and be discreetly informed that Hamilton was prepared to serve as inspector general, or second-in-command. It was safe to assume that Washington would remain a symbolic presence who never took the field, thereby placing the Provisional Army under Hamilton's control.

Coded letters from Hamilton to Pickering and McHenry then revealed a truly Napoleonic plan of breathtaking grandeur. Hamilton intended to march his army through Virginia, declare martial law in the Republican homeland, then arrest and jail those Jefferson disciples who refused to renounce their French sympathies. He would proceed south to seize Florida and the Gulf Coast, justifiable acquisitions because Spain was a French ally, then head west to occupy New Orleans and claim the vast Louisiana tract. If the campaigns went as well as he hoped, Hamilton thought he might decide to head south again and invade Mexico. All this should be accomplished in less than a year.[34]

How Hamilton could have seriously contemplated such a preposterous scheme, and how he could so cavalierly manage its implementation in defiance of all legal and constitutional considerations, challenges rational explanation. His most recent biographer acknowledges that this moment constituted "one of the most flagrant instances of poor judgment in Hamilton's career." He had become an American version of Talleyrand and Napoleon rolled into one, who was putting the entire American experiment with republican government at risk.[35]

As long as he had functioned within the orbit of Washington's authority, first as a trusted aide-de-camp and then as a cabinet officer, Hamilton's matchless powers of mind and energy had followed a disciplined course. Once Washington retired from the scene, however, Hamilton's unleashed and unchecked ambitions became wildly erratic, wholly imperious, and eventually self-destructive. He was setting a course that would soon carry the Federalist Party over the abyss and then place him before the fatal gaze of Aaron Burr on the plains of Weehawken.

John remained blissfully oblivious to Hamilton's brazen machinations throughout the summer of 1798. Abigail had always been more suspicious of Hamilton's motives than her husband, apprising a friend (with more accuracy than she realized) that "the man would in any mind become a Second Buonaparty if he was possessed of equal power." Over the ensuing months, however, as Hamilton focused his peerless energies on the creation of twelve new regiments—no detail escaped his attention, from the decorative stitching on the officers' uniforms to the location of latrines in the training camps—John began to grasp the outline of Hamilton's incredible scheme and the extent to which he had become a blind accomplice in its implementation.[36]

He spent two months back in Quincy that fall, digesting the growing realization that he had allowed Hamilton to wrest control of his presidency from him, but also tending to Abigail, who was bedridden with a serious attack of rheumatism and an equally debilitating "bilious disorder" that kept her awake most nights. For diversion, he began reading the collected works of Frederick the Great. At a deeper level he was processing his political options, fully aware, as Abigail apprised him, that Congress was expecting "a recommendation from the president of a declaration of war with France" upon his return to Philadelphia.[37]

His mind was moving in precisely the opposite direction. It would have been characteristic for him to share his thoughts with Abigail, but there is no evidence that he did, and in this instance her mind had been made up for months that war was unavoidable. Given her weak condition, he might have decided to keep his own counsel rather than risk an argument. At any rate, when the time came to leave for Philadelphia, he supported her decision to remain behind in Quincy. Writing from the road, he claimed to "miss my talkative wife" but agreed that she was in no condition to make the trip. He would have to make the defining decision of his presidency without her at his side.[38]

Even before he arrived in Philadelphia, the stunning news reached America that the French fleet, which was supposedly preparing for an invasion of the United States, had in fact sailed east rather than west and, more dramatic, had suffered a devastating defeat off the Egyptian coast at the hands of Horatio Nelson, the British naval hero who had thereby destroyed the myth of Napoleon's invincibility. It was now clear that the prospect of a French invasion was, and probably always had been, a mirage.

An interview with Elbridge Gerry, just back from France, also buttressed John's diplomatic instincts. Gerry had come under criticism for lingering in Paris after being ordered home, but he reported that his recalcitrance had paid dividends, permitting several conversations with Talleyrand in which the French minister expressed profuse regret about the XYZ fiasco and a strong desire to resume negotiations.

John Quincy also reported from his listening post in Berlin that the diplomatic corridors of Europe were filled with rumors about a major shift in French policy: "They are spreading abroad the idea that they wish reconciliation with the United States, and are extremely desirous of a new negotiation." The French were not to be trusted, John Quincy was quick to warn, and the words of both Talleyrand and Napoleon were inherently worthless. Nevertheless, it made realistic sense for Napoleon to end the undeclared war with America in order to consolidate his overextended military forces in Europe.[39]

With all these considerations in mind, John decided that a new American peace initiative had at least a decent chance of succeeding. On February 19, 1799, he apprised Congress that he intended to send William Vans Murray, currently American minister at The Hague, to reopen negotiations with the French government. Secretary of State Pickering, along with the Federalist leadership in Congress, claimed that they were "thunderstruck" by the decision, and began suggesting that John had lost his mind. Several commentators speculated that this apparent fit of temporary insanity was a function of Abigail's absence, an explanation that John relished and immediately reported to her as evidence of her reputation as the only sound mind in the family.[40]

Abigail responded in kind. She, too, had seen the stories from critics who thought that "if the old woman had been there . . . they did not believe it would have taken place." This was, as she put it, "pretty saucy, but the old woman can tell them they are mistaken, for she considers the measure a master stroke of policy, knowing as she did that the pulse had been feeling through that minister for a long time." This meant that the decision, instead of an impulsive act, as so many commentators claimed, was a highly deliberative judgment that John had been mulling over for several months.[41]

Abigail's unconditional support also signaled her realignment with his preference for peace at any cost, after arguing for over a year that another peace initiative was futile. John never doubted that Abigail's loyalty to their partnership would easily overwhelm her anti-French convictions. These were the kind of elemental presumptions on both their parts that required no conversation at this seasoned stage of their partnership. But John promised her a full recounting of his motives when they were next together. The mails could not be trusted, and "the Reasons which determined me are too long to be written."[42]

Pickering guessed at the reasons for both the decision and the apparently sudden manner in which it was made: "It was done without any consultation with any member of the government and for a reason truly remarkable—**because he knew we should all be opposed to the measure.**" This was an ironically shrewd assessment. John did not consult his cabinet because he had finally come to the realization that most of them were loyal to Hamilton. They would attempt to change his mind because they were co-conspirators in Hamilton's scheme to manipulate popular fear of the French threat into a national security crisis. But John's diplomatic initiative altered the political chemistry. It made the Provisional Army superfluous and Hamilton's grandiose plans irrelevant. And that was precisely the reason that John made the decision. He was not only avoiding war, a major achievement in its own right, he was also avoiding a prospective military dictatorship.[43]

BROODING TIME

Having delivered the decisive blow, John then proceeded to leave town, ensconce himself in Quincy with an ailing Abigail, and remain sequestered there for the next seven months. This behavior struck observers then, and most historians since, as bizarre. While Washington had periodically retreated to Mount Vernon, he had never remained away for that long, and he had never absented himself in the midst of an ongoing political crisis. John's decision had, in fact, provoked just such a crisis, because it caught Federalists and Republicans alike by surprise. As Abigail described the scene, his decision was "so unexpected that the whole community was like a flock of frightened pigeons; nobody had their story ready." A country that was eager to declare war was now being led in a different direction that raised a host of unresolved questions: What were the minimum terms the American peace delegation should demand from the French? Should planning for the Provisional Army, which was still only a skeleton force, go forward or stop? Was the buildup of an American navy, now at twenty-two frigates, still a priority? John had dropped a bombshell into the center of American politics and was walking away without even looking back at the debris.[44]

His explanation was Abigail. Her letters to family and friends had come to resemble medical reports: excruciating pain in her joints that kept her confined for eleven weeks and unable to sleep at night; chronic fevers, what she called "the ague," sufficiently severe to resemble malaria; mounting fear that her health would never recover, that she was either dying ("I hourly expect my own dissolution") or, worse, would become a permanent invalid. When informed that her youngest son, Thomas, was coming home after serving as John Quincy's secretary at The Hague and Berlin, she asked John to alert him about her appearance: "He must prepare to see his mother ten years older than when he left her; time and sickness have greatly altered her." At fifty-five, she felt seventy.[45]

John's stated motives for moving his presidency to Quincy, then, were not fabrications. He had always regretted his absence more than thirty years earlier, when Abigail delivered their stillborn daughter while he remained preoccupied with his wartime duties in the Continental Congress. He did not want to make that mistake again now that her physical condition, perhaps her very survival, appeared at risk. She had so often sacrificed her own personal agenda to the imperatives of his public career. It was now her turn to become his priority.

Over the ensuing months, as critics in Philadelphia continued to question his absence, he claimed that his administrative duties could be responsibly handled by letter. And he was, in fact, assiduous about responding to all cabinet requests—Pickering on American policy toward the slave insurrections in Santo Domingo; McHenry on rank squabbles in the army; requests for guidance from the newly appointed secretary of the navy, Benjamin Stoddert, on the deployment of recently commissioned frigates. All this routine business, he in-sisted, could be done from Abigail's bedside.[46]

Although he was unwilling to acknowledge it, perhaps even to himself, there were other motives for his extended absence. Once he finally realized that his cabinet, most especially Pickering and McHenry, were loyal disciples of Hamilton, he should have fired them and appointed his own subordinates. And once he rejected a declaration of war in favor of a new diplomatic initiative, he should have ordered all planning for the Provisional Army to stop. He did neither, which allowed Pickering and McHenry to resume their behind-the-scenes maneuvering, this time to scuttle additional appointments to the peace delegation, and Hamilton to proceed with planning for the Provisional Army as if nothing had really changed. John's hibernation in Quincy was part of a larger pattern of avoidance and procrastination whenever he was faced with the challenge of assuming direct control of the Federalist Party. On this score, instead of being impulsive—the major criticism directed at him— he was indecisive.

We are on treacherous ground here, since we are attempting to plumb the deeper recesses of John's mind and soul, where the historical evidence is at best circumstantial and more often nonexistent. But the best guess is that his elevated conception of the presidency, as an office that transcended party (and therefore partisan) interests, produced an acute case of paralysis when the office required a party leader. There was no longer any room for his preferred version of nonpartisan executive leadership, so his response was to escape. Being a president-above-party was no longer possible, and in the new context he did not know what to do.

When Secretary of the Navy Stoddert, the only loyal member of the cabinet, urged him to end his seclusion, warning that "artful and designing men" were scheming to destroy his prospects for reelection, John replied that the advice was welcome, except the very mention of "a certain election may be wholly laid out of this question and all others." In the political universe he chose to inhabit, the mere mention of partisan politics was inadmissible.[47]

By midsummer Abigail's health began to improve. She and John were able to take short walks around the farm, periodically joined by Nabby, who had come up from Eastchester with her three children to help care for her mother. Nabby's presence provided a painful reminder of another subject that both Abigail and John preferred to avoid, namely, that the husband they had so heartily approved for her, William Stephens Smith, had continued to flounder, thereby putting the fate of their daughter and grandchildren at the mercy of his growing number of creditors. John had lost all hope in Smith's capacity to salvage his life: "All the Actions of my Life and all the Conduct of my Children have not disgraced me so much as this Man," he lamented. "His pay will not feed his Dogs. And his Dogs must be fed if his children starve."[48]

An abject failure at everything he tried, Smith had decided to return to his original profession as a soldier, somewhat ironically seeing the new Provisional Army as a golden opportunity. John could only cringe at the poor man's flair for failure, since the golden opportunity was in the process of turning to dross—the Provisional Army was already being dismantled—as a result of the peace initiative toward France. (After Hamilton, Smith was apparently the last man to realize that the Provisional Army was an idea whose time had come and gone.) Desperate for a military career, Smith requested the president to appoint him commander of the American garrison at Detroit. John responded curtly, saying all such requests should be sent to the secretary of war, then concluding: "I will not interfere with the discipline and order of the army, because you are my son-in-law."[49]

Abigail tended to focus less on Smith's pathetic character than on Nabby's unhappy predicament. (She almost surely second-guessed herself about the abandonment of Royall Tyler, who was enjoying a flourishing legal career with a devoted family.) Though any discussion of John's prospects for reelection was taboo, Nabby's plight and the dismal future looming for her three children were prime candidates for extended family conversation. Besides worrying, the only thing Abigail and John could do was to remain ready for a rescue operation if and when Nabby's marriage collapsed.

But the most worrisome domestic crisis, more emotionally wrenching than Nabby's abiding unhappiness or even John's unresolved estrangement from his cabinet, was the sudden revelation that Charles had become an alcoholic. For several years he had managed to conceal his secret life of drink and promiscuity from both his parents and most of the world. His exposure, inevitable in the end, was triggered by the disclosure that he had lost all the money John Quincy had entrusted to him for investment—several thousand dollars—then bankrupted himself trying to recover the losses. Legal inquiries by his creditors revealed the sordid details of a double life: respectable lawyer and family man by day; barhopping drunk, drug addict, and adulterer by night. His wife, Sally, confirmed to Abigail that Charles had been spiraling downward for quite some time, but none of her pleas for his reform had any effect whatsoever.[50]

Neither Abigail nor John had seen this coming, and they were both stunned. John's initial reaction was to forbid mention of Charles's name in the home ever again: "A Being [Charles] who has violated a Trust committed to him by you," he wrote to John Quincy, "is a thorn in my flesh . . . Forlorn and undone, he has my unutterable indignation." Under Abigail's prodding, John backed off his hard-line position, and throughout the summer of 1799 both parents tried to understand how the designated charmer in the Adams family had collapsed into a heap of decrepitude, how they had remained oblivious to his descent for so long, and whether there was any way to bring the prodigal son back within the protective fold of the Quincy haven. Down in Philadelphia, as Federalists and Republicans were trying to guess what the absentee president was thinking about the evolving political landscape in France—Napoleon was rumored to be preparing for a military takeover of the government, as John Quincy had predicted more than a year earlier—both John and Abigail were primarily focused on their acute domestic dilemma.[51]

By September it had become painfully clear that no amount of worrying, hoping, or cajoling would make any difference: "But all has been lost upon him," Abigail lamented. "If only he would be penitent and reform, both parents would say my son was lost but now is found. But he remains unrepentant." In a life filled with more than its fair share of pain and tragedy, she thought, this was the deepest wound she had ever suffered, and she did not expect that she would ever recover from it fully.[52]

John decided to make one final effort. In October he ended his seven-month seclusion and began the long trip to Trenton, where the government had decamped until the yellow fever season ended in Philadelphia. On the way down, he stopped in New York to consult with Charles's wife in order to determine what, if anything, could be done to recover his lost son. The stories she shared with him were more lurid and thick with depravities than John had ever imagined. He wrote back to Abigail with his harsh and final verdict: Charles was "a Madman possessed by the Devil . . . I renounce him . . . as a mere Rack, Buck, Blood and Beast." He refused to visit him and never spoke to him again.[53]

SPLENDID ISOLATION

During John's seven-month seclusion, the most disloyal members of his cabinet, Pickering and McHenry, had been working assiduously to undermine his diplomatic initiative by delaying the departure of the two additional envoys Congress had required to ensure a more representative delegation. Hamilton had devoted his matchless energy to sustaining the illusion of a robust Provisional Army, now being called the New Army to imply a more permanent presence, despite the disappearance of any plausible rationale for its existence and without any recognition that the new name conjured up

Cromwell's dangerous precedent. John arrived at Trenton in a foul mood, having just renounced his son and knowing he would have to endure the smiling of Pickering and McHenry once again.

He did not realize that he would also have to encounter Hamilton, who rode over unannounced from his headquarters at Newark to make a face-to-face plea for a delay of the peace delegation and for presidential support for the New Army. There was never a remote possibility that John would agree to either request, but Hamilton's presumptive posture—he continued to believe that John should defer to his judgment—made the encounter a dramatic occasion.

John's later recollection of the conversation is not to be trusted, given his swollen hatred for Hamilton by then, but it is all we have. He claimed that "the little man" went on for two hours, lecturing him on the French threat and likely British retaliation if America signed a treaty with France. "Never in my life," John recalled, "did I hear a man talk so like a fool." When Hamilton urged delay in sending the envoys based on reports that the Bourbon monarchy was about to be restored to the throne, John countered caustically: "I should as soon expect that the sun, moon and stars will fall from their orbs." The peace mission would go forward, the navy would continue to grow, and the New Army would be allowed to expire. Though

Hamilton, clearly in denial, continued to resist the message, the meeting killed all prospects for his imperialistic agenda and firmly established John's control over American foreign policy. "I hope soon to hear that our Envoys have sailed," he wrote to Abigail, "that there may be no longer room for impertinent Paragraphs by busy bodies who are forever meddling with Things they understand not."[54]

That should have been the end of it. From any detached perspective at the time, even more from the perspective provided by hindsight, John had put American foreign policy on the realistic course recommended by Washington, a course that would serve the nation well over the next century. He had also blocked Hamilton's dangerous flirtations with a militarized version of republican government, which in fact possessed the potential to undermine the core values of republicanism itself. The leadership of the Federalist Party should have rallied around the presidential standard, which was planted firmly in the same solid ground that Washington had also chosen, and the future of Federalism as a mainstream political force would have been ensured.

The linkage with the Washington legacy proved impossible to ignore when word arrived from Mount Vernon that the great man, who had joked about making it into the next century, missed his mark by just over two weeks, the victim of a fatal throat infection. In his official message of mourning to the Senate, John struck a personal note: "I feel myself alone, bereaved by my lost brother."

Abigail had sufficiently recovered from her multiple ailments to be present in Philadelphia for the four-hour memorial service at the German Lutheran Church, where Henry "Light Horse Harry" Lee, Washington's old cavalry commander, gave the eulogy that was destined to echo through the ages, extolling Washington as "first in war, first in peace, first in the hearts of his countrymen." Abigail hosted a gathering for several hundred mourners after the ceremony, where she thought the men appropriately austere in their black suits, but the women inappropriately ornamental in their "epaulets of black silk . . . black plumes . . . black gloves and fans."[55]

As the new century began, tributes to Washington kept pouring in from across the land, demonstrating for the last time that he was truly, as the toasts in his honor put it, "the man who unites all hearts." John's speech to Congress, reporting that the American envoys had been courteously received in Paris, met with thunderous applause, which Abigail described as the most rousing response John had received during his presidency. A few weeks later word arrived from France that Napoleon had dissolved the Directory; named himself first consul, which made him de facto emperor; and declared the French Revolution ended. This was precisely the conclusion that John had always predicted, and a resounding refutation of Jefferson's blissful belief that "liberty, equality, and fraternity" would prove to be the French version of the American Revolution, all of which seemed to deliver a fatal blow to the central premise on which Republican prescriptions for American foreign policy had been based for nearly a decade. At the policy level, John could hardly have asked for more: the peace initiative was moving forward; funding for the New Army was stopped, making its dismemberment imminent; and the Republican commitment to the inevitable triumph of the French Revolution was exposed as an illusion.

At the personal level, history also seemed to be flowing in the Adams direction. Fears that Abigail might die or become permanently bedridden with her multiple ailments proved excessive. She was sufficiently recovered to take her place at John's side at the weekly levees and recover her role as his most trusted confidante. Moreover, they were joined by Thomas, fresh from four years of serving as John Quincy's secretary at The Hague and Berlin. Previously the most invisible of the Adams children, Thomas appeared quite suddenly as a conspicuously mature and supremely competent young man, an unexpected compensation delivered by the gods for the disgraced Charles. He afforded Abigail the opportunity to resume her old matchmaking skills, at one presidential ball guiding him toward a young beauty she described as "really fascinating," even though she wished her dress "had left more to the imagination and less to the eye."[56]

Thomas also brought firsthand reports of John Quincy's new wife, Louisa Catherine, a delicate orchid of a woman whom Abigail and John had never met, but who Thomas assured them brought a compelling new feminine presence into the Adams family. After a year of relentless worrying about Nabby's domestic predicament and Charles's alcoholism, it was consoling to know that two of their children were advancing nicely in wisdom, age, and grace.

Then the political winds shifted dramatically as the campaign season began. Neither John nor Abigail commented on the upcoming presidential election—to do so would have violated their classic pose of indifference—but the leadership in both the Federalist and Republican camps could talk of little else. Jefferson was the obvious choice on the Republican side, and as the incumbent, without doing or saying anything at all, John was the presumptive candidate for the Federalists. Then, in February 1800, John Marshall, an emerging Federalist leader, reported a discernible movement in the Hamiltonian wing of the party, which was "much dissatisfied with the President on account of the late mission to France [and] strongly disposed to desert him and to push some other candidate," presumably someone more amenable to Hamilton's agenda. Hamilton put out the word that anyone, even Jefferson, was preferable to the current incumbent: "If we must have an enemy at the head of government," he declared, "let it be one who we can oppose, and for whom we are not responsible."[57]

Hamilton's decision to focus his political firepower on John's defeat was nothing new. He had unsuccessfully attempted to manipulate the two preceding presidential elections in much the same way, believing as he did that his own political judgment was vastly superior to the shifting vagaries of the electorate, and loathing as he did a man who remained wholly immune to all forms of the dazzling Hamilton magic. But the political strategy Hamilton chose to pursue in the spring of 1800 was also a more far-reaching battle for the soul of the Federalist Party. For several years the editors of the **Aurora** had been accusing the Federalists of harboring monarchical ambitions, manipulating the popular hysteria about a prospective French invasion in order to justify censorship of the press and the creation of a massive military establishment. This, in fact, was precisely the direction that Hamilton still dreamed of taking the Federalist Party and the country.

No one had done more to block Hamilton's fantastic agenda than John Adams, which was the chief reason Hamilton was determined to remove him. For a time the Republicans were content to observe one of the few universal laws of political life; namely, never interfere when your enemies are engaged in flagrant acts of self-destruction. But eventually Jefferson decided that vanquishing the Federalists meant targeting the only man who stood between him and the prize. And so he commissioned a talented scandalmonger, James Callender, to do the requisite hatchet job.

In **The Prospect Before Us** Callender claimed that John's peace initiative toward France was wholly disingenuous, that the choice was "between Adams and war, or Jefferson and peace." This was an outright lie, but then Callender was being paid to deliver the goods. As Jefferson succinctly put it: "Such papers cannot fail to produce the best effects." Most of Callender's effort was devoted to vilifying John in generic terms as "a repulsive pedant, . . . a gross hypocrite, . . . a wretch that has neither the science of a magistrate, the politeness of a courtier, nor the courage of a man."[58]

Federalist critics, prompted by Hamilton, completed the cross fire by spreading rumors that the president was slightly out of his mind, a judgment they found incontrovertible because any peaceful accommodation with France struck them as lunacy. Writing to John Quincy, Abigail lamented the two-sided attack on her husband: "The Jacobins are so gratified to see the federalist split to pieces that they enjoy in Silence the game," she observed, "whilst in the Southern States they combine to bring Mr. Jefferson in as President." She felt certain that the open breach in the Federalist camp made John's re-election highly unlikely.[59]

Results from state elections in New York in May confirmed this judgment. Skillful behind-the-scenes work by Aaron Burr, who was angling to become Jefferson's running mate, and who was rumored to have spent $50,000 to seduce undecided voters, produced a new Republican majority in the New York legislature, which would choose twelve presidential electors the following fall. "It is generally supposed that New York would be the balance in the ~~Scaile~~, ~~Scale~~, ~~Skaill~~, Scaill (is it right now? it does not look so)," Abigail asked her sister. While she was not sure how to spell **scale**, she knew a Republican sweep of New York's electoral votes made Jefferson essentially unbeatable.[60]

Abigail was the designated vote counter on the Adams team, while John felt obliged to cultivate at least the posture of studied indifference toward such mundane matters. But the realization that his electoral prospects were remote seemed to lift a burden from his shoulders. Right after the New York results were confirmed, he did what he should have done long ago, that is, demand the resignations of McHenry and Pickering. When Pickering refused to resign, claiming among other things that he needed the salary, John fired him outright and then appointed John Marshall as his new secretary of state. McHenry's account of the occasion described it as the impulsive act of a raving lunatic, whereas John's chief mistake had been to delay the decision much too long. Hamilton urged McHenry to comb the cabinet files on the way out for any documents that could be used to question John's competence.[61]

When Congress adjourned in late May, John headed down to survey the new capital on the Potomac, still very much a work in progress that was nonetheless scheduled to become the seat of government the following fall. There were as yet no clearly marked roads into the capital, prompting John to label it a "wilderness city" and then joke about losing his way: "Rolling, rolling, rolling," he wrote Abigail, "till I am very near rolling into the bosom of Mother Earth." His spirits were obviously up.[62]

They were buoyed even higher upon receiving a letter from Abigail, who had stopped at Newark on the way back to Quincy in order to serve as John's surrogate at the ceremony for disbanding the New Army. She stood alongside Hamilton amid the pomp and circumstance as they witnessed the final parade of troops that Hamilton had hoped to lead on a grand and glorious adventure. Hamilton behaved gallantly, despite his pain, Abigail reported, and "I acted as the **Aurora** says, as your proxy, praised and admired." Then she added "and regretted," referring to Hamilton's obvious discomfort at her awkward presence as the death knell sounded on the chief instrument of his extravagant ambitions.[63]

If the political battle between John and Hamilton had become a duel to the death—and it had—then John could only relish the realization that, despite his own gloomy political prospects, he was taking Hamilton down with him. As he wandered through the Maryland woods on the way back to Abigail at Quincy, he had placed himself in a familiar position that fit squarely into the dominant pattern of his public life.

He invariably focused his fire on opponents who achieved satanic status for blocking his path, such as Thomas Hutchinson, Benjamin Franklin, Vergennes, and now Alexander Hamilton, the latest entry in his rogues' gallery. (Jefferson kept slipping on and off the list.) He was deeply attuned to the ambitions of his enemies, which he understood intuitively because the same ambitions were stirring in his own soul, so by eviscerating them he was assuming control of himself. His deepest energies were mobilized in defense of worthy causes that appeared lost, against enemies who embodied the formidable strengths of his own darker side.

As he began the long trek back to Quincy, then,

even though the forces aligned against him constituted a political version of the perfect storm, the interior forces of the Adams soul were perfectly
aligned in their most potent pattern. The fact that
the Republicans and ultra-Federalists had deployed
their forces to defeat him was a reassuring sign that
his own course was correct. The fact that he was
likely to lose the election was also greatly satisfying,
since it meant that political motives had played no
role in shaping his policies, which had only the
long-term interests of the American republic as a
guide. Singular acts of defiance had become his
trademark from the day he decided to defend the
British troops after the Boston Massacre. So now he
would be going out as he came in, like a cannonball
aimed at the center of American history, primed for
one final explosion.

EXIT

Soon after he had settled in at Quincy, John received an extraordinary letter from Hamilton: "It
has been repeatedly mentioned to me," wrote Hamilton,

> that you have on different occasions
> asserted the existence of a **British Faction**
> in this Country, embracing a number of

leading or influential characters of the
Federal Party (as usually denominated)
and that you have named me . . . As one
of this description of persons . . . I must
Sir take it for granted that you cannot have
made such assertions without being willing
to avow them and to assign reason to a
party who may conceive himself injured
by them.[64]

As John surely recognized, this was the language of an affair of honor, the preliminary verbal etiquette that preceded a challenge. Hamilton had obviously crossed another line in his headlong descent toward self-destruction, carrying his political competition with the president of the United States to the brink of a duel.

A few weeks later a series of essays began appearing in the newspapers entitled **Letter from Alexander Hamilton, Concerning the Public Conduct and Character of John Adams, Esq. President of the United States.** Although it stopped short of calling John crazy, it did accuse him of being mentally unstable and unfit to serve as president. Hamilton described his nemesis as "a man of imagination sublimated and eccentric; propitious neither to the regular display of sound judgment or to steady perseverance in a systematic plan of conduct . . . that to this defect are added the unfortunate foibles of a vanity without bounds, and a jealousy capable of discoloring every subject." Material that McHenry and Pickering had confided to Hamilton was cited to document John's irritable and volatile behavior in cabinet meetings and "the disgusting egotism, the distempered jealousy, and the ungovernable indiscretion of Mr. ADAMS' temper."[65]

The dominant reaction, even among Hamilton's most devoted disciples in the Federalist camp, was that the pamphlet was conclusive evidence that Hamilton himself had lost his mind. (The Republicans were overjoyed to see the Federalists engaged in public bloodletting that clinched Jefferson's election.) John's somewhat disingenuous reaction was to express regret: "I am confident it will do him more harm than me." Abigail regarded the episode as confirmation of her original assessment of Hamilton as a diabolical egomaniac, who was, in fact, "a mere Sparrow," and further evidence that the electoral politics of the infant republic had become an intellectual swamp fit only for scandalmongers and ideological fanatics. It would be an enormous relief to be free of this increasingly toxic atmosphere, she claimed, and leave Jefferson to navigate among the floating piles of muck, which he would surely describe as "a turbulent Sea of Liberty."[66]

When John left for Washington in October, the only question was whether Abigail should risk the difficult trip to join him. They had obviously talked at some length about the looming public and private tribulations coming their way: the near-certain loss of the presidency, and the deteriorating condition of Charles, which raised domestic questions about their obligations to his wife and children. It was clearly time for the Adams family to circle the proverbial wagons in preparation for the imminent blows.

In early November John wrote from the still unfinished presidential mansion, urging Abigail to join him: "It is fit and proper," he explained, "that you and I should retire together." (In the same letter he penned the words later inscribed into the mantel of the fireplace at the White House: "May none but honest and wise Men ever rule under this roof.") Thomas volunteered to accompany his mother on the final leg of the trip from Philadelphia to Washington. They arrived at the fledging capital on November 16, 1800, Abigail pronouncing that "the country is romantic but wild, a wilderness at present."[67]

Her chief task was to make the presidential mansion habitable. As it turned out, this was not easy. The plaster on the walls was still drying, the staircases were unfinished, there was not enough wood to keep the twelve fireplaces going sufficiently to dry the paint on the walls, and the roof leaked so badly that twelve tubs were needed to catch the water during a storm. The grounds around the building, a huge mud pile, were being landscaped by slaves: "I have amused myself from day to day in looking at the labour of 12 negroes from my window loading dirt in carts," she observed, but working at a leisurely pace that two hardy New England laborers would easily outstrip. Washington was a decidedly southern city, she reported to Nabby, which meant that it was cursed by the stain of slavery, the unmentionable centerpiece of Jefferson's "true Republicanism."[68]

The expected bad news came all at once in the first week of December. The tandem of Jefferson and Burr had received seventy-three electoral votes to sixty-five for John and sixty-four for Pinckney. It was actually much closer than Abigail and John had expected. John ran ahead of the Federalist candidates for Congress and, apart from the New York vote, ahead of his margin in the previous election. "The deflection of New York has been the source," Abigail observed, adding that "at my age and with my bodily infirmities I shall be happier at Quincy." John chimed in with a similar sentiment: "I feel my shoulders relieved from a burden," he informed Thomas. "The short remainder of my days will be the happiest of my life." They had been preparing themselves for this moment for several months, and now that it had arrived, they both were eager to move past it.[69]

The second blow arrived almost simultaneously with the election results, and although they had been anxiously anticipating it as well, the news that Charles had died on December 1 produced emotional tremors that shook both parents to the core. "The melancholy death of your brother is an affliction of a more serious nature to this family than any other," John apprised Thomas. "Oh! That I had died for him if that would have relieved him from his faults as well as his disease." Having renounced Charles while he was still alive, now that he was gone John felt free to express his love for him again.[70]

Abigail feared this was so deep a wound that it would never completely heal. Political defeat was a bitter pill, to be sure, but the loss of a son was a tragedy beyond words. She intended to banish from her mind "all the frailties and offences of my dear departed son" and to focus her memories on the young child whose beguiling personality had made him the most popular boy in the neighborhood and "a favorite where ever he went." She kept asking herself if there was something she could have done as a mother to avert the tragedy, but kept reaching the conclusion that Charles was the victim of his own demons. She informed Charles's widow that she and John stood ready to assist with the two children in whatever way seemed appropriate. The political defeat was actually a godsend on this score, because it meant that they would now have the time and energy to become dutiful grandparents.[71]

A piece of splendid news cast at least one beam of light into the prevailing darkness. Secretary of State Marshall had kept John apprised of the dispatches from France, which suggested that the peace negotiations were proceeding apace. Soon after the election results became known, official word arrived that a new Franco-American treaty, named the Treaty of Morfontaine, had been signed ending the "quasi-war." Although the French had refused to pay compensation to American merchants for losses suffered, an unnecessary war that threatened to undermine the entire American government was now avoided. And since this had been the central goal of his presidency, John could plausibly say that he had steered the American ship of state through stormy seas and into a safe port.

As it turned out, while it was clear that John had lost the election of 1800, it was not clear who had won. The same flaw in constitutional procedure that had made Jefferson his vice president in 1796 this time permitted Jefferson and Burr to tie in the Electoral College at seventy-three votes apiece. The decision was therefore thrown into the House of Representatives, as mandated by the Constitution, and eventually required six weeks and thirty-six highly contentious ballots to resolve.

Both Abigail and John assumed that Jefferson

would win and that he was the vastly preferable candidate. (So, ironically, did Hamilton, who lobbied against Burr behind the scenes, which helped pave the way to their deadly encounter nearly four years later.) Abigail thought that Burr had "risen upon Stilts," meaning that none of the voters had intended to elect him as president, and that if he were to sneak in, "God save the United States of America." John concurred, describing Burr as "ambitious, insinuating, a voluptuary . . . and a much more dangerous Man than Mr. Jefferson." John came under some pressure to make a public statement on Jefferson's behalf, but he refused, claiming that such interference would be inappropriate. Moreover, his own mind had already moved on to planning his retirement, he claimed somewhat disingenuously. Jefferson's fate, he joked, was of less concern to him than the fruit trees, cucumbers, and new potato field he was contemplating as "The Farmer of Stoneyfield."[72]

At Abigail's urging, they did make a social statement of sorts in Jefferson's behalf by inviting him to dinner in early January. "Mr. Jefferson dines with us," she informed Thomas, "and in a card of replie to the President's invitation, he begs him to be assured of his **Homage** and **high consideration**." Although neither member of the Adams team was yet prepared to forgive Jefferson's duplicities during the campaign, Jefferson was apparently disposed to forget them. Abigail was surprised during their dinner conversation that he seemed less informed about the provisions of the new French treaty than she was, and that she had to introduce him to members of the House, fellow guests, who, in fact, would soon determine his fate. Jefferson could only laugh when Abigail joked that he obviously needed her to serve as his political manager.[73]

While it was somewhat true that John had little to do as a lame-duck president other than daydream about fruit trees and cucumbers, circumstance presented him with the opportunity to make one final decision that turned out to be one of the most consequential acts of his presidency. Chief Justice Oliver Ellsworth chose to resign, creating a vacancy that John was still empowered to fill. He then offered the post to John Marshall, who had impressed John with his uncommon sense, massive probity, and total loyalty.

Marshall went on to serve for thirty-four years, without much question the most towering and influential chief justice in American history and, beyond any question, the most relentlessly effective opponent of Jefferson's state-centered view of the Constitution. Marshall was even more of a Trojan horse, planted squarely in the Jefferson administration, than Jefferson had been in the Adams administration.

Abigail decided that she should leave the capital

before John, despite his wish that they go out together. The roads and rivers between Washington and Philadelphia were notoriously difficult to negotiate in winter. (The absence of bridges meant that riders had to travel out onto the ice, crash through, then move on to locate safer crossings.) She dreaded this adventure and wanted to get it behind her. Jefferson visited her before her departure, a gracious gesture, "more than I expected," she declared, and she kept the conversation focused on practical matters like rugs and furniture in the presidential mansion. It was the last time they saw each other. She began the trek back to Quincy on February 13. The House elected Jefferson as the next president three days later.[74]

The **Aurora** chose to treat John in the same abusive way it had treated Washington when he prepared to exit the office. The editors described him as a pathetic malingerer who "needed to be cast like polluted water out the back door, and who should immediately leave for Quincy, that Mrs. Adams may wash his befuddled brains clear." He could certainly be forgiven for cringing at such stings, for he had, in the space of four years, lost his mother, a son, and the presidency, and almost lost his wife. (One might add that he had also supervised the suicide of the Federalist Party, but that was really Hamilton's work.) He was, in several senses of the term, a beaten man.[75]

But, rather remarkably, he did not feel beaten so much as buoyant. When a fire broke out at the Treasury Department building next door to the presidential mansion, the local newspapers described the scene: "Through the exertions of the citizens, animated by the example of the President of the United States (who on this occasion fell into the ranks and aided in passing the buckets), the fire was at length subdued." It was a trademark Adams act, defiantly energetic when most wounded, at his best when the situation was at its worst. For beyond the litany of losses, there were two overarching victories: his policy of neutrality and peace, which he was confident would become the keystone of his presidential legacy over the years, had been vindicated; and Abigail had neither died nor become a permanent invalid, but was waiting for him at Quincy at something approaching full force. These were the true essentials, and they were both in place.[76]

On March 4, 1801, the day of Jefferson's inauguration, John boarded the four o'clock morning stage out of town. His absence at his successor's installation attracted criticism then, and has ever since, as a petulant gesture. More likely, he did not think he was supposed to be present. There was no precedent for a defeated candidate to attend the inauguration of his successor, and he wished neither to complicate Jefferson's moment of triumph nor to lend a hand in its celebration.

Matters of ceremony were the furthest thing from his mind, an unfortunate fact given that his presence would have added symbolic significance to the first peaceful and routine transfer of power from one party to another in American history. But his mind was elsewhere: on the awkward realization that he had outlived a son; on the best design for his potato field; on the melting ice in the rivers that would delay his trek back to Quincy; mostly, on the time remaining to him, which he presumed would be brief, and the woman with whom he wished to spend it.

CHAPTER SEVEN

1801–18

"I wish I could lie down
beside her and die too."

FOR MORE THAN TWENTY YEARS Abigail had been urging her husband to retire from public life and join her beside the hearth at Quincy. Now, at last, he was finally doing so, albeit at the insistence of the American electorate rather than by any choice of his own. John Quincy, writing from Berlin, observed that his father should not be surprised at being hurled from office, since such was the fate that, by his own analysis, awaited all public servants determined to lead rather than listen to popular opinion. "I knew he was aware that in contributing to found a great republic," John Quincy noted to his mother, "that he was not preparing a school for public gratitude . . . and that he himself in all probability would be one of the most signal instances of patriotism sacrificed to intrigue and envy." Indeed, as John Quincy himself was destined to discover, a conspicuous flair for alienating voters while acting in their long-term interest, much like premature baldness, was bred into the genes of all prominent male members of the Adams line.[1]

At least publicly, John claimed to realize that his political defeat had been inevitable: "I am not about to write lamentations or jeremiads over my fate nor panegyrics upon my life and conduct," he told a friend. "You may think me disappointed. I am not. All my life I expected it." He also knew that, according to the Ciceronian code, he was supposed to affect the posture of a world-weary pilgrim who had at last reached the Promised Land that was his Quincy farm, where blessedly bucolic rhythms would replace the frenzied and often frantic pace of political life. John, for his part, preferred to sound a more irreverent note: "I found about a hundred loads of sea weed in my barnyard," he joked. "I thought I had made a good exchange . . . of honors and virtues for manure."[2]

Abigail shared his joking mood. All the well-coiffed and turned-out ladies of Washington would surely be impressed to see her skimming milk at dawn in her nightgown. It had been a cold, wet, and sour spring in Quincy, she added: "They call it Jeffersonian weather here."[3]

John sustained the frivolous face to the world, announcing that his Quincy estate, initially named Peacefield but now referred to more simply as the

Old House, needed a grander title in order to do justice to his new status as an elder statesman. Jefferson had his Monticello, so he must have his Montezillo, which he said meant "little mountain," apparently not realizing that Monticello meant the same thing. As one who had been accused of an affinity for aristocratic titles, he announced that he now wished to be identified as "the Monarch of Stony Field, Count of Gull Island, Earl of Mount Ararat, Marquis of Candlewood Hill, and Baron of Rocky Run."[4]

Whatever one wished to call it, the Quincy homestead had grown over the years to six hundred acres, a product of both Abigail's and John's assiduous pursuit of any proximate lots that came on the market. There were in fact three farms, one at the main house and two near Penn's Hill, which included the building where John had been born. While hardly a match for Jefferson's five thousand acres at Monticello, by New England standards it was a handsome estate that, upon John's death, was valued at almost $100,000.

Nor were they retiring to the proverbial empty nest. The household staff included John and Esther Brisler, loyal servants who had been with them for nearly thirty years; Louisa Smith, Abigail's niece, who had come aboard as a child and now grown into a proper New England spinster, regarded by all as a fully vested member of the family; and finally

Phoebe Abdee, the black servant whose regal bearing purportedly reflected her descent from African chiefs. The only new member of the Quincy household was Juno, a Newfoundland puppy, who was a gift from John Quincy to his father, though Juno preferred to follow Abigail around the house on her daily rounds.

This little congregation of household help was not caring just for Abigail and John. During that first summer Sally Adams, widow of Charles, moved in with her two children, soon joined by Nabby and her three toddlers. Shortly thereafter, Thomas, having failed at the law in Philadelphia, moved back to Quincy, married a local girl named Ann Harrod, and immediately began to demonstrate a proficiency at producing children that he could never achieve in a job, eventually fathering seven grandchildren for Abigail and John. Within a year, John Quincy and Louisa Catherine arrived home from Berlin and purchased a house in Boston, but because John Quincy's career carried him to Washington, St. Petersburg, and then back to Washington, two and sometimes all three of their children were deposited in Quincy to be raised by their grandparents.[5]

To be sure, there were so many comings and goings that any account of the number of residents in the Old House (or Montezillo) was always a snapshot of a moving picture. But on several occasions Abigail reported seating twenty-one people for dinner. From the very start, then, the image of Abigail and John living out their last chapter together in secluded serenity was a complete distortion. Their retirement home was also a hotel, an orphanage, a child-care center, and a hospital.

This seemed wholly natural to them, in part because they were accustomed to providing the home base for all the wounded and derelict members of the extended Adams family, in part because they presumed that the family was supposed to perform the multiple functions now assigned to a variety of different institutions. They also agreed that John, whatever his title, was the acknowledged master of Montezillo, though day-to-day management of the domestic dominion belonged to Abigail. She had spent so many years joining him on his turf; they would now live out the remainder of their time on hers.

In a strictly legal sense, John Quincy became the owner of all the Quincy properties, and John and Abigail became his tenants only a few years into their retirement. In 1803 their life savings in stocks and bonds, about $13,000, disappeared when the London bank Bird, Savage & Bird, in which John Quincy had invested their only liquid assets, inexplicably collapsed. Ever the super-responsible son, John Quincy sold his Boston house and used the proceeds to purchase all the various pieces of Quincy land. In effect, he bought his own inheritance, then gave his parents title to the land for life. The legal transactions were all in the family, where John remained the unquestioned patriarch and Abigail his equal partner, but the arrangement was an early sign of how much their sought-after serenity would come to depend on their only nonprodigal son.[6]

Even John Quincy unwittingly disappointed his father by naming his eldest son George Washington Adams. "I am sure your brother had not any intention of wounding the feelings of his father," Abigail reported to Thomas, "but I see he has done it . . . Had he called him Joshua, he would not have taken it amiss." Apparently John stomped around the house, murmuring obscenities for several days in the summer of 1801, furious that his brilliant son had been so stupid as to memorialize in the Adams line the only American hero with a stronger claim on posterity's admiration. Years later, John attempted to compensate by making George his favorite and most indulged grandson.[7]

There were obviously still demons darting about John's bruised psyche, lingering resentments that resisted his best efforts to make them the butt of self-deprecating jokes. Abigail spied him working in the fields alongside the hired help one summer day, swinging his scythe in rhythmic strokes, looking like the epitome of the retired statesman in his agrarian paradise. She also reported that he appeared to be talking or mumbling to himself with each swing, though she could not make out the words. If his correspondence at that time is any indication, he was probably cursing Jefferson.[8]

RAVAGES OF TIME

It was clear from the start that John was emotionally incapable of sitting serenely beneath his proverbial vine and fig tree. Idyllic images failed to take account of his obsession with posterity's judgment of his role in America's founding, his brooding memories of the political shenanigans by both Jefferson and Hamilton that had denied him a second term as president, and, finally, his impulsive vivacity, which rendered a stoic posture virtually impossible.

This is not to mention the inevitable vicissitudes of aging, which had rendered him hairless and almost toothless—his speech had grown increasingly slurred—and the shaking of his palsied hands, which he referred to as "quiverations," a word he claimed to have "borrowed from an Irish boy [and] an improvement of our language worthy of a place in Webster's dictionary." These "quiverations" sometimes required him to grip his pen with both hands while writing letters. And his poor eyesight—he somewhat melodramatically claimed that he had been going blind for almost twenty years—meant that Abigail often read out loud to him at night. These physical ravages of time imposed the kind of daily burdens that Cicero's idealistic account of elderly bliss had somehow neglected to mention.[9]

Although nine years younger than John, Abigail was actually in worse physical shape. Her congenital rheumatism and associated rheumatic fevers flared up more frequently. And when they did she was often confined to her bed for weeks at a time, which required the household staff to gather in her bedroom each morning to receive her instructions for the day. Even when the rheumatism was in remission, she seldom left the house and could only accompany John on his daily ride around the farms in a cushioned carriage. Her hair had turned completely white and, in conjunction with her deepening wrinkles, led her to observe that the woman depicted in Gilbert Stuart's portrait of 1800 was no longer recognizable a few years later.[10]

She was also, albeit in a different way than John, emotionally invested in the Adams legacy. For John, the concern about his place in the history books was painfully personal. For Abigail, on the other hand, the focus was on the family, her role as the matriarch who helped lay the foundation on which succeeding generations of Adams descendants could make future contributions to the unfolding American story.

Quite obviously, John was still her highest domestic priority. In retirement, that meant helping him to navigate past the sharp edges of his vanities and remaining calm when he was in mid-eruption, listening patiently to his passionate denunciations of partisan politics, Jefferson's misguided foreign policy, or the suicidal tendencies of the New England Federalists. She had been performing this essential task for their entire life together, and it was even more essential that she continue to perform it now, since once John was removed from the public arena his ambitious energies had no outlet and simmered away inside him with greater ferocity.

The heir apparent, just as obviously, was John Quincy, who had been groomed for greatness almost from the moment he exited Abigail's womb. All prospects for an Adams dynasty now rested wholly on the eldest son, since Charles had already carried their hopes to a besotted early death, and Thomas had established a pattern of inexplicable ineptitude sufficiently severe that he was forced to move back to Quincy under the eye and within the orbit of his parents.

John Quincy's return from Berlin in 1801, most especially his return to Quincy in December, was a landmark event. For then Abigail met her "new daughter" for the first time. Louisa Catherine was an elegantly statuesque, delicately boned young woman who spoke with a slight British accent. Very much at home in the European salon set—she had been the sensation of the Berlin court—Louisa Catherine was up for inspection, since Abigail regarded her as the crucial partner that John Quincy would need by his side in the long march toward public triumph. She was also the biological fountainhead for the third generation of Adams descendants, heir apparent to Abigail's role as matriarch.

First impressions on both sides were not encouraging. Abigail was alarmed at her sickly condition, "which confined her almost the whole time she was here." More basically, Louisa Catherine struck her as precariously refined: "Her frame is so slender and her constitution so delicate that I have many fears that she will be of short duration."[11]

For her part, Louisa Catherine remembered the Quincy introduction as an unmitigated catastrophe: "Had I stepped onto Noah's Ark I do not think I could have been more utterly astonished." She also sensed Abigail's disapproval, not that any wife of John Quincy would have passed muster in Abigail's eyes. "Do what I would," Louisa Catherine recalled, "there was a conviction on the part of others that I could not suit, however well inclined."[12]

Abigail saw it differently. From that day until her final illness, she resolved to make Louisa Catherine her special project. She was not the woman Abigail would have chosen for John Quincy, but she was the woman he had chosen for himself, and therefore the essential link with future generations of Adams progeny who must be cultivated, encouraged, folded into the dynastic network.

Finally, it merits attention that the extended Adams family over which Abigail was supposed to exercise her legendary prowess bore no relationship at all to the idyllic domestic world described in the Latin classics. Abigail was attempting to manage what, by any measure, qualified as a dysfunctional family: Nabby and her little brood were living on the edge of poverty in a marriage sustained only by her unconditional loyalty; Sally Adams, widow of Charles, had become a permanent casualty of life, frequently breaking down in tears for no apparent reason; Thomas, upon his return to Quincy, retreated into self-doubt, chronic dissipation, and eventually a losing battle with alcoholism. Although the magic between Abigail and John remained intact, they were in fact surrounded by the kind of human debris subsequently depicted in the plays of Eugene O'Neill.

VOLCANIC ERUPTIONS

Though the Old House was Abigail's designated domain, she did her best to create a secluded space for John, where he could do his daily reading and writing with a minimum of interruption. Given the sheer size of the resident population, and the fact that so many of them were infants and young children often running from room to room, this was not an easy task. It was rendered even more difficult by John's habit of plopping himself down at the parlor table after dinner, which was usually served between three and four o'clock, and commencing his work in what was, in effect, the center of the wind tunnel. John had developed impressive powers of concentration over the years, and Abigail made a point of reminding the grandchildren that the patriarch, often referred to as "the president," was not to be disturbed. But interruptions were inevitable, whether it was young George climbing onto his lap, or Susanna, the somewhat precocious daughter of Charles, asking him to read her a book.

John apparently welcomed the periodic interruptions as a relief from the burdensome thoughts about his problematic place in the history books that had become his all-consuming obsession. "How is it that I, poor, ignorant I, must stand before Posterity as differing from all the other great Men of the Age?" he asked. And why was it that even when his name was admitted onto the list with those of Franklin, Washington, Jefferson, and Madison, it was always accompanied by an asterisk describing him as "the most vain, conceited, imprudent, and arrogant Creature in the World?"[13]

He had begun his career as a young lawyer aiming for fame more than fortune. And then history had presented him with the chance to play a major role in leading a revolution and establishing a new nation, a truly remarkable opportunity that came around only once every few centuries. But now, with his work done, his achievement was being airbrushed out of the story, and others were being accorded prominent places in the American pantheon while he was required to languish in obscurity, or worse, being described as an erratic, slightly deranged curmudgeon who did not fit comfortably into the proper heroic mold.

For the first twelve years of his retirement John spent a portion of most days seated at the parlor table amid the buzz of grandchildren, and most nights by the fire alongside Abigail, who was often reading a book while he did battle with his emotions. First in his somewhat pathetic attempt at an autobiography, then in a caustic exchange with Mercy Otis Warren, then in a nearly interminable series of weekly essays for the **Boston Patriot,** and throughout in an extraordinary correspondence with Benjamin Rush—easily the most candid and colorful letters he ever wrote—John released the pent-up energies of his tortured soul. These separate venues were really parts of a single project, namely, to claim his proper place in American history, or, if that proved problematic, to smash all the other statues currently being enshrined in the American pantheon. He was, to put it charitably, slightly out of control.

In November 1804 John Quincy, by then serving as the senator from Massachusetts, encouraged his father to write his memoirs: "I have heretofore requested you, if you find it consistent with your leisure, to commit to writing an account of the principle incidents of your own life . . . It would afford a lasting and cordial gratification to your children, and I have no doubt, be ultimately a benefit to your Country. It might also amuse many hours which otherwise may pass heavily." John effectively threw up his hands at the suggestion: "You have recommended to me a Work, which . . . would engage my feelings and enflame my Passions. In many Passages it would set me on fire and I should have occasion for a Bucket of Water constantly by my side to put it out."[14]

He spoke from experience, since, unbeknownst to John Quincy, he had been working on his memoirs in fits and starts for more than two years. His self-defeating message was announced at the start: "As the lives of Philosophers, Statesmen or Historians written by themselves have generally been suspected of vanity, and therefore few People have been able to read them without disgust; there is no reason to expect that any sketches I may leave of my own

Time would be received by the Public with any favour, or read by individuals with much interest."[15]

As the editors of the modern edition of the **Adams Papers** acknowledge, to call John's autobiography chaotic would be generous. Its disorderly and often incoherent shape was in part a function of the fitful, stop-and-start manner of its composition. Initially he worked solely from memory; then it occurred to him to consult his own diaries and letter books, then volumes he had in his library on sessions of the Continental Congress, which he began to quote verbatim for long stretches without commentary, thereby losing any semblance of narrative control.[16]

But another source of incoherence was the periodic explosions that went off throughout the text when John encountered a character who conjured up painful memories. Predictably, Hamilton produced a major detonation, even though he had recently died in a duel with Aaron Burr: "Nor am I obliged by any Principles of Morality or Religion to suffer my character to lie under infamous Calumnies," John argued, "because the Author of them, with a Pistol Bullet through his Spinal Marrow, died a Penitent." The venom poured out: "Born on a Speck more obscure than Corsica . . . with infinitely less courage and Capacity than Bonaparte, he would in my Opinion, if I had not controlled the fury of his Vanity . . . involved us in all the Bloodshed and distractions of foreign and Civil War at once." There was score-settling with Franklin, Paine, and Jefferson as well, all of whom ended up with Hamilton in the Adams rogues' gallery. One can almost see him hunched over the table, scribbling away despite his palsied hand, gleefully eviscerating his enemies into the night.[17]

In 1807 he shifted his guns to Mercy Otis Warren, who had recently published a three-volume **History of the American Revolution** (1805) in which, as John saw it, his own role in making independence happen was not sufficiently appreciated. Actually, Abigail had fired the first shot two years before Warren's **History** was published, declaring to her old friend that "the sacred deposit of private confidence has been betrayed, and the bonds of Friendly intercourse swept asunder, to serve the most malicious purposes . . . I have been ready to exclaim with the poet [Shakespeare] 'What sin unknown dipt you in Ink.'" Abigail was apparently referring to critical remarks that Warren had made about John because he had refused to give her son a job in his administration.[18]

The appearance of Warren's **History** clinched the breakdown of communication between the families. The most offensive passage echoed the charges of the Republican press that John was a closet monarchist, that during his eight-year tour of duty in Europe, "living long near the splendor of courts and courtiers" had caused him to become "beclouded by a partiality for monarchy [and] a lapse from his former republican principles." This was a long-standing accusation, not really true, but now enshrined in one of the first serious histories of the American Revolution by none other than a life-long friend of the Adams family. Worse yet, it was sure to influence all subsequent histories, because it came at the start and because Warren herself possessed impeccable revolutionary credentials.[19]

The initial salvo from Abigail, which effectively announced that her friendship with Warren was seriously compromised, was followed by ten letters from John that verged on hysteria. No one in the revolutionary generation, he claimed, had "done more labor, run through more and greater dangers, and made greater sacrifices." He had done more than "any man among my contemporaries living or dead, in the service of my country." In the Continental Congress he had been the singular voice insisting on American independence. In the peace negotiations in Paris he alone had insisted on a separate treaty with England despite instructions to the contrary. These were, in truth, plausible claims, but he was the last person to make them on his own behalf without sounding like an arrogant fool, which is pretty much what Warren called him: "What is Mrs. Warren to think of your comments?" she asked rhetorically. "I readily tell you she thinks them the most captious, malignant, irrelevant compositions that have ever been seen." All communication between the two families then ceased for several years.[20]

Although Abigail had actually led the assault on Warren, and in that sense made herself a full partner in the defense of the Adams legacy, she almost surely recognized that John's outbursts only damaged his reputation by seeming to document the long-standing charge, first enshrined in the public record by Franklin, then amplified in Hamilton's notorious pamphlet, that his thought process was a series of volcanic eruptions. Even John himself acknowledged that he was making a fool of himself, but he could not help it: "A man never looks so silly as when he is talking or writing about himself," he admitted, "but Mrs. Warren's severity has reduced me to the necessity of pouring out all myself." Once he began pouring, however, his emotions flowed into an interior Adams zone where no one, not even Abigail, could reach him. She had learned from years of experience that when that happened, the only thing to do was to let him go until the flow subsided.[21]

From Abigail's perspective, the only positive feature of the exchange with Warren was that no one knew about it beyond the two families, so that

John's embarrassing behavior remained a private affair. But once his sluices had opened, the surge of painful memories and score-settling accusations needed somewhere else to go, so in 1809 John decided to publish a series of weekly essays in the recently established **Boston Patriot.** He was obviously in full flight: "Let the jackasses bray or laugh at this, as they did at the finger of God," he shouted at the start of the series. "I am in a fair way to give my critics food enough to glut their appetites." In one of the first **Patriot** pieces he compared himself to "an animal I have seen take hold of the end of a cord with his teeth, and be drawn slowly up by pulleys, through a storm of squils, crackers, and rockets, flashing and blazing around him every moment . . . and although the scorching flames made him groan, and mourn, and roar, he would not let go."[22]

John did not let go for three years and more than a thousand pages, most of them directed at the defining decision of his presidency, sending a peace commission that avoided war with France. He went out of his way to describe the duplicitous behavior of Vice President Jefferson, the disloyalty of his cabinet, and most especially the grandiose scheming of Hamilton to wrest control of the Federalist Party for his own traitorous purposes. All this was, in fact, historically accurate, but it came off to readers as special pleading, and at times as the ranting of a sore loser afflicted by some combination of paranoia and dementia.

The tortured remembering that John was attempting to write about in his autobiography, then the prideful and almost pugilistic vindications of his historical significance spewed out to Warren and, more endlessly, to the **Boston Patriot,** could be construed as forms of therapy, if that term meant the effort to bring latent emotional anger that had been previously suppressed to the surface for more conscious and explicit scrutiny. But the conspicuously self-serving character of John's version of therapy, plus the often incoherent and always frenzied form of its expression, only enhanced the charge that he was, as his critics had claimed, a one-man bonfire of vanities. This was not quite fair, as became clear in the freewheeling correspondence with Benjamin Rush in which his ghosts and goblins became the butt of jokes and, at least momentarily, he could laugh at himself.

Rush had been a friend for over thirty years, but they had drifted apart over the last decade, when Rush had sided with Jefferson. The correspondence, then, represented the recovery of a friendship rooted in a personal affinity that both men recognized as deeper than politics: a common instinct for a level of candor that bordered on irreverence; a mutual disregard for any kind of conventional wisdom that deterred their rollicking, almost daredevil style; and their recognition that, at this late stage in their lives, they were like gamblers with nothing to lose.[23]

Quite coincidentally, Rush had recently decided to conclude his medical career by focusing his attention on mental illness, a decision that eventually earned him the title "father of American psychiatry." As part of that project, he proposed that he and John engage in a high-stakes game of honesty in which they reported to each other on their respective dreams.

John leapt at the offer, vowing to match Rush "dream for dream." He dreamed that he was "mounted on a lofty scaffold in the center of the great plain in Versailles, surrounded by an innumerable congregation of five and twenty millions." But then the crowd became a collection of animals—lions, elephants, rats, squirrels, even sharks and whales. When he attempted to lecture this weird menagerie on "the unadulterated principles of liberty, equality, and fraternity among all living creatures," the menagerie became a violent mob, tearing one another to pieces, then forcing him to flee for his life "with my clothes torn from my back and my skin lacerated from head to foot." This was simultaneously a joke about the naïveté of the French philosophes and a fable about his own fate at the hands of the American electorate.[24]

The mad-hatter character of the correspondence encouraged free association, and the Versailles scene made John remember a phrase used by a French barber in Boston, "a little crack," meaning slightly crazy, which described the entire British ruling class and all the utopian thinkers of the French Revolution. "I must tell you," he confided to Rush, "that my wife, who took a fancy to read this letter upon my table, bids me to tell you that she thinks my head too, a little cracked, and I am half of that mind too."[25]

Apparently their wives were often sitting nearby while Adams and Rush wrote their letters, and periodically commented on their giddy tone. Rush reported to John that "my saucy wife says that you and I correspond like two young girls about their sweethearts." And when Rush proposed, to John's horror, that colleges eliminate the study of Latin and Greek for more practical subjects, it turned out, so John claimed, that Abigail agreed with him: "Mrs. Adams says she is willing you should discredit Greek and Latin, because it will destroy all the pretensions of the gentlemen to superiority over the ladies and restore liberty, equality, and fraternity between the sexes." Or when Rush described a special "tranquillizing chair" that he had designed for interviews with his mental patients, Abigail suggested in jest that John could benefit from such seating. John countered that he already had his own proper chair, for if Samuel Johnson pontificated from his tavern stool, John did the same from his "throne at my fireside."[26]

With Rush, instead of engaging in endless lamentations about the scandalmongers who had vilified him, he claimed that he "would subscribe 100 guineas for a complete edition of all the scandal against me from 1789 to 1801, then have it bound in an expensive leather binder for preservation." It was actually his own fault for failing to hire what he called "puffers" to answer the ridiculous accusations: "These puffers, Rush, are the only killers of scandal . . . and you and I have never employed them, and therefore scandal has prevailed against us." When Rush reminded John that one such "puffer," William Cobbett, had defended the Adams presidency, John countered with self-mockery: "Now I assure you upon my honor and the faith of the friendship between us," he vowed, "that I never saw the face of Cobbett, and that I should not know him if I met him in my porridge dish."[27]

And instead of bemoaning his failure to fit comfortably into the stoic mold that history seemed to require, he went on the offensive, mocking the presumption that stoic serenity was anything but a theatrical posture. The Virginians were especially good at such posing, Washington the best of the lot, but then "Virginian geese were all Swans." Rather than make the point in a defensive way, he made his critique of the stoic style into a bawdy joke: "Deceive not thyself," he told Rush. "There is not an old friar in France, not in all Europe, who looks on a blooming young virgin with **sang-froid.**"[28]

The dream-driven correspondence with Rush drew on John's lifelong habit of introspection, itself a secular version of the venerable New England tradition in which the aspiring Puritan saint searched his soul for signs of God's grace. But as John himself seemed to be aware, the therapeutic technique that Rush brought to the conversation, by insisting on dreams as the subject matter, permitted fresh emotional insights and connections by bypassing the defense mechanisms of the conscious mind. "Dream, you know, is a mighty Power," he observed to Rush. "It is not shackled with any rules of Method in Arrangement of Thoughts . . . Time, Space and Place are annihilated; and the free independent Soul darts from Suns to Suns, from Planets to Planets . . . to all the Milky Way, quicker than rays of Light." He was beginning to learn how to round up those "raging Bulls" that he felt stampeding inside him when he was a young man.[29]

At the same time that he was being tortured by his demons in his embarrassingly vain letters to Mercy Otis Warren and his hopelessly self-serving essays in the **Boston Patriot**, John was conquering those demons, or at least bringing them under a measure of control, in his correspondence with Rush. Only to Rush, and perhaps in conversations with Abigail that left no trace, could he acknowledge that the personal crusade on behalf of his rightful place in the history books was a fool's errand: "There have been many times in my life when I have been so agitated in my own mind," he confessed to Rush, "as to have no considerations at all of the light in which my words would be considered by others . . . The few traces of me that remain, I believe, must go down to posterity with much confusion." Although Abigail had learned to cope with the childlike tantrums of the aggrieved seeker of fame, this less frantic creature was the man she loved. It was good to get him back.[30]

ABIGAIL'S AGENDA

Abigail's duties were her demons, at least in the sense that the extended family that flocked to Quincy in fits and starts in the early years of her alleged retirement put her prowess as the legendary matriarch of the Adams dynasty to a strenuous test. For, as we have seen, the Old House became either the final destination or the temporary depository for a sizable congregation of near and distant relatives, all bearing young children and most carrying heavy emotional baggage. As a result, she faced an even more sprawling set of domestic challenges in her retirement than she did as a young mother coping with four children in John's absence. She was the irrepressible center of gravity for the Adams family, and now all the accumulated loose ends floated into her domestic orbit.

Ironically, it was her powerful domestic instinct that led her into an extraordinary exchange of letters with Jefferson, in which she became the most ardent and effective defender of John's political legacy. It began in May 1804, when she learned that Jefferson's younger daughter, Maria Jefferson Eppes, whom she had known and nurtured as Polly in London, had died of complications during childbirth. Her deep parental empathy—she had by then lost three of her own children—compelled her to offer consolation to Jefferson regardless of the political chasm that had opened up between them: "It has been some time I conceived of any event in this Life," she somewhat poignantly observed, "which would call forth feeling of mutual sympathy." But a daughter's death was just such a rare occasion.[31]

Jefferson normally had perfect pitch in such exchanges, but he misread Abigail's intentions, thinking she sought to use Maria's death as an opportunity to restore diplomatic relations between Monticello and Quincy. After thanking her for the gesture of empathy, he proceeded to minimize the Adams-Jefferson conflict, blaming it on partisan journalists, claiming that their quite real political differences had never threatened the personal friendship. This was revisionist history of the charitable sort, designed to recover the friendship by denying it had ever been lost.

But then Jefferson made a fatal blunder. He had but one personal criticism of John's behavior as president, he wrote, which was his appointment of John Marshall as chief justice during the latter weeks of his presidency, thereby burdening Jefferson with an entrenched and alien presence. Jefferson characterized this decision as "personally unkind," almost a slap in the face by John before departing. Over time, however, in an elegant turn of phrase, Jefferson concluded that the Marshall appointment "left something for friendship to forgive," so that "after brooding it over for some time, I forgave it cordially."[32]

Jefferson was extremely adept in verbal jousts of this sort, usually establishing a genteel tone that made any form of conflict or confrontation seem inappropriate. He should have known that his tactics would not work with Abigail, who had reprimanded him in no uncertain terms as a delinquent parent of the very child who had just died. "You have been pleased to enter upon some subjects which call for a reply," she ominously observed. "And now Sir, I freely disclose to you what has severed the bonds of former friendship and placed you in a Light very different from what I had viewed you in."

The notion that John's appointment of Marshall was a personal affront defied the obvious fact, so Abigail argued, that he was legally obliged to make the appointment. (She did not reveal that she had strongly supported the decision.) But the most preposterous and presumptive claim was Jefferson's assumption of the moral high ground—this from the same man who had "spread the blackest calumny and foulest falsehoods" against both her husband and her eldest son by paying James Callender to assault their integrity in the newspapers in order to ensure his own election, all the while denying that he had done so. "This, Sir, I considered as a personal injury," she wrote, "and the sword that cut the Gordion Knot." If there was any sin for friendship to forgive, all the forgiving rested on the Adams side of the ledger. The fact that Callender had subsequently turned on Jefferson and exposed his affair with the mulatto slave Sally Hemings was a delectable irony: "The serpent you cherished and warmed," she caustically observed, "bit the hand that nourished him." She closed with a quote from Proverbs: "Faithful are the wounds of a friend."[33]

Jefferson's response was both deft and duplicitous. He argued that partisans on both sides had engaged in wild distortions during the presidential campaign, and that scandalmongers on the Federalist side had vilified him beyond recognition. (This was true.) But he also claimed that "any person who knew either of us could not possibly believe that either meddled in the dirty work." In effect, he was contesting the claim that he had personally paid Callender to libel John. (This was a lie.)[34]

Abigail called his bluff. Jefferson's payments to Callender were well documented, exposed by Callender himself after the election, when he complained about the meager level of compensation he had received and then went after Jefferson for his liaison with Sally Hemings. Jefferson's response to these revelations had been some subtle combination of silence and denial. Abigail was the only person on the historical record to confront Jefferson with the charge that he was a bald-faced liar. She did it with almost Jeffersonian deftness, recalling her previous respect for him, observing that "the Heart is long, very long in receiving the conviction that is forced upon it by reason." But there was no denying that he had mortgaged his honor to win an election against her husband. His critics had always accused him of being slippery, disingenuous, and dishonorable. "Pardon me, Sir," Abigail concluded, "that I fear you are." In the vast Jefferson correspondence, no one had ever put it to him so directly.

Jefferson presumed that this volley of letters with Abigail had occurred with John's knowledge and consent. In fact, Abigail had conducted the correspondence on her own, never informing John of the exchange until several months later, when she showed all the letters to him. "The whole of this correspondence was begun and conducted without my Knowledge or Suspicion," John wrote in the margins of the last letter. "I have no remarks to make upon it at this time and in this place." Always his most ardent advocate, Abigail had delivered a decisive blow to his most elusive enemy, done with a level of controlled anger that John himself could never have mustered. All communication between Quincy and Monticello subsequently ceased for the next eight years.[35]

The blow delivered to Jefferson, no matter how satisfying, was a wholly private triumph, invisible to the public. It was also an exception to the main pattern of Abigail's focus during the retirement years, which was more domestic than political. If John's chief ambition was to live forever in the memory of future generations, Abigail's was to create the hard nucleus of a family that would do the same. Her immortality was more derivative; she would live on in the memories and genes of her children, her grandchildren, and their progeny. It was also more maternal, frequently taking the form of a personal campaign to gather as many members of the extended family as possible to her Quincy haven, where they would come under her direct supervision and matriarchal gaze.

Her major projects were Louisa Catherine and Nabby. Quincy was probably the last place where

Louisa Catherine wished to reside, since she was temperamentally incapable of matching Abigail's domestic competence, and in her presence felt like a hummingbird to Abigail's eagle. But Abigail made a heroic effort to cultivate her trust, writing her on nearly a weekly basis and insisting that she regarded the wife of John Quincy as her own daughter. Her efforts to be helpful, however, frequently backfired, in part because of her own commanding style, in part because Louisa Catherine was predisposed to collapse into heaps of sobbing insecurity whenever Abigail's advice seemed to question her own effectiveness as a wife and mother.

Soon after John Quincy, in keeping with his destiny, was elected to the Senate, for example, Abigail began a bombardment of maternal wisdom that Louisa Catherine, somewhat understandably, deeply resented: "I regret to hear that my dear son's health is not good," Abigail began. "I wish you would not let him go to Congress without a cracker in his pocket. The space between Breakfast and dinner is so long, that the stomach gets filled with flatuencies, and his food when he takes it neither digests or nourishes him." Some newspaper reports had called attention to his careless and even slovenly attire, which Abigail found embarrassing, prompting her to urge Louisa Catherine "to prevail upon him to pay more attention to his personal appearance." By almost any standard, this was maternal overkill and intrusive, no matter how well-intentioned.[36]

On the other hand, even a harmless suggestion by Abigail could send Louisa Catherine into a tearful collapse. For example, when Abigail mentioned that a relative living in Washington had expressed regret at not hearing from the wife of the newly elected senator, Louisa Catherine interpreted the remark as a personal affront "that gave me pain as it obliquely insinuated a reflection on my family," meaning that she had not been raised properly and was obviously ill-equipped to fulfill the social obligations of her station. Abigail had said no such thing, but that is what the precariously perched and always vulnerable Louisa Catherine heard. Emotionally and temperamentally, the two women were worlds apart.[37]

Yet they were also inextricably connected, not only by the link with John Quincy but also by two young grandchildren, George and John, who did much of their growing up under Abigail's care at Quincy, where they were deposited for most of John Quincy's term in the Senate and then again when he was appointed ambassador to Russia. Louisa Catherine frequently fretted about her role as absentee mother, and Abigail did due diligence as a hovering grandmother who tried to reassure her that the boys had her fullest attention: "I told him [John, then two years old] that I was writing to you," she wrote

Louisa Catherine, "and asked him what I should say. Shall I say John is good? No. Shall I say John is Naughty? No. He stood a moment and his little Eyes glistened. Say John has got a Beauty new Hat."[38]

Abigail's only concern was that grandparenting was almost by nature a more permissive and indulgent role than parenting, which might bode badly for the boys down the line. John apparently gave the matter no thought whatsoever. He encouraged the boys to crawl into bed with him, "disarrange all the Papers on my writing Table," and whenever they said they were hungry, "devour all my Strawberries, Cherries, Currants, Plumbs, Peaches, Pears and Apples." The children of John Quincy, it seems safe to say, were not raised in the same superdisciplined way as their father and pretty much had the run of the house. Although both boys eventually attended Harvard, neither lived long enough to make a contribution to the Adams line, and George committed suicide at twenty-nine.[39]

Nabby was Abigail's other priority, more a rescue operation like Thomas, designed to limit losses in the current generation rather than cultivate prospects for the future. She wrote to Nabby more than anyone else, most often pleading with her to leave her hopelessly insolvent and dissolute husband and bring her three children back to the safe haven at Quincy: "I am writing by candle-light, whilst all around me are fast bound in sleep . . .

Even faithful Juno lies snoring beside me . . . You must come to live with us." It was a difficult command for Nabby to hear, since it contradicted all her previous education about a wife's obligations to her husband. Nabby adopted a compromise position, which fit her core disposition to please all parties, by spending three or four months a year at Quincy and the remainder of the time in Lebanon, New York, with her husband, at one point even joining him in jail, where he was detained for his complicity in a wild-eyed scheme—his specialty—to invade and liberate Venezuela.[40]

This prevailing pattern changed dramatically in the fall of 1811. Nabby was in residence at Quincy with her daughter, Caroline, a spirited girl who reminded Abigail of herself at the same age, when she detected a tumor in her breast. John immediately wrote to Rush for advice, and he provided an unequivocal diagnosis: "From her account the remedy is the knife . . . I repeat again, let there be no delay in flying to the knife . . . It may be too late." In November, three physicians performed a full mastectomy of her right breast in the parlor of the Old House, without anesthesia, while Abigail and John held each other in an adjoining room.[41]

"My own bosom has been lacerated by wound upon wound," Abigail wrote to John Quincy. "I can scarcely trust my pen to describe them." She was primarily referring to Nabby's surgery, but her sister, Mary Cranch, and Mary's husband, Richard, had died a day apart at almost the same time. Sally Adams seemed on the verge of death with pleurisy, and John had seriously gashed his shin while attempting to view the transit of a comet a few nights earlier. Her Quincy haven had become a hospital.[42]

Nabby remained in Quincy for six months to recover from the surgery, then returned to her husband. But, as Rush feared, the cancer had spread. Two years later, in July 1813, she arrived back at Quincy to die, emaciated, almost unrecognizable: "She is indeed a very sick woman," Abigail reported to John Quincy. "Cannot take food . . . How she got here is a marvel to me." Three weeks later Nabby died in her father's arms with Abigail sobbing at the bedside.[43]

While resilience was a trademark Abigail trait, she never fully recovered: "To me the loss is irreparable," she confided to John Quincy. "The wound . . . cannot be healed." She had used similar words at the death of Charles, but Nabby's death clinched a new level of prevailing sorrow that she could never completely dispel. Her grief poured out in gushes in her letters for a full year after Nabby's passing, which Abigail described as the sudden departure of "my closest companion." She had conceived of her matriarchal role as the preparation of future generations for greatness. But now it seemed that her primary task was to watch her own children die or, in Thomas's case, slide gradually into alcoholism.[44]

NORTH AND SOUTH POLES

The cloud of despair that descended upon Abigail after Nabby's death coincided, ironically, with the lifting of the cloud that had been shadowing John since his retirement. Perhaps the deuces-wild correspondence with Rush had helped him to exorcise his demons. Or perhaps the interminable rantings in the **Boston Patriot** had served as a catharsis that purged his tortured soul of anxieties about posterity's judgment. Whatever the cause, starting in 1812, and growing steadily thereafter, his letters reflect an emerging recognition of his own foibles and follies, a flair for self-deprecating humor, a capacity to laugh at his own eccentricities.

Inquiries about his physical and mental condition, for example, became occasions to make fun of himself: "I have one head, four limbs and five senses," he told one curious stranger. "My temper in general has been tranquil except when any Instance of extraordinary Madness, Deceit, Hypocrisy, Ingratitude, Treachery or Perfidy has suddenly struck me. Then I have been irascible enough, and in three or four Instances too much so." His expanding girth, he explained, had forced him to adopt a strict diet: "No veal cutlets, no old hock, no old or young madeira, no meat, no spirits, nothing but Indian porridge, water gruel . . . and five and twenty cigars." There was no question, however, that time had taken its toll: "My constitution is a glass bubble or a hollow icicle . . . A slight irregularity or one intemperate dinner might finish the catastrophe of the play."[45]

What did he think of Jefferson's decision to mothball the ships-of-the-line that he, as president, had built up into a respectable American navy? Well, Jefferson would live to regret that decision, John observed, since war with Great Britain was probably inevitable, despite Jefferson's futile policy of an embargo. (This was in 1811.) And when war began we would quickly discover that the American navy "was so Lilliputian that Hercules after a hasty dinner would sink it by setting his foot on it." Or, even more irreverently: "I had like to say that Gulliver might bury it in the deep by making water on it."[46]

How did it feel to be an American icon? Well, somewhat strange: "It is become fashionable to call me 'The Venerable.' It makes me think of the venerable Bede . . . or the venerable Savannarola," icons of the past whom John thought undeserving. He considered all efforts to mythologize him or the founding generation as a whole misguidedly reverential: "But to tell you the truth," he wrote one young admirer, "as far as I am capable of comparing the merit of different periods, I have no reason to believe we were better than you are."[47]

Did he have any serious reservations about the Christian doctrine of life after death? Well, such questions were inherently unanswerable, but he had presumed that God would afford him the opportunity to debate Franklin in heaven. On the other hand: "If it should be revealed or demonstrated that there is no future state, my advice to every man, woman, and child would be . . . to take opium."[48]

These flashes of self-possessed irreverence suggested that the great volcano of American politics was at last in remission. The clinching evidence came in 1812, when he allowed Rush to manipulate him into a correspondence with Jefferson: "I perceive plainly enough, Rush," he observed, "that you have been teasing Jefferson to write to me, as you did me to write to him." Abigail's earlier exchange with Jefferson had appeared to deliver the coup de grâce to any resumption of the old friendship. But Rush was relentless in his efforts to bargain a breakthrough: "I consider you and him," he told John, "as the North and South Poles of the American Revolution. Some talked, some wrote, and some fought to promote and establish it, but you and Mr. Jefferson thought for us all." Moreover, Rush reported that he had a dream in which the two great patriarchs resolved their differences, restored their famous friendship, and then "sunk into the grave nearly at the same time." As it turned out, Rush's dream proved eerily prophetic.[49]

Over the course of fourteen years, from 1812 to 1826, Adams and Jefferson exchanged 158 letters, with the flow from Quincy more than double the output from Monticello. Since John had made no secret of his animus against Jefferson during the past decade, several friends expressed surprise that he would agree to a reconciliation with that man from Monticello. But John claimed that he could no longer remember what disagreements he had with Jefferson, except that they had once argued about the proper length of a man's hair: "It was only as if one sailor had met a brother sailor after twenty-five years absence," he joked, "and had accosted him, 'how fare you, Jack?'"[50]

His more revealing, and more honest, explanation came a few years later:

> I do not believe that Mr. Jefferson ever
> hated me. On the contrary, I believe that
> he always liked me, but he detested
> Hamilton and my whole administration.
> Then, he wished to be President of the
> United States, and I stood in his way. So he
> did everything he could to pull me down.
> But if I should quarrel with him for that,
> I might quarrel with every man I have had

anything to do with in my life. This is
human nature.

Was this merely bravado? Or did he mean what he
said, that he genuinely had forgiven Jefferson for his
multiple duplicities?[51]

The clearest answer came more than a year into
the correspondence, when Abigail appended a note
to one of John's letters: "I have been looking for
some time for a space in my good Husband's Letters
to add the regards of an old Friend," she jotted at
the bottom of the page, "which are still cherished
and preserved through all the changes and vicissitudes which have taken place . . . and will I trust
remain as long as, A. Adams." As Jefferson surely
knew, Abigail was the ultimate protector of her husband's reputation, as the volleys she had fired at
Monticello a decade earlier made abundantly and
painfully clear. Her endorsement meant that the
wounds Jefferson had inflicted on the Adams family
had healed, or at least been forgiven. His chief sin
had been to place political interest above friendship.
Abigail, speaking for the Adams family, had made
the recovery of friendship their highest priority.
They were the ones making the magnanimous
gesture.[52]

Unlike the correspondence with Rush, which resembled free verse, John's letters to Jefferson, especially at the beginning, were more self-consciously

classical occasions in which both men assumed the role of philosopher-king in the Ciceronian mode: "But wither is senile garrulity leading me?" Jefferson asked rhetorically. "Into politics, of which I have taken final leave. I think little of them and say less. I have given up newspapers in exchange for Tacitus and Thucydides, for Newton and Euclid, and I find myself much happier." John responded in the same elegiac manner: "I have read Thucydides and Tacitus, so often, and at such distant periods of my life," he observed, "that elegant, profound and enchanting is their style, I am weary of them." Fully aware that their letters would eventually become part of the historical record, both men were posing for posterity.[53]

Posing was a natural act for Jefferson, who regarded argument as a dissonant noise that created static instead of his preferred harmonies. For John, on the other hand, argument was the ideal conversation. He could no more stay on script in his dialogue with Jefferson than he could impersonate Franklin-like diplomacy with Vergennes. Such etiquette was not in him, since all his instincts were argumentative: "You and I ought not to die," he proposed to Jefferson, "before We have explained ourselves to each other." A graphic depiction of the correspondence, then, would have Jefferson standing erectly in a stately pose with arms folded across his chest while John paced back and forth, periodically pausing to pull on Jefferson's lapels or poke a finger into his chest. It was the closest thing that history allowed for the two sides of the American Revolution to engage in a dialogue.[54]

There were several safe subjects on which both sages could easily agree and in the process display their patriarchal wisdom. For example, here is Jefferson on aging: "But our machines have now been running for 70 or 80 years, and we must expect that, worn as they are, here a pivot, there a wheel, now a pinion, next a spring, will be giving way. And however we may tinker them up for a while, all will at last surcease motion." John retorted that he was "sometimes afraid that my 'Machine' will not 'surcease motion' soon enough; for I dread nothing so much as 'dying at the top,' and thereby becoming a weeping helpless object of compassion for years." He had seen this happen to Sam Adams, and feared dementia more than death.[55]

After a year of polite foreplay, John began to raise more controversial issues. He chided Jefferson for failing to prepare the nation for the War of 1812, most especially in dismantling the American navy, which had always been John's hobbyhorse. Jefferson never responded directly but instead parried the thrust by noting recent American victories against the British fleet on the Great Lakes, graciously observing that "these must be more gratifying to you than most men, as having been an early and constant advocate of wooden walls."[56]

Jefferson was even more conciliatory when it came to their differences over the French Revolution: "Your prophecies . . . proved truer than mine," he acknowledged, "and yet fell short of the fact, for instead of a million, the destruction of 8 or 10 millions of human beings has probably been the effect of the convulsions. I did not, in 89 believe they would have lasted so long, nor have cost so much blood." What's more, John had predicted that Great Britain would eventually win the competition for European supremacy with France, and the recent defeat of Napoleon at Waterloo had proved him right.[57]

This was a huge concession. For Jefferson was not only admitting that his optimistic estimate of events in revolutionary France had proved misguided. He was also acknowledging that on the dominant foreign policy issue of John's presidency, the insistence on neutrality toward France, which Jefferson and the Republicans had used as a political club to beat him out of office, history had vindicated John's policy. John recognized the implications of Jefferson's admission immediately: "I know not what to say of your Letter," he wrote, "but that it is one of the most consolatory I have ever received."[58]

On two equivalently seminal disagreements,

however, Jefferson stood his ground, and the exchange exposed the underlying reasons for the political chasm that had opened between them in the 1790s. Because the correspondence was more like a conversation that bounced off one topic after another without a moderator to reel in extraneous diversions, core differences between the two patriarchs remained somewhat blurry and elliptical. However, with the advantage of hindsight (the historian's only advantage), two elemental differences emerged more clearly than ever before.

First, in an exchange in the summer of 1813 prompted by Jefferson's insistence that the distinction between "the few and the many" was an eternal political division, it became clear that the two founders disagreed about what had, in fact, been founded. John believed that the creation of a nation-state at the Constitutional Convention was the culmination and political fulfillment of "the spirit of '76." Jefferson believed that it was a betrayal of that spirit and had created a central government with powers akin to the despotic Parliament and king that he and John together had so eloquently and effectively opposed. There were, in effect, two founding moments. John regarded both as essential; Jefferson regarded only the first as legitimate.[59]

Second, in a nearly simultaneous exchange over the role of "the aristoi" (aristocracies or elites) throughout history, Jefferson argued that the American Revolution had "laid the axe to the root of the Pseudo-aristocracy . . . founded on wealth and birth without either virtue or talents." In that sense, the American Revolution represented a clean break with the vestiges of European feudalism and had thereby cleared the ground for a new kind of egalitarian society in the United States based on merit and equality of opportunity.

John disagreed, arguing that the problem was not European feudalism but human nature itself, which had not undergone any magical transformation in crossing the Atlantic. Jefferson's vision of a classless American society was, therefore, a romantic pipe dream. "After all," John observed, "as long as property exists, it will accumulate in Individuals and Families and . . . the Snow ball will grow as it rolls." Pretending that the new American republic would be immune to the social inequalities of Europe was Jefferson's seductive version of the grand illusion. And at the political level, elites would always exist here as well as in Europe, and exercise disproportionate influence unless managed by government.[60]

Again, with hindsight as the guide, one could argue that John's position on the first disagreement was vindicated by the Civil War; his position on the second, by the New Deal. But in the crucible of the moment, such prescience was unavailable, and Jefferson's more optimistic forecast enjoyed a decided rhetorical advantage. The more historically correct conclusion would be that the Adams-Jefferson correspondence had exposed the two conflicting versions of America's original intentions, each passionately embraced by founders with unmatched revolutionary credentials.

INDIAN SUMMER

Although John's recovered friendship with Jefferson eventually became famous, even legendary, for its symbolic significance, his all-time dearest friend—no one else came close—was Abigail. And the feeling was mutual. When her sister somewhat mischievously asked her if she would marry John if she could live her life over, Abigail responded with an unambiguous declaration: "Yet after half a century, I can say my first choice would be the same if I again had my youth and opportunity to make it." This was in February 1814, when she was still recovering from Nabby's death, another bout with rheumatism had confined her to bed, and her sister Mary and the ever-faithful Juno had just passed away. But the dominant Adams pattern, for Abigail as well as for John, was to rally in the face of adversity. "I bend to disease, totter under it," she explained, "but rise again . . . feel grateful for the reprieve and wish so to number my days as to apply my mind to wisdom." She and John had not only lived so much life together, they had also suffered so much pain together that it was impossible to imagine doing it with anyone else.[61]

Unlike the renewed friendship with Jefferson, which was recorded in letters, no correspondence between Abigail and John was necessary because they were together all the time. And, in fact, the routine intimacies that did not make it into the historical record were the most emotionally important moments: John reading a recent letter from Jefferson by the fireside while Abigail sorted laundry; Abigail reading to John from Shakespeare, her favorite writer, late at night, when the candles could not compensate for John's failing eyesight; John fulminating over Mary Wollstonecraft's romantic delusions about the French Revolution while Abigail silently shelled beans and eventually announced it was time for bed.[62]

As their friends, close relatives, even their own children died around them, as the irrevocable aging process and accompanying physical failures made each look into the mirror a moment of horror, as the extended family that surrounded them at Quincy came to resemble a menagerie of wounded animals, Abigail and John remained resolute, infinitely resilient, the invulnerable center that would always hold. If love, like leadership, could never be defined, only recognized when it presented itself in its most ideal form, they embodied it. The long melody played on.

Their mutual obsession was John Quincy, who now single-handedly carried the prospects of the Adams family for the next generation. For this reason, they wanted him to have a brilliant political career, presumably culminating in the presidency. Yet the more they aged, the more dependent they became on his proximity. And so his appointment as American ambassador to Russia in 1809, which should have been greeted as another step toward his appointment with destiny, became a bittersweet occasion: "I find it very difficult to reconcile my mind to it," Abigail lamented. "At the advanced years both of his father and myself, we can have very little expectation of meeting again upon this mortal theatre . . . Both his father and I have looked to him as the prop and support of our advanced and declining years." For the next seven years, Abigail claimed to be clinging to life until her eldest son returned home.[63]

John Quincy was gone so long because history seemed to have a larger claim on him than his family obligations. (Louisa Catherine also opposed the Russian posting, deeply resenting that George and John had to be left behind with their grandparents at Quincy.) His presence lent stature to the American mission at St. Petersburg, where the British minister observed that "he sat among us like a bull-dog among spaniels." In 1815 he was ordered from St. Petersburg to Ghent, where he negotiated the treaty with Great Britain that ended the War of 1812, repeating his father's triumph thirty years earlier in the Treaty of Paris. Then, again like his father, he was dispatched to London as America's first postwar ambassador to the Court of St. James's. Then his star rose even higher in 1816, when President James Monroe tapped him to serve as secretary of state, which had become the acknowledged stepping-stone to the presidency.[64]

One would expect Abigail and John to be thrilled that their child prodigy was fulfilling his promise, and at some level they obviously were. But they also wanted him nearby during their own last chapter, as John forcefully apprised him in 1816: "One thing is clear in my mind, and that is you ought to be home . . . My sphere is reduced to my Garden and so must yours be. The wandering life that you have lived, as I have done before you is not compatible with human nature. It was not made for it." As if John Quincy had not gotten the point, John wrote him again two weeks later: "You must return to Montezillo, renounce all public employment forever, and lay down your bones here with your Ancestors. "[65]

This was not going to happen, as John surely realized, since John Quincy had been programmed for success on the public stage from early child-hood, and the same lust for fame that had propelled his father to answer every call also consumed the son. While John's request—almost an order—had a somewhat selfish sound, his primary motive was protective. He saw John Quincy following in his own footsteps, and he worried that his son would suffer the same bitter disappointment in the end.

On August 10, 1817, John declared that "Yes-terday was one of the most uniformly happy days of my whole life." He had just learned that John Quincy, Louisa Catherine, and their three boys had landed at New York and the whole entourage would be arriving at Quincy in about a week. The joyous homecoming on August 18 was the highlight of their retirement years, a festive occasion to which Abigail invited a host of local dignitaries. She put on one of her best dresses and insisted that her fa-mous son sit at the head of the table for dinner. The minister from Salem described her as the model of competence, seated on the sofa, sorting laundry while answering questions about Madison's con-duct of the recent war: "She had a distinct view of our public men and measures," he reported, "and had her own opinions."[66]

She also had her own property, or at least prop-erty that she regarded as her own. According to Massachusetts law, all family property was legally owned by the male head of household. But in January 1816 Abigail prepared a will, parceling out to her children, grandchildren, and niece, Louisa Smith, her silk gowns, jewelry, a lace shawl, beds, blankets, and $4,000, which was the nest egg that resulted from war bonds purchased during the 1770s. She also distributed to John Quincy and Thomas two parcels of land she had inherited from her family. Though a clear violation of the law, neither Abigail nor John regarded her will as an especially defiant act. It simply reflected the underlying assumption of Abigail's personal independence that had been the basis of their life together for over fifty years. John endorsed the terms of her will as a statement by the saucy woman he loved, but who never belonged to him or anyone else. No legal official in the commonwealth dared to challenge her claims in court.[67]

The will also reflected Abigail's looming sense that the end was near, that her nearly miraculous ability to recover from each bout with debilitating illness, almost to reclaim her life by sheer act of will, would eventually run its course. Blessedly, for the year following John Quincy's triumphant return she enjoyed excellent health, which permitted her to join John in carriage rides over the Quincy hills to visit friends and relatives. She even made two trips to Boston, where they were feted and fussed over as New England's most venerable couple and one of the last surviving links to a glorious but bygone era.

It was a kind of Indian summer for the now legendary partnership, a final fling celebrating their central satisfaction of being together. John's only complaint was that Abigail's overly assiduous devotion to her domestic duties sometimes prevented them from spending more time together. He lamented her "uncontrollable attachment to the superintendence of every part of her household," despite the obvious reality of "how few minutes either of us have to live." For almost a full year, however, they recovered the old rhythms, walking the gardens, riding the fields, reading aloud to each other at night—Abigail was particularly intrigued by a biography of an emerging American hero named Andrew Jackson—relishing together the seasoned quality of their ongoing conversation.[68]

It all came to a sudden end in October 1818. Abigail collapsed with typhoid and probably suffered an accompanying stroke that made it difficult for her to speak. Interestingly, John first reached out to Jefferson, who had lost his own wife many years earlier: "The dear partner of my life for fifty-four years and for many years more as a lover, now lies in extremis, forbidden to speak or be spoken to." Abigail was in great pain and at one point murmured to John that she knew she was dying, that it was just a matter of time. After leaving her bedside in tears, John was inconsolable: "I wish I could lie down beside her and die too . . . I cannot bear to see her in this state." Despite Abigail's chronic ailments, as almost ten years her senior, John had always expected to go first. With John at her bedside, Abigail died on October 28. She was seventy-four. The music they had made together for so long finally stopped.[69]

Of the many eulogies, Louisa Catherine's was the best: "She was the guiding planet around which all revolved, performing their separate duties only by the impulse of her magnetic power." John remained adrift and in mourning for nearly a year: "My House is a Region of Sorrow," he explained to one friend. "Inhabited by a sorrowful Widower . . . burdened with Multitudes of Letters from total strangers, teasing me with impertinent inquiries." He felt strangely alone, like a dancer without a partner: "The bitterness of death is past," he told John Quincy. "The grim spider so terrible to human nature has no sting left for me." The time that remained for him was just an earthly limbo while he waited to join her, either in heaven or under the ground, whatever providence decreed. He had no way of knowing that he had eight years left.[70]

1818–26

**"Have mercy on me Posterity,
if you should see any of my letters."**

JOHN DID NOT THINK of the years that remained as a final chapter so much as an epilogue. With his partner of fifty-four years gone, he waited for the summons to join her and resume their conversation in the hereafter. (If it turned out there was no such place, his bodily remains would at least rest beside hers in the cemetery of Quincy's First Congregational Church.) As he told Nabby's daughter, he was ready to go at a moment's notice, and growing increasingly impatient with "my distemper, Old Age, which I will not say with Franklin is incurable, because the ground will soon cure it."[1]

He missed the daily banter with Abigail: the routine exchanges about children and grandchildren, Jefferson's latest letter, John Quincy's achievements as secretary of state, the annual manure shortage, Thomas's embarrassing slide into alcoholism and permanent depression—the whole motley mix of large and small interests that, taken together, had filled their well-lived life together. He felt empty.

No one could replace Abigail, but the closest approximation became Louisa Catherine, another highly intelligent and well-read woman, not as saucy or self-confident as Abigail, though formidable despite her frailties. He had grown accustomed to being in constant contact with a woman's voice, so he initiated a correspondence with Louisa Catherine to fill the void.

"The world falls to pieces around me," he confessed to her in his most candid mode, "my friends and my enemies disappear." This was the kind of emotional honesty that he had formerly reserved for conversations with Abigail. Louisa Catherine responded with equivalent candor, sending John drafts of her poetry and her translations of Greek and Roman classics, requesting his advice about how to handle the delinquency of her eldest son, George, now at Harvard, and—this was risky—exposing her own discomfort with the social and political obligations of a wife whose husband wished to become the next president of the United States. John was all commiseration: "You will find in no department of public life any exemption from frequent twinges," he explained from deep experience. "You must retire to Montezillo . . . for perfect serenity."[2]

He confided to Louisa Catherine his frustration at never quite fitting into the Ciceronian mode of retirement. She responded by suggesting that he should not even try, since the role did not fit him: "You, my dear Sir, have ever possessed a nature too ardent . . . to sink into the cold and thankless state of stoicism." Abigail could not have put it better.[3]

From Louisa Catherine's perspective, John's heartfelt letters conveyed a level of unconditional acceptance that she had always wanted but never received from Abigail, whose matriarchal stature seemed so forebidding and whose efforts at intimacy often struck Louisa Catherine as thunderbolts hurled from atop Mount Abigail. If John needed to be in regular contact with a woman's voice and mind, Louisa Catherine needed endorsement from the family headquarters at Quincy. John gave it to her: "The old gentleman took a fancy to me," she recalled in her autobiography, "and was the only one [to whom] I was literally and without knowing it a fine lady."[4]

John had always worried about "dying at the top," but just the opposite aging process was happening to him: most of his teeth were now gone, and his "quiverations" made it impossible to hold a pen, so he had to dictate all letters to different grandchildren. He could ride a horse three miles but could not walk without a cane, and stairs had become insurmountable mountains. On the other hand, his mind remained hyperactive, at times almost child-like in its reckless release of innocent energy and endless curiosity.

An ice storm in the early spring of 1820, for example, caused him to conjure up the frozen rain on the trees as nature's equivalent of a diamond necklace that was "more striking than all the dia-monds worn by the Queen of France." He was con-vinced that "all the glitter of her jewels did not make an impression upon me equal to that pre-sented by every shrub." Or when rereading Cicero's **De Senectute**, the classical handbook for retired statesmen, his mind took flight while contemplat-ing the punctuation: "I have never delighted much in contemplating commas or colons," he observed, "or in spelling or measuring syllables, but now, while reading Cato, if I look at these little objects, I find my imagination . . . roaming in the Milky Way." As his body shriveled, his mind soared.[5]

In 1820 he was named a special delegate to the Massachusetts Constitutional Convention, which had assembled to revise the document he had single-handedly drafted more than forty years earlier. He claimed to feel like a witness to his own second com-ing: "I feel not much like a maker or mender of con-stitutions in my present state of imbecility," he told

Louisa Catherine, "but I presume that we will not be obliged to carry windmills by assault."[6]

He rose to speak on two occasions, first to argue for the retention of the property qualification to vote, then to urge the removal of any religious requirement. He was outvoted on both occasions, prompting him to observe that he was simultaneously too far behind and too far ahead of popular opinion to win an election: "I boggled and blundered more than a young fellow just rising to speak at the bar," he apprised Jefferson. "I believe the Printers have made better speeches than I made for myself," meaning that his own toothless mumblings had been rendered more cogent by newspaper editors than they deserved, perhaps the only occasion in his political career, he claimed, when the press seemed disposed to protect him from himself.[7]

It was not clear whether he ever conquered his demons or simply outlived them. Clinching evidence that all had either been forgiven or forgotten with Jefferson came in 1823. One of his old letters to a friend, castigating Jefferson for his multiple duplicities, had found its way into print, threatening the recovered friendship with an explosive blast from the past. Jefferson's response was Monticellian gallantry in its most lyrical form: "Be assured, my dear Sir," he wrote John, "that I am incapable of receiving the sightest impression from the effort now made to plant thorns on the pillow of age, worth, and wisdom, and to sow tares between friends who have been such for nearly half a century. Beseeching you then not to suffer your mind to be disquieted by this wicked attempt to poison its peace, and praying you to throw it by."[8]

John was overjoyed, only wishing that Abigail were there to read the letter alongside him. Instead, he insisted that it be read aloud to the entire extended family at the breakfast table, calling it "the best letter that ever was written . . . just such a letter as I expected, only it was infinitely better expressed." He promised Jefferson that he would join him in all-out war against "the peevish and fretful effusions of politicians," then signed off as "J.A. In the 89 year of his age, still too fat to last much longer."[9]

Both men were also able to share the sense that they had become living statues. Jefferson, for example, entrusted his last letter to his grandson, Thomas Jefferson Randolph, who was traveling to Boston and planned a visit with the Sage of Quincy: "Like other young people," Jefferson explained, "he wishes to be able, in the winter nights of old age, to recount to those around him what he has learnt of the Heroic age preceding his birth, and which of the Argonauts particularly he was in time to have seen." Most Americans coming of age in the 1820s regarded the American Revolution as a sacred moment in the distant past, when a gallery of greats had been privileged to see God face-to-face. It was disconcerting to realize that two of the most prominent heroes of that bygone era were still alive.[10]

In 1825 the American sculptor John Henri Isaac Browere visited both sages with a proposal to produce "life masks" designed to yield realistic likenesses of their faces and heads, so that subsequent generations could see an accurate rendering of the American icons. The process required pouring several coats of a hot, plasterlike liquid over the head, allowing it to harden, then breaking it off in chunks. "He did not tear my face to pieces," John explained, "though I sometimes thought that he would beat my brains out with a hammer."[11]

The bronze casting that resulted made John look like a metallic cadaver clad in a Roman toga, what he himself described as the "life mask" for a corpse. The most accurate and inspired rendering of the elder statesman proved to be the last portrait by Gilbert Stuart, painted in 1823, which managed to capture the wrinkled and rumpled body encasing an ever-glowing spirit. As John's neighbor Josiah Quincy put it, Stuart caught the old man "at one of those happy moments when the intelligence lights up the wasted envelope." John himself sounded the same note: "I enjoy life and have as good spirit as I ever had," he wrote to Charles Carroll, "but my fabric has become very weak, almost worn out." His body was ready to join Abigail's in the ground, but his mind kept up a running mockery of his wrinkled frailties with regular flashes of vivacity.[12]

One such flash occurred when he received a visit from Mrs. Ebenezer Storer, a widow who in her earlier incarnation as Hannah Quincy had been John's old flame in the pre-Abigail days. John startled her and the other visitors by declaring, "What! Madam, shall we not go walk in Cupid's Grove together?" (Cupid's Grove was the lover's lane where John and Hannah had strolled over sixty years before.) Initially taken aback, Mrs. Storer quickly recovered her old coquettish form: "Ah, sir, it would not be the first time we have walked there." Josiah Quincy, who witnessed the exchange, observed that "the flash of old sentiment was startling for its utter unexpectedness . . . It is a surprise to find a great personage so simple, so perfectly natural, so thoroughly human."[13]

Quincy also provided what is perhaps the best description of the elder statesman's personality in full flight near the end. In June 1823, despite a bad gash on his ankle, John walked over a mile to Quincy's house in order to share company and conversation. He held forth for more than two hours, recalling his negotiation with the ambassador from Tripoli, when he blew smoke rings in a competition to reduce the size of the required ransom of American prisoners, and then proceeded to demonstrate his proficiency by duplicating the feat for Quincy's guests. He speculated, incorrectly as it turned out, that John Jay had actually written Washington's Farewell Address. (It was Hamilton, still the last person that John could stoop to honor.) He also surmised that John Dickinson's opposition to American independence in the Continental Congress was due to the influence of his wife and mother, both devout Quakers and resolute pacifists. "If I had such a mother and such a wife," John concluded, "I believe I should have shot myself."

His last story was about Judge Edmund Quincy, Josiah's grandfather, who had once beaten off a robber with his cane. John lifted up his own cane to demonstrate how the old judge had defended himself, but accidentally struck and demolished a picture hanging on the wall behind him. John began to laugh uncontrollably at his blunder, announcing that he had not had such a good time in months: "If I was to come here once a day," he declared, "I should live half a year longer." One of the guests responded that John might consider coming "twice in a day, and live a year longer." John found that to be a splendid suggestion and, to the applause of the crowd, vowed to return that evening.[14]

There are several other evocative scenes of the sage in his twilight phase: the day the entire Corps of Cadets from West Point assembled on the Old House lawn, where John delivered a speech to them on Washington's commitment to civilian control of the military; or the afternoon that Lafayette and his huge entourage visited Quincy as a mandatory stop on his American tour, and both patriarchs left the interview muttering that age had so changed the other that they found themselves unrecognizable. But the most poignant and historically suggestive scene occurred without witnesses in the privacy of John's library.

It was prompted by John Quincy's out-of-the-blue announcement that he intended to write a biography of his father. "Tell Mr. A," John wrote to Louisa Catherine, "that I am assiduously and sedulously employed in Exertions to save him trouble, by collecting all my Papers. What a Mass!" He had dipped into the unedited Adams archives while writing his autobiography and the **Boston Patriot** series, but he had never before taken the full measure of the historical record that he and Abigail had generated and preserved, which was so vast that the modern editors of the **Adams Papers**, after sixty years of scholarly effort, still have no end in sight.[15]

"I am deeply immersed in researches," he wrote John Quincy, "after old Papers. Trunks, Boxes, Desks, Drawers locked up for thirty years have been broken open because the Keys are lost. Nothing stands in my Way." In one of his last letters to Rush after renewing their candid correspondence, he had shouted out his fear: "Have mercy on me Posterity, if you should ever see any of my letters." Now, however, sitting in his library amid the enormous cache of family history, he began to realize that he and Abigail had created the most comprehensive and intimate portrait of a prominent family living through America's founding.[16]

The abiding candor of the correspondence still left him uneasy, as he explained to John Quincy: "Every scrap shall be found and preserved for your Affliction [or] for your good," he warned. "I shall leave you with an inheritance sufficiently tormenting [to] make you Alternately laugh and cry, fret and fume, stamp and scold, as they do me." He knew, deep down, that his letters would render him ineligible as an American hero who fit the mythical mold that all new nations required. But he began to glimpse, for the first time, that the full exposure of his edges and imperfections might eventually, over the long stretch of time, endear him to posterity as the most fully revealed member of the revolutionary generation. These letters, spread all around him, were his ticket into the American pantheon as the original postmythical hero. And he was the only one who would be admitted with his wife alongside him. It turned out to take more than a century and a half for history to rediscover him.[17]

He could no longer write letters to Abigail, but he almost certainly conferred with her spirit on a daily basis. And as the presidential election of 1824 approached, he surely shared his concern about the looming fate of their eldest son, who was generally regarded as one of the leading candidates—along with Henry Clay, William Crawford, and Andrew Jackson—for the highest office in the land. "What a rattling & crackling and clattering there is about the future presidency," John observed to a friend. "It seems like a Conclave of Cardinals intriguing for the Election of the Pope."[18]

The more explicit style of political campaigning offended John's personal sensibilities, which had been formed in an earlier era when any overt expression of political ambition was regarded as inadmissible. Even more paternally, he worried about the fate of John Quincy, and his worries were maddeningly double-barreled: first that he would lose, and then that he would win.

At first blush the second worry seems strange. After all, it is not often that a father grooms his son from birth for public office at the highest level of achievement, monitors every phase of his upbringing and education to focus on that goal, lives long enough to witness his son's imminent arrival at the providential destination, then hopes it does not happen. But, in fact, John had been sending precisely that signal to John Quincy for more than a decade: "Political claims cannot be of long duration in this Country," he worried in a typical plea. "My advice . . . is to be always prepared and ready to retire at a moment's warning." Multiple letters to Louisa Catherine carried the same message, which only intensified as the election approached.[19]

Although he never said so explicitly, it seems clear that John feared that his son would repeat his own painful pattern. So much of John Quincy's political and diplomatic career had already followed an arc that seemed eerily reminiscent of his father's course. (Only a member of the Adams family, it appeared, could negotiate the end of a war with Great Britain.) John worried that the pattern would continue with the presidency, which would end like his, after one term, in frustration and disappointment. And, in fact, it did.

The pattern was so predictable because John Quincy had been educated in the Adams political tradition, which harbored only hatred for all forms of partisan politics and skepticism toward the shifting winds of popular opinion. Almost by definition, an Adams felt most comfortable defying the illusion that there was such a harmonious thing as "the people," which knew where history was headed. An Adams, again by definition, distrusted the wild political swings of democracy and relished alienation from its superficial certainties. It was the trademark conviction of the Adams family, given its classic formulation in **The Education of Henry Adams** by John Quincy's grandson. John put it most concisely in what was to be his last letter to Jefferson: "Our American Chivalry is the worst in the World. It has no laws, no bounds, no definitions, it seems to be all a caprice." Any political leader who embraced such a conviction, it turned out, was running against the grain of the emerging American democracy, which was the major reason why John Quincy, like his father, would be a one-term president.[20]

By the summer of 1826 John's physical condition had declined beyond the point where another surge of his indomitable spirit could rescue it. He had already apprised Jefferson that the end was near: "The little strength of mind . . . that I once possessed appears to be all gone," he acknowledged, "but while I breathe I shall be your friend. We shall meet again, so wishes and so believes your friend, but if we are disappointed we shall never know it." He was still hedging his bets on the hereafter, and had come to regard heaven as a putative place where Abigail was waiting. The Christian doctrine of the Beatific Vision struck him as insipid and boring. Gazing upon God was less interesting than embracing Abigail and resuming his arguments with Franklin and Jefferson. That for him was the true paradise.[21]

He knew that his powers of thought and speech

were permanently diminished, so when a delegation from Quincy visited him on June 30, requesting some statement from the patriarch for the looming Independence Day celebration, he refused to cooperate: "I will give you 'Independence forever,'" he declared. Asked if he might like to elaborate, he declined: "Not a word." He had finally learned, at the very end, the gift of silence. Abigail would have approved. Physicians and other visitors came away from his bedside convinced that the end was near.[22]

On the morning of July 4 John lay in his bed, breathing with difficulty, apparently unable to speak. But when apprised that it was the Fourth, and the fiftieth anniversary of Independence Day, he lifted his head and, with obvious effort, declared: "It is a great day. It is a **good** day."[23]

Late in the afternoon he stirred in response to a severe thunderstorm—subsequently described in eulogies as "the artillery of Heaven"—and was heard to whisper, "Thomas Jefferson survives," by several bedside observers. But by a coincidence that defied the probabilities of history and even the parameters of fiction, Jefferson had died earlier that afternoon. Both patriarchs, each possessed of indomitable willpower, seemed determined to die on schedule.[24]

John drew his last breath shortly after six o'clock. Witnesses reported that a final clap of thunder sounded at his passing, and then a bright sun broke through the clouds. An estimated four thousand people attended the funeral at the First Congregational Church three days later as his body was laid to rest alongside Abigail's. They have remained together ever since.

ACKNOWLEDGMENTS

As every author can attest, a book that has only one name on the cover is really a child with multiple parents, or at least several midwives who have nurtured it into the world. In my case, four readers provided wisdom, a critical eye for both style and substance, and savvy about how to tell the story.

Edmund S. Morgan, my long-ago mentor at Yale, and beyond much doubt the most distinguished historian of early American history over the last half century, heartily endorsed the project, caught many gaffes, and urged me to have the courage of my convictions.

Robert Dalzell, who continues to stalk the classrooms of Williams College dispensing wit and wisdom, provided suggestions about the role of family dynasties in American history and pushed me on what makes for a happy marriage.

Stephen Smith, currently editor of the **Washington Examiner,** is a journalist who takes American history seriously. He is also a peerless critic, capable of showing you why this word is better than that, or persuading you that what you want to say is not quite what you have said.

C. James Taylor, editor of the **Adams Papers,** not only read and commented on a late draft, but also made available the unpublished letters between Abigail and John assembled by his staff for subsequent volumes of the **Adams Family Correspondence.**

This is my fifth book with Ash Green, who is officially retired from Knopf but remains my editor and friend until one of us goes to the hereafter. If Abigail and John had unconditional love, Ash and I have unconditional trust. Andrew Miller, his successor at Knopf, ushered the completed manuscript through the several stages of editorial wizardry that transformed it into a book.

My agent, Ike Williams, negotiated the contract with a minimum of fuss, then called periodically to see how things were going. Our conversations invariably became passionate digressions into the prospects of the Red Sox, Patriots, and Celtics.

Although I had no research assistants—I have this stubborn conviction that reading the sources with my own eyes is the only way—Linda Fernandes was my assistant in all the other ways, including technological, clerical, and therapeutic. I wrote the drafts in longhand on the blank back sides of junk mail, sometimes late at night, when the slant of my scrawl defied translation. Linda put it all into printed form on a disk, periodically offering suggestions that I could not afford to ignore.

Twenty students at Mount Holyoke took a research seminar with me on Abigail and John in the spring of 2008. Our conversations and their papers influenced my thinking about Abigail as a proto-feminist, the perils of parenting, and, most important, what to leave out. Undergraduates are supposed to be incapable of irony, but that was the interpretive edge they insisted upon.

As I took notes and wrote words in my study, I was accompanied by an aging golden retriever, a young Labradoodle, a feisty Jack Russell terrier, and a defiant cat. They offered no advice that I could understand, but their sheer presence created serenity.

My wife, Ellen Wilkins Ellis, as the dedication suggests, merely provided the ballast. I have a hunch that this was essential.

Joseph J. Ellis
Amherst, Massachusetts

NOTES

The notes below represent my attempt to provide documentation for all quotations in the text, the vast majority of which come from the published and yet unpublished correspondence between Abigail and John. When the story I try to tell crosses over contested historical terrain that has spawned a formidable scholarly literature, I have tried to cite books and articles that strike me as sensible and seminal. But my accounting on this score is far from exhaustive, in part because such a standard would burden the book with notes that outweighed the text itself, in part because I think the conversation between Abigail and John should take precedence over the conversation among several generations of historians.

That said, previous biographers of John and Abigail have blazed the trail in ways that have influenced my reading of the primary sources and, therefore, deserve mention at the start. For John there are three distinguished predecessors: Page Smith, **John Adams,** 2 vols. (New York, 1962); John Ferling, **John Adams: A Life** (Knoxville, 1995); and David McCullough, **John Adams** (New York, 2001). For Abigail there are also three biographical pioneers: Lynn Withey, **Dearest Friend: A Life of Abigail Adams** (New York, 1981); Phyllis Lee Levin, **Abigail Adams: A Biography** (New York, 1987); and Edith Gelles, **Portia: The World of Abigail Adams** (Bloomington, 1992). A new biography by Woody Holton, **Abigail Adams** (New York, 2009), appeared just in time to influence my final draft.

Because the relationship between Abigail and John was so seamless, any biographer of one almost automatically ends up writing about both. And all the biographers mentioned above do just that. But there is a difference between a biographer who leans in the direction of the partner and a historian of the partnership itself. I aspire for the latter.

P.S.—While this book was being copyedited, a study appeared of the Adams partnership, entitled

Abigail & John: Portrait of a Marriage (New York, 2009), by Edith B. Gelles. Gelles is a distinguished student of Abigail and a friend. I look forward to comparing her version of the story with mine.

ABBREVIATIONS

TITLES

AFC   Lyman H. Butterfield et al., eds., **Adams Family Correspondence,** 9 vols. to date (Cambridge, Mass., 1963–).

AJ   Lester G. Cappon, ed., **The Adams–Jefferson Letters,** 2 vols. (Chapel Hill, 1959).

AP   **The Microfilm Edition of the Adams Papers,** 608 reels (Boston, 1954–59).

DA   Lyman H. Butterfield et al., eds., **The Diary and Autobiography of John Adams,** 4 vols. (Cambridge, Mass., 1961).

EDJA   Lyman H. Butterfield, ed., **The Earliest Diary of John Adams** (Cambridge, Mass., 1966).

HP   Harold Syrett, ed., **The Papers of Alexander Hamilton,** 26 vols. (New York, 1974–92).

JCC   Worthington C. Ford, ed., **The Journals of the Continental Congress, 1774–1789,** 34 vols. (Washington, D.C., 1904–37).

JM   James Morton Smith, ed., **The Republic of Letters: The Correspondence Between Thomas Jefferson and James Madison, 1776–1826,** 3 vols. (New York, 1995).

JP   Julian Boyd et al., eds., **The Papers of Thomas Jefferson,** 28 vols. to date (Princeton, 1950–).

NEQ   **New England Quarterly**

PA   Robert J. Taylor et al., eds., **The Papers of John Adams,** 11 vols. to date (Cambridge, Mass., 1983–).

UFC   Unpublished correspondence of the Adams family transcribed by the editors of the **Adams Papers.**

WMQ   **William and Mary Quarterly,** 3rd series.

Works   Charles Francis Adams, ed., **The Works of John Adams,** 10 vols. (Boston, 1850–60).

PERSONS

AA   Abigail Adams

AA(2)   Abigail Adams Smith

AS   Abigail Smith (before marriage to John)

CA   Charles Adams

CFA   Charles Francis Adams

JA   John Adams

JQA   John Quincy Adams

LCA   Louisa Catherine Adams

TBA   Thomas Boylston Adams

TJ   Thomas Jefferson
WSS William Stephens Smith

CHAPTER ONE. 1759–74

1. **DA** 1:108.
2. **DA** 1:109, for the derogatory quotation about the Smith sisters.
3. JA to AS, 4 October 1762, **AFC** 1:2.
4. JA to AS, 14 February 1763, **AFC** 1:3.
5. AS to JA, 11 August 1763, **AFC** 1:6.
6. JA to AS, 30 December 1761, **AFC** 1:1; AS to JA, 12 September 1763, **AFC** 1:8.
7. AS to JA, 19 April 1764, **AFC** 1:44–46; JA to AS, 9 May 1764, **AFC** 1:46–47.
8. AS to JA, 4 October 1764, **AFC** 1:50–51.
9. **DA** 3:256–61, for John's autobiographical account of his family history and childhood.
10. All of John's biographers cover these early years, but see David McCullough, **John Adams** (New York, 2001), 37–53, for the most recent and comprehensive account.
11. **DA** 3:272–76, for the start of his legal career and the decision to delay marriage.
12. Phyllis Lee Levin, **Abigail Adams: A Biography** (New York, 1987), 3–9.
13. **DA** 1:21.
14. **DA** 1:26–27, 57.
15. **DA** 1:63, 95.

16. **DA** 1:6–8.
17. **DA** 1:13–14.
18. **DA** 1:25.
19. **DA** 1:33.
20. **EDJA,** 73; John Ferling and Lewis E. Braverman, "John Adams's Health Reconsidered," **WMQ** 55 (January 1998), 82–104.
21. Edith B. Gelles, "The Abigail Industry," **WMQ** 45 (October 1988), 656–83, for a cogent assessment of the scholarly literature on Abigail's primary identity as a traditional wife and mother.
22. For Abigail's upbringing, I find Lynn Withey, **Dearest Friend: A Life of Abigail Adams** (New York, 1981), 1–10, most sensible. The "wild colts" quotation is from a letter to John Quincy in 1804, when Abigail recalled her grandmother's advice.
23. JA to AA, 20 April 1763, **AFC** 1:4–5, for John's clearest acknowledgment that Abigail possessed a personal serenity that he envied and would never be able to match.
24. Editorial note on the smallpox epidemic in Boston, **AFC** 1:14; JA to AS, 11 April 1764, **AFC** 1:22.
25. AS to JA, 12 April 1764, **AFC** 1:25–27.
26. AS to JA, 8 April 1764, **AFC** 1:19.
27. The best and most recent synthesis of the scholarship on the constitutional crises is Gor-

don S. Wood, **The American Revolution: A History** (New York, 2002), 3–62.

28. AA to JA, 14 September 1767, **AFC** 1:62; JA to AA, 23 May 1772, **AFC** 1:83; JA to AA, 29 June 1774, **AFC** 1:111.

29. **PA** 1:46–48, for the moralistic essays; **DA** 1:172–73, for John's diary account of tavern life.

30. **PA** 1:58–94.

31. **DA** 3:284, for the composition of **Dissertation.**

32. **PA** 1:103–28.

33. **PA** 1:132–35, 152.

34. **DA** 1:263.

35. JA to AA, 6 July 1774, **AFC** 1:128–29; AA to Mary Smith Cranch, 31 January 1767, **AFC** 1:60–61.

36. **DA** 3:294–95.

37. AA to Isaac Smith Jr., 20 April 1771, **AFC** 1:76–77.

38. **DA** 3:276.

39. **PA** 1:155–73.

40. **PA** 1:174–211.

41. **PA** 1:252–309.

42. **DA** 1:324, JA to William Tudor, 15 May 1817, **AP,** reel 123. For a more sympathetic portrait of Hutchinson, see Bernard Bailyn, **The Ordeal of Thomas Hutchinson** (Cambridge, Mass., 1974).

43. **DA** 3:287–88; JA to AA, 9 July 1774, **AFC** 1:135.
44. JA to AA, 1 July 1774, **AFC** 1:119.
45. **DA** 3:291–94; the authoritative study is Hiller B. Zobel, **The Boston Massacre** (New York, 1970); on the role of Sam Adams behind the scenes, see Mark Puls, **Samuel Adams: Father of the American Revolution** (New York, 2006), 99–111.
46. JA to AA, 7 July 1774, **AFC** 1:131; **DA** 3:292.
47. JA to Isaac Smith Jr., [1771?], **AFC** 1:82.
48. JA to AA, 12 May 1774, **AFC** 1:107.
49. JA to AA, 6 July 1774, **AFC** 1:126–27, for John's sense that there was no turning back.
50. JA to AA, 2 July 1774, **AFC** 1:121; also JA to AA, 12 May 1774, **AFC** 1:107.
51. Editorial note, **AFC** 1:136–37.
52. JA to AA, 23 June 1774, **AFC** 1:108–9.
53. Editorial note, **AFC** 1:140.

CHAPTER TWO. 1774–78

1. AA to JA, 22 October 1775, **AFC** 1:310; JA to AA, 23 October 1775, **AFC** 1:311–12.
2. AA to JA, 29 August 1776, **AFC** 2:112–13.
3. JA to AA, 28 April 1776, **AFC** 1:400; JA to AA, 22 May 1776, **AFC** 1:412.
4. JA to William Tudor, 7 October 1774, **PA** 2:188.

5. AA to JA, 16 July 1775, **AFC** 1:247, 250.
6. JA to AA, 2 June 1776, **AFC** 2:3.
7. JA to James Warren, 25 June 1775, **PA** 2:99. See also, in the same vein, **DA** 2:134–35.
8. **DA** 2:150.
9. **DA** 2:121, 173, 182; JA to AA, 25 September 1774, **AFC** 1:163. See also JA to AA, 9 October 1774, **AFC** 1:166.
10. JA to William Tudor, 29 September 1774, **PA** 2:177.
11. On Macauley's view of English history, see Lucy M. Donnelly, "The Celebrated Mrs. Macauley," **WMQ** 6 (April 1949), 173–207.
12. On Mercy Otis Warren, see Katherine Anthony, **First Lady of the Revolution: The Life of Mercy Otis Warren** (New York, 1958).
13. AA to Catharine Sanbridge Macauley, [1774], **AFC** 1:177–79; AA to Mercy Otis Warren, 2 May 1775, **AFC** 1:190–91. See also AA to Mercy Otis Warren, 14 August 1777, **AFC** 2:313–14.
14. JA to AA, 17 June 1775, **AFC** 1:216.
15. See the editorial note on John's role in the First Continental Congress, **PA** 2:144–52. For his own somewhat melodramatic version of his role, see **DA** 2:124–54. His contribution to the Declaration of Rights and Grievances is recorded in **JCC** 1:54–55.

16. See the editorial note on **Novanglus, PA** 2:216–26. For the thirteen essays, see **PA** 2:226–387.

17. JA to AA, 2 May 1775, **AFC** 1:192; JA to AA, 8 May 1775, **AFC** 1:195–96.

18. AA to JA, 18 June 1775, **AFC** 1:22–24.

19. See the editorial note on John Quincy's latter-day recollections in 1843, **AFC** 1:224; JA to AA, 7 July 1775, **AFC** 1:242; AA to JQA, 13 March 1802, **UFC**.

20. AA to JA, 8 September 1775, **AFC** 1:276–78; AA to JA, 16 September 1775, **AFC** 1:278–79. See also Elizabeth A. Fenn, **Pox Americana: The Great Smallpox Epidemic of 1775–82** (New York, 2001).

21. AA to JA, 3 June 1776, **AFC** 2:4; AA to Mercy Otis Warren, January 1776, **AFC** 1:422.

22. JA to AA, 26 September 1775, **AFC** 1:285–86; JA to AA, 19 October 1775, **AFC** 1:302.

23. JA to AA, 7 October 1775, **AFC** 1:295.

24. AA to JA, 12 November 1775, **AFC** 1:324.

25. Paul C. Nagel, **Descent from Glory: Four Generations of the John Adams Family** (New York, 1983), is the best survey of the subject, though I find his treatment of Abigail unduly harsh. See also David F. Musto, "The Youth of John Quincy Adams," American Philosophical Society **Proceedings** 113 (1969), 269–82.

26. JQA to JA, 13 October 1774, **AFC** 1:167; AA to JA, 5 November 1775, **AFC** 1:322.
27. AA to JA, April 1777, **AFC** 2:229.
28. JA to TBA, 6 May 1774, **AFC** 1:234; AA to JA, 7 May 1776, **AFC** 1:403.
29. JA to AA, 22 May 1776, **AFC** 1:412–13.
30. JA to AA, 8 July 1777, **AFC** 2:277.
31. **DA** 3:355; the fellow delegate was none other than Thomas Jefferson, quoted in my **American Sphinx: The Character of Thomas Jefferson** (New York, 1997), 242.
32. JA to Moses Gill, 10 June 1775, **PA** 3:21.
33. JA to AA, 1 October 1775, **AFC** 1:290.
34. JA to AA, 17 June 1775, **AFC** 1:215; AA to JA, 16 July 1775, **AFC** 1:246.
35. JA to AA, 15 April 1776, **AFC** 1:383.
36. JA to John Trumbull, 13 February 1776, **PA** 4:22; for the arrival of news about the Prohibitory Act, see Jack N. Rakove, **The Beginnings of National Politics: An Interpretive History of the Continental Congress** (New York, 1979), 91–92.
37. AA to JA, 27 November 1775, **AFC** 1:329–30.
38. **PA** 4:65–73, for the text and an editorial note on John's later comments on **Thoughts**. I have discussed the significance of **Thoughts** at greater length in **American Creation: Triumphs and Tragedies at the Founding of the Republic** (New York, 2007), 46–49.

39. AA to JA, 31 March 1776, **AFC** 1:370.

40. JA to AA, 14 April 1776, **AFC** 1:382.

41. AA to Mercy Otis Warren, 27 April 1776, **AFC** 1:396–98; AA to JA, 7 May 1776, **AFC** 1:402.

42. AA to JA, 14 August 1776, **AFC** 2:94; JA to AA, 25 August 1776, **AFC** 2:108.

43. JA to James Sullivan, 26 May 1776, **PA** 4:208–12.

44. For the style and message of **Common Sense,** see Eric Foner, **Tom Paine and Revolutionary America** (New York, 1776). For Paine as the ultimate advocate for implementing the radical implications of the revolutionary agenda, see Harvey J. Kay, **Thomas Paine and the Promise of America** (New York, 2005).

45. **AP** 4:185; JA to James Warren, 15 May 1776, **AP** 4:186.

46. JA to AA, 17 May 1776, **AFC** 1:410.

47. AA to JA, 2 March 1776, **AFC** 1:352–56; AA to JA, 16 March 1776, **AFC** 1:358.

48. JA to AA, 3 July 1776, **AFC** 2:27–31. He wrote Abigail two separate letters on this day.

49. For a longer exegesis of this point, as well as the primary sources on which it was based, see my **Passionate Sage: The Character and Legacy of John Adams** (New York, 1991), 64.

50. JA to AA, 3 July 1776, **AFC** 2:30.

51. For the best synthesis of this crowded moment, see Pauline Maier, **American Scripture: Mak-**

ing the Declaration of Independence (New York, 1997), 97–153.

52. JA to Benjamin Rush, 21 June 1811, quoted in Ellis, **Passionate Sage**, 64.

53. For John's appointment as chair of the Committee on War and Ordnance and the difficult logistical and strategic problems he faced, see JA to AA, 26 June 1776, **AFC** 2:23–24.

54. AA to JA, 20 September 1776, **AFC** 2:129.

55. JA to AA, 16 July 1776, **AFC** 2:50–51.

56. AA to JA, 29 July 1776, **AFC** 2:65–67; AA to JA, 14 August 1776, **AFC** 2:93; AA to JA, 17 August 1776, **AFC** 2:98.

57. AA to JA, 19 August 1776, **AFC** 2:101; JA to AA, 27 July 1776, **AFC** 2:63.

58. JA to AA, 28 August 1776, **AFC** 2:111.

59. AA to JA, 1 August 1776, **AFC** 2:72–73; AA to JA, 25 August 1776, **AFC** 2:106.

60. JA to AA, 30 August 1776, **AFC** 2:114–15; JA to AA, 8 October 1776, **AFC** 2:140.

61. AA to JA, 2 September 1776, **AFC** 2:116; AA to JA, 29 September 1776, **AFC** 2:134–36.

62. **JCC** 5:723–35, for the conference with Howe. See also the editorial note in **AFC** 2:124–25.

63. John's latter-day recollection of the episode with Franklin is in **DA** 3:414–30.

64. **PA** 4:260–302, for the Plan of Treaties.

65. Ira D. Gruber, **The Howe Brothers and the American Revolution** (New York, 1972),

127–57, and Kevin Phillips, **The Cousins'**
Wars: Religion, Politics, and the Triumph of
Anglo-America (New York, 1999), 291–99,
provide different but compatible interpreta-
tions of Howe's fateful decision.

66. JA to AA, 7 October 1776, **AFC** 2:139; JA to
AA, 11 October 1776, **AFC** 2:141.

67. JA to AA, 10 February 1777, **AFC** 2:159; JA
to AA, 3 February 1777, **AFC** 2:152–53.

68. AA to Mercy Otis Warren, [January?] 1777,
AFC 2:150–51; all previous accounts are
superceded by David Hackett Fischer's **Wash-**
ington's Crossing (New York, 2004).

69. AA to JA, 8 February 1777, **AFC** 2:157; JA to
AA, 3 April 1777, **AFC** 2:199–200.

70. AA to JA, March 1777, **AFC** 2:173.

71. JA to AA, 22 May 1777, **AFC** 2:245; JA to
AA, 21 February 1777, **AFC** 2:166.

72. JA to JQA, 16 March 1777, **AFC** 2:177–78;
JA to TBA, 16 March 1777, **AFC** 2:178; JA to
AA, 17 March 1777, **AFC** 2:178–79; JA to
CA, 17 March 1777, **AFC** 2:179–80.

73. JA to AA, 13 April 1777, **AFC** 2:209.

74. JA to AA, 16 March 1777, **AFC** 2:175–77.

75. JA to AA, 15 May 1777, **AFC** 2:238–39.

76. AA to JA, 1 June 1777, **AFC** 2:250–51.

77. AA to JA, 30 July 1777, **AFC** 2:295.

78. JA to AA, 6 April 1777, **AFC** 2:201; JA to AA,
10 July 1777, **AFC** 2:278.

79. AA to JA, 9 July 1777, **AFC** 2:278.
80. JA to AA, 18 July 1777, **AFC** 2:284–85; JA to AA, 30 July 1777, **AFC** 2:296–97.
81. AA to JA, 10–11 July 1777, **AFC** 2:278–80; AA to JA, 16 July 1777, **AFC** 2:282–83; AA to JA, 23 July 1777, **AFC** 2:287.
82. JA to AA, 28 July 1777, **AFC** 2:292.
83. AA to JA, 5 August 1777, **AFC** 2:301; JA to AA, 25 October 1777, **AFC** 2:360.
84. JA to AA, 30 September 1777, **AFC** 2:349–50.
85. JA to AA, 14 November 1777, **AFC** 2:366.

CHAPTER THREE. 1778–84

1. Mercy Otis Warren to AA, 8 January 1778, **AFC** 2:379.
2. AA to James Lovell, 15 December 1777, **AFC** 2:370–77.
3. AA to John Thaxter, 15 February 1778, **AFC** 2:390; see also the editorial note on the question of Abigail's thinking prior to John's departure.
4. **DA** 4:6–35, for John's diary account of the voyage.
5. AA to Hannah Quincy Lincoln Storer, 7 March 1778, **AFC** 2:397–98; AA to JA, 8 March 1778, **AFC** 2:402; AA to JA, 18 May 1778, **AFC** 2:22–24; AA to JA, 18 June 1778, **AFC** 3:46–47.

6. AA to JA, 30 June 1778, **AFC** 3:51–53.

7. This is a very rough guess. More letters were lost during the early stage of their separation than during the latter.

8. JA to AA, 2 December 1778, **AFC** 3:124–26; AA to JA, 30 June 1778, **AFC** 3:51–53; AA to JA, 12–23 November, **AFC** 3:118–20.

9. AA to JA, 15 July 1778, **AFC** 3:59–62; AA to John Thaxter, 19 August 1778, **AFC** 3:76–77; AA to JA, 29 September 1778, **AFC** 3:94–96; AA to JA, 21 October 1778, **AFC** 3:108–9; AA to JA, 27 December 1778, **AFC** 3:139–40.

10. AA to JA, 25 October 1778, **AFC** 3:110–11; AA to JA, 2 January 1779, **AFC** 3:146–47.

11. **DA** 1:288, for a sketch of Lovell. There is some evidence that Lovell's quarters in Philadelphia were located in a brothel.

12. On the correspondence between Abigail and Lovell, see the editorial note in **AFC** 3:xxxiv; James Lovell to AA, 13 June 1778, **AFC** 3:43–44.

13. AA to James Lovell, February–March 1779, **AFC** 3:184–86.

14. **DA** 4:36, for the Adam and Eve story.

15. **DA** 4:47.

16. JA to AA, 25 April 1778, **AFC** 3:17.

17. **DA** 4:69–71; for John's assessment of Arthur Lee and Silas Deane, **DA** 4:86–87; see the correspondence John generated while performing

all the mundane diplomatic duties in **DA** 4:36–172.

18. JA to AA, 9 February 1779, **DA** 2:347.

19. See Walter Isaacson, **Benjamin Franklin: An American Life** (New York, 2003), 333–36, for the most recent account of the spy nest in Franklin's household. His documentation of Bancroft's inspired duplicity (ibid., 550–51) includes an unpublished case study done by the CIA.

20. JA to AA, 27 November 1778, **AFC** 3:122–23, where John recounts his recommendation to the Continental Congress; for the debate in the congress, see **JCC** 12:908.

21. JA to AA, 21 February 1779, **AFC** 3:176–78; the "wedged in the Waiste" quotation is from **AFC** 3:229.

22. Three recent biographies of Franklin have informed my interpretation: Isaacson, **Benjamin Franklin**; Edmund S. Morgan, **Benjamin Franklin** (New Haven, 2002); and Gordon S. Wood, **The Americanization of Benjamin Franklin** (New York, 2004).

23. **DA** 4:69, 77, 118.

24. AA to JQA, 10 June 1778, **DA** 4:37.

25. JQA to AA, 20 February 1779, **DA** 4:175–76.

26. For the voyage home, see the editorial note in **DA** 4:183, and JA to AA, 14 May 1779, **DA** 4:195–96.

27. See the long editorial note on John's role in drafting the Massachusetts Constitution in **DA** 4:225–33. The quotation is in **DA** 4:228.
28. Another lengthy editorial note, in **PA** 8:228–36, provides more context on the contents of the document, which is reproduced in **PA** 8:237–61. The quotation is in **PA** 8:237.
29. JA to Elbridge Gerry, 4 November 1779, **PA** 8:276.
30. These are my interpretive conclusions, indebted to the work of earlier scholars, most especially Robert J. Taylor, "Construction of the Massachusetts Constitution," American Antiquarian Society **Proceedings** 90 (1980), 317–46.
31. **JCC** 13:487, for the official reprimand of Dean and the absolution of Franklin and John; Henry Laurens to JA, 4 October 1779, **PA** 8:188–91.
32. **PA** 8:199–201, for letters urging speed from James Lovell and Benjamin Rush.
33. JA to Henry Laurens, 4 November 1779, **PA** 8:279.
34. JA to AA, 13 November 1779, **AFC** 3:224.
35. AA to JA, 14 November 1779, **AFC** 3:233–34.
36. John described the overland journey through Spain and southern France in **DA** 2:415–33 and 4:218–38; JA to AA, 11 December 1779, **AFC** 3:243–44.

37. JA to AA, April–May, 1780, **AFC** 3:332–33; JA to AA, 12 May 1780, **AFC** 3:342.

38. JA to AA, 6 April 1780, **AFC** 3:319; AA to JA, 13 April 1780, **AFC** 3:320–21.

39. AA to JA, 23 August 1780, **AFC** 3:400–1; AA to Mercy Otis Warren, 1 September 1780, **AFC** 3:402–3; AA to JA, 25 December 1780, **AFC** 4:40; JA to AA, 2 December 1781, **AFC** 4:251.

40. AA to JA, 10 April 1782, **AFC** 4:305–8.

41. The effort by Vergennes to have John recalled is summarized in two editorial notes, **AFC** 3:390–95 and 4:174–76. For John's version, see **DA** 3:103–5. The quotation is in **DA** 2:446. The debate and vote in the Continental Congress is in **JCC** 20:746.

42. Benjamin Franklin to Continental Congress, 9 August 1780, **AFC** 3:395; Benjamin Franklin to R. R. Livingston, 23 July 1780, reproduced in **AFC** 5:251–52.

43. Elbridge Gerry to JA, 30 July 1781, **AFC** 4:189.

44. AA to James Lovell, 30 June 1781, **AFC** 4:165.

45. AA to JA, 17 March 1782, **AFC** 4:293.

46. AA to JA, 25 May 1781, **AFC** 4:128–31; JA to AA, 14 May 1782, **AFC** 4:323. John's Dutch initiative, if recounted fully, would require a separate volume of its own. My account here

is, and only intends to be, a brief summary, its brevity necessitated by the need to sustain the focus on the relationship between Abigail and John. The editorial note in **AFC** 3:390–95 describes John's multiple movements and machinations in the Netherlands during 1780 and 1781.

47. AA to JA, 9 December 1781, **AFC** 4:255–61; AA to JA, 5 August 1782, **AFC** 4:356–59.

48. AA to JQA, 19 January 1780, **AFC** 3:268–69.

49. JA to AA, 18 December 1780, **AFC** 4:34–35.

50. John's rather terrifying injunction to John Quincy dates from a later time, though it represents his consistent paternal posture. Obviously, when he was a young boy, John Quincy was not expected to become president, because no such office existed. But he was expected to lead a life of public service that culminated at the top. See Ellis, **Passionate Sage**, 195; AA to JQA, 26 December 1783, **AFC** 5:284. For a psychiatric interpretation of the pressure placed on John Quincy, see David F. Musto, "The Youth of John Quincy Adams," American Psychological Society **Proceedings** 113 (1969), 269–82.

51. JA to JQA, 14 May 1781, **AFC** 4:114.

52. JQA to AA, 21 December 1780, **AFC** 4:38–39; JA to JQA, 23 December 1780, **AFC** 4:47; JA to JQA, 28 December 1780, **AFC** 4:55.

53. AA to CA, 26 May 1781, **AFC** 4:135; JA to AA, 16 March 1780, **AFC** 3:305; JA to AA, 25 September 1780, **AFC** 3:424.

54. JA to AA, 2 December 1781, **AFC** 4:249.

55. AA to JA, 23 December 1782, **AFC** 5:54–59; AA to JA, 30 December 1782, **AFC** 5:61–63.

56. JA to AA, 22 January 1783, **AFC** 5:75–76; JA to AA, 4 February 1783, **AFC** 5:88–89; AA to JA, 7 May 1783, **AFC** 5:151–52.

57. Royall Tyler to JA, 13 January 1784, **AFC** 5:297–98; JA to Royall Tyler, 3 April 1784, **AFC** 5:316–17.

58. G. Thomas Tanselle, **Royall Tyler** (Cambridge, Mass., 1967).

59. JA to AA, 22 March 1782, **AFC** 4:300; JA to AA, 29 March 1782, **AFC** 4:303.

60. JA to AA, 22 March 1782, **AFC** 4:301.

61. JA to AA, 15 August 1782, **AFC** 4:360–61.

62. It is possible, indeed probable, that John's account of the number of letters lost at sea was inflated.

63. JA to AA, 12 October 1782, **AFC** 5:15–16.

64. JA to Edmund Jenings, 20 July 1782, **AP** 13:188–90.

65. JA to AA, 8 November 1782, **AFC** 5:28–29, in which John describes how he and Jay pressured Franklin to accept the concept of a separate peace.

66. **DA** 3:81. The story of the negotiations leading

up to the Treaty of Paris has more twists and turns than this brief summary can possibly capture. The authoritative history is Richard B. Morris, **The Peacemakers: The Great Powers and American Independence** (New York, 1965). See also Ronald Hoffman and Peter J. Albert, eds., **Peace and Peacemakers: The Treaty of 1783** (Charlottesville, 1986). The scholarship on this auspicious moment in American diplomatic history tends to divide along pro-Franklin or pro-Adams lines, with the former position enjoying a clear hegemony, invariably at the expense of Adams's reputation. See, for example, James H. Hutson, **John Adams and the Diplomacy of the American Revolution** (Lexington, Ky., 1980). More recently, however, Adams advocates have become more numerous. See, for example, John Ferling, "John Adams, Diplomat," **WMQ** 51 (April 1994), 227–52. While, like Ferling, I lean in the Adams direction, my deepest conviction is that the scholarly debate needs to free itself of the partisan prejudices of the participants and recognize that the success of the American negotiating team depended on the complementary strengths of both Franklin and Adams, but also on the extremely weak hand that history had dealt the British side.

67. The correspondence and draft articles that paved the way for the Provisional Treaty are in **PA** 14:2–102. The treaty itself is in **PA** 14:103–9.

68. AA to JA, 7 April 1783, **AFC** 5:116–17; JA to AA, 4 December 1782, **AFC** 5:46–47.

69. JA to AA, 30 May 1783, **AFC** 5:167.

70. JA to AA, 7 April 1783, **AFC** 5:119–21; JA to AA, 11 April 1783, **AFC** 5:121; JA to AA, 16 April 1783, **AFC** 5:125–27.

71. AA to JA, 30 June 1783, **AFC** 5:188–90.

72. JA to AA, 11 April 1783, **AFC** 5:121–22; **DA** 3:41–43, 50.

73. JA to AA, 16 April 1783, **AFC** 5:125–27.

74. AA to JA, 15 December 1783, **AFC** 5:280.

75. AA to JA, 7 December 1783, **AFC** 5:276–78.

76. JA to AA, 8 November 1783, **AFC** 5:265–66; AA to JA, 20 November 1783, **AFC** 5:271.

77. AA to Elbridge Gerry, 19 March 1784, **AFC** 5:311–12; Elbridge Gerry to AA, 16 April 1784, **AFC** 5:320–21.

78. AA to JA, 3 January 1784, **AFC** 5:291–92; AA to JA, 11 February 1783, **AFC** 5:302–3.

79. Editorial note, **AFC** 5:350–51, for the voyage and arrival in London; **DA** 4:154–67, for Abigail's diary. See also Levin, **Abigail Adams,** 167–73.

CHAPTER FOUR. 1784–89

1. Abigail kept a journal of her voyage and early weeks in London, written in the form of a long letter to her sister Mary Smith Cranch. The Copley portion of her commentary is in **AFC** 5:373–74.

2. **AFC** 5:382; JA to AA, 1 August 1784, **AFC** 5:416; JA to JQA, 1 August 1784, **AFC** 5:416–17; AA to Mary Smith Cranch, 30 July 1784, **AFC** 5:382.

3. **AFC** 5:430, 433–35, 439–40; AA to Cotton Tufts, 8 September 1784, **AFC** 5:456–59. Howard C. Rice, **The Adams Family in Auteuil, 1784–1785** (Boston, 1956).

4. AA to Elizabeth Smith Shaw, 14 December 1784, **AFC** 6:29.

5. AA to Mercy Otis Warren, 5 September 1784, **AFC** 5:446–51.

6. AA to Lucy Cranch, 5 September 1784, **AFC** 5:436–38.

7. AA to Hannah Quincy Lincoln Storer, 20 January 1785, **AFC** 6:65.

8. **AFC** 6:66–67.

9. AA to Elizabeth Smith Shaw, 13 December 1784, **AFC** 6:5–6; AA to Cotton Tufts, 2 May 1785, **AFC** 6:103–9.

10. AA to JQA, 20 March 1786, **AFC** 7:97.

11. AA to Elizabeth Smith Shaw, 11 January 1785,

AFC 6:56–57; AA to Mary Smith Cranch, 20 February 1785, **AFC** 6:67; AA to Mary Smith Cranch, 15 April 1785, **AFC** 6:84.

12. AA to Mary Smith Cranch, 20 February 1785, **AFC** 6:67–68.

13. AA to Cotton Tufts, 3 January 1785, **AFC** 6:43; AA to Mary Smith Cranch, 15 April 1785, **AFC** 6:84.

14. My effort here to recover the daily interactions of the Adams family at Auteuil represents a distillation of multiple letters from Abigail in 1784–85, in which the ordinary conversations are usually mentioned as asides. The last scene is described in AA to Royall Tyler, 4 January 1785, **AFC** 6:45. The fact that Abigail's fullest account of a domestic scene was written to Tyler suggests that she still, at this stage, regarded him as a potential member of the Adams family.

15. JA to James Warren, 27 August 1784; JA to Elbridge Gerry, 12 December 1784, **PA** 7:382–83.

16. AA to TJ, 6 June 1785, **AFC** 6:169–73; JA to TJ, 22 January 1825, **AJ** 2:606.

17. More specific documentation of Jefferson's visionary views of international trade appears in subsequent notes. This preliminary assessment of his mental habits is based on my earlier effort (in **American Sphinx**, 64–117) to capture his mentality at this stage of his career.

18. JA to TJ, 4 September 1785, **AJ** 1:61.
19. Lord Dorset to American Commissioners, 13 April 1785, **JP** 7:55–56; JA to TJ, 6 June 1786, **AJ** 1:133–34.
20. TJ and JA to American Commissioners, 28 March 1786, **JP** 9:357–59.
21. Editorial note, "Jefferson's Proposed Concert of Powers Against the Barbary Pirates," July–December 1786, **JP** 10:560–66.
22. JA to TJ, 3 July 1786, **AJ** 1:142–43; JA to John Jay, 15 December 1784, **Works** 8:217–19; JA to TJ, 6 June 1786, **AJ** 1:133.
23. JA to TJ, 31 July 1786, **AJ** 1:146; JA to TJ, 17 February 1786, **AJ** 1:121.
24. The extensive correspondence between Abigail and Jefferson that documents my interpretation here can be found in **AFC** 6:223–24, 262–65, 333–34, 346–47, 390–92, 414–15, 422–23, 437–39, 441–42, 466–68, 488–89, 495–97.
25. TJ to AA, 9 August 1786, **AFC** 7:312–13; AA to TJ, 19 October 1785, **AFC** 6:437–39.
26. TJ to AA, 25 September 1785, **AFC** 6:390–92; AA to TJ, 7 October 1785, **AFC** 6:414–15.
27. TJ to AA, 9 August 1786, **AFC** 6:312.
28. TJ to AA, 22 February 1787, **AFC** 6:468–69; AA to TJ, 29 January 1787, **AFC** 6:455.
29. AA to TJ, 26 June 1787, **AFC** 8:92–93.
30. AA to TJ, 6 July 1787, **AFC** 8:107–9.
31. AA to TJ, 10 July 1787, **AFC** 8:109–10.

32. TJ to JA, 21 June 1785, **AJ** 1:34; JA to TJ, 22 May 1785, **AJ** 1:21.

33. AA to Mary Smith Cranch, 24 June 1785, **AFC** 6:192.

34. **DA** 3:184.

35. JA to John Jay, 2 June 1785, **Works** 8:255–59.

36. AA to Mary Smith Cranch, 24 June 1785, **AFC** 6:190; AA to JQA, 26 June 1785, **AFC** 6:196.

37. AA to Mary Smith Cranch, 24 May 1786, **AFC** 7:197–98; AA to Elizabeth Smith Shaw, 19 July 1786, **AFC** 7:264.

38. AA to Elizabeth Smith Shaw, 2 September 1785, **AFC** 6:327–30; **DA** 3:184–86.

39. AA to Mary Smith Cranch, 30 September 1785, **AFC** 6:393.

40. **DA** 3:187, 193, where an editorial note provides the Jefferson quotation.

41. AA to Elizabeth Smith Shaw, 21 November 1786, **AFC** 7:392.

42. Jefferson's correspondence to American friends after meeting with John provides the most succinct statement of the diplomatic futility for an American ambassador in London: "With this nation nothing is done; and it is now decided that they intend to do nothing with us." See TJ to James Madison, 25 April 1786, **JP** 9:433–34.

43. AA to TJ, 6 September 1785, **AFC** 6:346–47.

44. AA to Charles Storer, 23 March 1786, **AFC** 7:113–14.
45. AA to JQA, 20 March 1786, **AFC** 7:98.
46. JA to AA, 25 December 1786, **AFC** 7:412.
47. JA to TJ, 22 May 1785, **AJ** 1:21; Jefferson's analysis of African American inferiority in **Notes** is most conveniently available in Merrill Peterson, ed., **The Portable Jefferson** (New York, 1975), 186–93.
48. AA to JQA, 16 February 1786, **AFC** 7:62–63.
49. AA to WSS, 18 September 1785, **AFC** 6:366.
50. AA to JQA, 21 July 1786, **AFC** 7:276; AA to CA, 1 February 1786, **AFC** 7:60–61; JA to CA, 2 June 1786, **AFC** 7:208.
51. JA to JQA, 26 May 1786, **AFC** 7:205; JA to JQA, 23 January 1788, **AFC** 8:219–20.
52. AA to JQA, 28 February 1787, **AFC** 7:474–75.
53. For a sensitive and sensible discussion of Abigail's recognition that gender equality was a clear consequence of the ideology used to justify the American Revolution, but that its arrival lay far in the future, see Elaine Forman Crane, "Political Dialogue and the Spring of Abigail's Discontent," **WMQ** 56 (October 1999), 745–74.
54. AA to Mary Smith Cranch, 15 August 1785, **AFC** 6:276–80; editorial note on the end of the Tyler courtship, **DA** 3:192.

55. AA to Mary Smith Cranch, 26 February 1786, **AFC** 7:77–80. See **DA** 3:183, for an editorial note on William Stephens Smith.

56. WSS to AA, 5 September 1785, **AFC** 6:340–42; WSS to AA, 29 December 1785, **AFC** 6:508–9; AA to Mary Smith Cranch, 21 March 1786, **AFC** 7:101.

57. AA to Mary Smith Cranch, 24 April 1786, **AFC** 7:147; AA to Mary Smith Cranch, 25 February 1787, **AFC** 7:471; AA to Mercy Otis Warren, 14 May 1787, **AFC** 8:47.

58. JA to Cotton Tufts, 27 August 1787, **AFC** 8:149. For news of the purchase, see Cotton Tufts to AA, 20 September 1787, **AFC** 8:162–63.

59. AA to AA(2), 15 August 1786, **AFC** 7:318–20; AA to Cotton Tufts, 10 October 1786, **AFC** 7:359–64.

60. John Jay to JA, 4 July 1787, quoted in editorial note, **AFC** 8:153.

61. There is no modern edition of **Defence,** though there are selections from the text published in several anthologies of John's political thought. The only place to find the unabridged version is in **Works,** vols. 4–6.

62. The most favorable modern-day assessment of **Defence** is C. Bradley Thompson, "John Adams and the Science of Politics," in Richard

A. Ryerson, ed., **John Adams and the Founding of the American Republic** (Boston, 2001), 257–59.

63. The hostile review in the **London Monthly Review** is quoted in an editorial note, **AFC** 8:79.

64. AA to JQA, 20 March 1787, **AFC** 8:12; **Works** 4:290, for the quotations from **Defence.** The scholarly debate over John's stature as a political thinker, based in part on his arguments in **Defence,** tends to focus on his dependence on classical categories of analysis (i.e., monarchy, aristocracy, democracy). Gordon S. Wood, in **The Creation of the American Republic** (Chapel Hill, 1969), 567–92, makes the strongest case for reading **Defence** as an anachronistic work that was irrelevant to the more egalitarian context of the American republic. John P. Diggins, in **The Lost Soul of American Politics: Virtue, Self-Interest, and the Foundations of Liberalism** (New York, 1984), 69–99, on the other hand, sees **Defence** as prescient for its recognition that the absence of hereditary aristocracy in America did not mean the absence of class divisions or the hegemonic influence of political elites. I have offered my own interpretation of the issues at stake in **Passionate Sage: The Character and**

Legacy of John Adams (New York, 1993), 143–73, where I tend to agree with Diggins.

65. AA to Cotton Tufts, 6 November 1787, **AFC** 8:203.
66. TJ to JA, 20 February 1787, **AJ** 1:172.
67. TJ to JA, 5 March 1788, **JP** 12:638.
68. JA to TJ, 12 February 1788, **AJ** 1:224–25.
69. AA to JA, 23 March 1788, **AFC** 8:247–48.
70. TJ to JA, 13 November 1787, **AJ** 1:212; JA to TJ, 10 November 1787, **AJ** 1:210; JA to TJ, 6 December 1787, **AJ** 1:213–14.
71. **DA** 3:215.

CHAPTER FIVE. 1789–96

1. Editorial note, quoting report in the **Massachusetts Centennial, AFC** 8:216–17.
2. AA to AA(2), 7 July 1788, **AFC** 8:277–78.
3. AA(2) to JA, 27 July 1788, **AFC** 8:282; AA(2) to JQA, 28 September 1788, **AFC** 8:299.
4. JA to AA, 2 December 1788, **AFC** 8:312.
5. JA to AA(2), 11 November 1788, **AFC** 8:305; AA to Mary Smith Cranch, 24 November 1788, **AFC** 8:308.
6. AA to JA, 15 December 1788, **AFC** 8:318–19; JA to AA, 28 December 1788, **AFC** 8:325.
7. AA to JA, 3 December 1788, **AFC** 8:313–14; JA to TJ, 2 January 1789, **AJ** 1:234.

8. JA to AA, 19 December 1793, **AFC**, vol. 9. The editors of the **Adams Papers** granted me access to the unpublished galleys of the forthcoming volume of the **Adams Family Correspondence** before pagination was finalized. Subsequent references to this volume will provide the date of the letters without pagination.

9. Editorial note, 16 March 1789, **AFC** 8:340.

10. AA to Mary Smith Cranch, 28 June 1789, **AFC** 8:379; AA to Mary Smith Cranch, 12 July 1789, **AFC** 8:391.

11. JA to AA, 14 May 1789, **AFC** 8:352.

12. AA to Mary Smith Cranch, 9 August 1789, **AFC** 8:397.

13. Editorial note, 21 April 1789, **AFC** 8:340; JA to JQA, 9 July 1789, **AFC** 8:387.

14. Linda Grant De Pauw, et al., eds., **Documentary History of the First Federal Congress**, 15 vols. (Baltimore, 1972–84) 9:3–13; James H. Hutson, "John Adams' Title Campaign," **NEQ** 41 (January 1968), 30–39.

15. AA to Mary Smith Cranch, 5 January 1790, **AFC**, vol. 9. There is no modern, easily accessible edition of **Discourses on Davila;** I have relied on the old edition in **Works,** vol. 6.

16. JA to AA, 24 November 1792, **AFC**, vol. 9, where John describes a conversation that he overheard containing these accusations.

17. **Works** 6:258–62.

18. **Works** 6:237, 245; see also JA to JQA, 7 May 1794, **UFC**, and JA to TBA, 19 September 1795, **UFC**.
19. AA to JA, 31 December 1793, **AFC**, vol. 9.
20. JA to AA, 12 March 1794, **UFC**.
21. JA to AA, 11 November 1789, **AFC** 8:342.
22. AA to Cotton Tufts, 18 April 1790, **AFC**, vol. 9.
23. Woody Holton, "Abigail Adams, Bond Speculator," **WMQ** 64 (October 2007), 821–38; editorial note, AA to Cotton Tufts, 6 February 1790, **AFC**, vol. 9.
24. AA to Cotton Tufts, 7 March 1790, **AFC**, vol. 9.
25. AA to JQA, 11 July 1790, **AFC**, vol. 9; AA to Cotton Tufts, 1 September 1789, **AFC** 8:405; AA to AA(2), 21 November 1790, **AFC**, vol. 9.
26. I have discussed the issues surrounding the treaty with the Creek Nation at greater length in **American Creation: Triumphs and Tragedies at the Founding of the Republic** (New York, 2007), ch. 4.
27. AA to Mary Smith Cranch, 8 August 1790, **AFC**, vol. 9.
28. TJ to JA, 10 May 1789, **AJ** 1:237.
29. JA to TJ, 29 July 1791, **AJ** 1:247–48.
30. TJ to JA, 17 July 1791, **AJ** 1:246.
31. JA to TJ, 29 July 1791, **AJ** 1:249–50. John Quincy's eleven essays appeared in the **Columbia Centinel** in June and July 1791.
32. AA to JA, 7 January 1793, **AFC**, vol. 9.

33. AA to JA, 27 May 1794, **UFC**; JA to AA, 11 March 1796, **UFC**.
34. AA to Martha Washington, 25 June 1791, **UFC**; AA to Mary Smith Cranch, 20 March 1792, **UFC**.
35. AA to Mary Smith Cranch, 28 April 1790, 25 October 1790, **UFC**; AA to JQA, 7 November 1790, 5 November 1792, **UFC**.
36. JA to JQA, 26 April 1795, **UFC**.
37. JA to AA(2), 31 January 1796, **UFC**; JA to AA, 28 December 1794, **UFC**.
38. JA to AA, 13 February 1796, **UFC**.
39. JA to AA, 2 February 1796, **UFC**.
40. AA to JA, 26 February 1794, 8 March 1794, **UFC**; JA to AA, 16 January 1795, **UFC**.
41. AA to AA(2), 14 December 1795, 21 February 1791, **AFC**, vol. 9.
42. WSS to JA, 21 October 1791, **AFC**, vol. 9; JA to AA, 2 March 1793, **AFC**, vol. 9.
43. JA to AA, 21 January 1794, **UFC**.
44. JA to JQA, 4 October 1790, **AFC**, vol. 9; JA to JQA, 8 September 1790, 17 October 1790, **AFC**, vol. 9.
45. JA to Thomas Welsh, 13 September 1790, **AFC**, vol. 9; JA to AA, 19 May 1794, **UFC**.
46. AA to Mary Cranch Smith, 12 March 1791, **AFC**, vol. 9; JA to AA, 14 January 1794, **UFC**.
47. JA to JQA, 30 May 1794, **UFC**; Martha Washington to AA, 19 July 1794, **UFC**; JA to JQA,

19 September 1795, **UFC**, in which John provides the quotation from Washington.

48. JA to JQA, 25 August 1795, **UFC**.

49. AA to JA, 22 April 1789, **AFC** 8:334; JQA to William Cranch, 27 May 1789, **AFC** 8:361. See also AA(2) to JQA, 30 March 1789, **AFC** 8:363.

50. AA to JA, 20 October 1789, **AFC** 8:427; AA to Mary Smith Cranch, 9 January 1790, **AFC**, vol. 9; JA to JQA, 8 September 1790, **AFC**, vol. 9.

51. The correspondence started on 23 December 1793 and ended on 17 May 1794. The early letters are in **AFC**, vol. 9, the remainder in **UFC**. The question is from JA to CA, 11 May 1794, **UFC**.

52. JA to CA, 25 December 1794, **UFC**.

53. JA to CA, 7 February 1795, **UFC**. My interpretation here cannot be proved conclusively, but strikes me as the most plausible explanation based on a considerable body of circumstantial evidence.

54. JA to AA, 8 December 1792, **AFC**, vol. 9. John took offense at the support for Clinton, calling him "a mere cipher, a logroller in New York politics, a man of mere ambition and no virtue." JA to AA, 19 December 1792, **AFC**, vol. 9.

55. JA to AA, 4 February 1794, 8 February 1794, **AFC**, vol. 9.

56. JA to AA, 19 November 1794, **UFC**; JA to AA, 23 November 1794, **UFC**; AA to JA, 13 February 1795, **UFC**.

57. AA to Mary Smith Cranch, 20 April 1792, 25 March 1792, **AFC**, vol. 9.

58. JA to AA, 26 January 1794, **UFC**; JA to AA, 14 January 1793, **AFC**, vol. 9.

59. The best secondary account of this crowded moment is in Stanley Elkins and Eric McKitrick, **The Age of Federalism** (New York, 1993), 330–84. See also my **American Creation,** ch. 5, and CA to JA, 29 July 1793, **AFC**, vol. 9; JA to AA, 12 December 1793, **AFC**, vol. 9; JA to AA, 17 February 1793, **AFC**, vol. 9.

60. JA to AA, 28 December 1792, **AFC**, vol. 9.

61. JA to AA, 3 February 1793, **AFC**, vol. 9.

62. JA to JQA, 3 January 1794, **UFC**. See also JA to AA, 6 January 1794, **UFC**.

63. Jerald A. Combs, **The Jay Treaty: Political Battleground of the Founding Fathers** (Berkeley, 1970), is the standard account. Elkins and McKitrick, **The Age of Federalism,** 406–50, is superb on the diplomatic twists and turns.

64. JA to CA, 13 December 1795, **UFC**; AA to JQA, 15 September 1795, **UFC**.

65. JA to AA, 9, 14, 23, and 29 June 1795, **UFC**, for John's report on the debate in the Senate. AA to JQA, 10 February 1795 and JA to CA, 20 April 1796, **UFC**, for the quotations.

66. JA to AA, 21 and 26 April 1796, **UFC,** for John's description of the melting Republican majority. JA to AA, 28 April 1796, **UFC,** for reference to Madison's condition.
67. JA to JQA, 29 November 1795, **UFC.**
68. JA to AA, 5, 7, and 20 January 1796, **UFC.**
69. AA to JA, 21 January and 14 February 1796, **UFC.**
70. JA to AA, 15 February 1796, 10 February 1796, **UFC.**
71. AA to JA, 20 February 1796, **UFC;** JA to AA, 1 March 1796, **UFC.**
72. AA to JA, 28 February 1796, **UFC.**
73. JA to AA, 9 April 1796, **UFC;** AA to JA, 4 December 1796, **UFC.**
74. JA to AA, 8 December 1796, 7 December 1796, **UFC.**
75. AA to JA, 1 January 1797, **UFC.**
76. JA to AA, 27 December 1796, **UFC.**
77. AA to JA, 31 December 1796, **UFC.**
78. AA to JA, 15 January 1797, **UFC.**

CHAPTER SIX. 1796–1801

1. TJ to James Madison, 8 January 1797, **JM** 2:955; **Aurora,** 6 March 1797; William Duane, "A Letter to Washington" (Philadelphia, 1796); AA to JA, 23 December 1796, **UFC.**
2. AA to JA, 15 January 1797, **UFC;** AA to JA,

31 December 1796, **UFC**; AA to JA, 28 January 1797, **UFC**. The standard account of the Adams presidency is Stephen G. Kurtz, **The Presidency of John Adams: The Collapse of Federalism, 1795–1800** (Philadelphia, 1957).

3. JA to Elbridge Gerry, 20 February 1797, **AP**, reel 117; TJ to James Madison, 1 January 1797, 22 January 1798, **JM** 2:953, 959–60.

4. TJ to JA, 28 December 1796, **JM** 2:961–62; JA to AA, 1 and 3 January 1797, **UFC**; AA to JA, 18 March 1797, **UFC**.

5. James Madison to TJ, 15 January 1797, **JM** 2:956–58.

6. I have told this story in somewhat greater detail in **Founding Brothers: The Revolutionary Generation** (New York, 2000), 184; John's recollection of the episode is in **Works** 9:285.

7. JA to AA, 13 March 1797, **UFC**; AA to JA, 2 March 1797, **UFC**; JA to JQA, 3 November 1797, **UFC**. On Jefferson's machinations, see Elkins and McKitrick, **The Age of Federalism**, 566.

8. JA to AA, 17 March 1797, **UFC**.

9. JA to AA, 5, 9, 17, and 27 March 1797, **UFC**.

10. JQA to JA, 3 February, 4 March, and 20 May 1797, **UFC**, for John Quincy's quite extraordinary analysis of French policy toward the United States.

11. JQA to JA, 21 May 1797, **UFC**.

12. AA to JA, 26 April 1797, **UFC**.

13. Alexander Hamilton to James McHenry, 21 April 1797, **HP** 20:574–75. An excellent account of Hamilton's behind-the-scenes behavior is in John Ferling, **John Adams: A Life** (Knoxville, 1995), 343.

14. AA to Mary Smith Cranch, 23 June 1797, **UFC**.

15. **Aurora,** 16 June 1798.

16. George Washington to JA, 28 February 1797, **Works** 8:529–30.

17. JA to JQA, 25 October and 3 November 1797; AA to JQA, 3 November 1797, **UFC**; JQA to AA, 28 December 1797, **UFC**.

18. **Aurora,** 17 May 1797, 26 May 1797.

19. AA to Mary Smith Cranch, 6 June 1797, **UFC**; AA to Mercy Otis Warren, 1 October 1797, **UFC**.

20. AA to Mary Smith Cranch, 20 and 27 March 1798, **UFC**; AA to Hannah Cushing, 9 March 1798, **UFC**.

21. JQA to AA, 29 December 1797, **UFC**; JA to Cotton Tufts, 18 November 1797, **UFC**.

22. AA to Mary Smith Cranch, 20 March 1798, **UFC**.

23. AA to TBA, 4 April 1798, **UFC**.

24. AA to TBA, 1 May 1798, **UFC**.

25. AA to Mary Smith Cranch, 10 May 1798, **UFC**.

26. JQA to JA, 15 April 1798, **UFC.**
27. AA to WSS, 8 April 1798, **UFC;** AA to Norton Quincy, 12 April 1798, **UFC;** AA to Mary Smith Cranch, 13 April 1798, **UFC.**
28. AA to Mary Smith Cranch, 22 April and 26 May 1798, **UFC;** AA to JQA, 26 May 1798, **UFC.**
29. The standard work is James Morton Smith, **Freedom's Fetters: The Alien and Sedition Laws and American Civil Liberties** (Ithaca, 1956). For a somewhat less harsh assessment of Adams, see Elkins and McKitrick, **The Age of Federalism,** 590–93, which cautions against imposing our modern notion of civil liberties on an era that was still groping toward a more expansive version of First Amendment protections.
30. AA to Mary Smith Cranch, 21 May 1798, **UFC;** AA to Cotton Tufts, 25 May 1798, **UFC;** AA to WSS, 20 March 1798, **UFC.**
31. JA to George Washington, 7 July 1798, **Works** 8:575.
32. JA to James McHenry, 22 October 1798, **Works** 8:612–13.
33. **HP** 21:381–447.
34. Ron Chernow, **Alexander Hamilton** (New York, 2004), 546–68, provides the fullest and fairest account.
35. Ibid., 568.

36. AA to WSS, 7 July 1798, **UFC**.

37. AA(2) to JQA, 28 September 1798, **UFC**, for a description of Abigail's ailments; AA to JQA, 20 July 1798, **UFC**.

38. JA to AA, 1 February 1799, **UFC**.

39. JQA to JA, 25 September 1798, **UFC**.

40. JA to AA, 25 February 1799, **UFC**.

41. AA to JA, 27 February 1799, **UFC**.

42. JA to AA, 22 February 1799, **UFC**.

43. Pickering's comment is in **HP**, 22:494–95.

44. AA to JA, 3 March 1799, **UFC**.

45. AA to JQA, 15 November 1998; AA to JA, 25 January 1799, **UFC**.

46. The correspondence with his cabinet during the Quincy seclusion is in **Works** 8:626–69.

47. JA to Benjamin Stoddert, 21 September 1799, **Works** 9:32–34.

48. JA to AA, 5 January 1799, **UFC**.

49. JA to WSS, 22 May 1799, **Works** 8:652.

50. AA to JA, 14 February 1799, **UFC**, for the first explicit mention of Charles's condition, prompted by the loss of John Quincy's money.

51. JA to JQA, 28 February 1800, **UFC**.

52. AA to WSS, 6 September 1799, **UFC**.

53. JA to AA, 12 October 1799, **UFC**.

54. **Works** 9:254–55, for John's recollection in 1809; JA to AA, 30 October 1799, **UFC**.

55. **Works** 9:154–55; AA to Mary Smith Cranch, 30 December 1799, **UFC**.

56. AA to Mary Smith Cranch, 24 April 1800, **UFC.**

57. Marshall quoted in Elkins and McKitrick, **The Age of Federalism,** 728; Alexander Hamilton to Charles Carroll, 1 July 1800, **UFC.**

58. James T. Callender, **The Prospect Before Us** (Philadelphia, 1800), 12–14, 47–48, 67; TJ to James Monroe, 26 May 1800, quoted in Ellis, **American Sphinx,** 219.

59. AA to JQA, 1 September 1800, **UFC.**

60. AA to Mary Smith Cranch, 24 April 1800, **UFC.**

61. Chernow, **Alexander Hamilton,** 612–14, provides the fullest treatment of McHenry's hyperbolic account of the incident. Hamilton was especially upset at the firings because he believed that McHenry and Pickering worked for him.

62. JA to AA, 13 June 1800, **UFC.**

63. AA to JA, 22 May 1800, **UFC.**

64. Alexander Hamilton to JA, 1 August 1800, **HP** 25:51.

65. **HP** 25:187–88, 190, 208–9.

66. JA to Uzal Ogden, 3 December 1800, **HP** 25:183; AA to TBA, 12 October 1800, **UFC.**

67. JA to AA, 2 November 1800, **UFC;** AA to Mary Smith Cranch, 21 November 1800, **UFC.**

68. AA to AA(2), 21 and 28 November 1800, **UFC.**

69. AA to TBA, 13 December 1800, **UFC**; JA to TBA, 11 December 1800, **UFC**.

70. JA to TBA, 18 December 1800, **UFC**.

71. AA to Sarah Smith Adams, 8 December 1800, **UFC**.

72. AA to TBA, 3 January 1801, **UFC**; JA to TBA, 25 January 1801, **UFC**; JA to Cotton Tufts, 26 December 1800, **UFC**.

73. AA to TBA, 3 January 1801, **UFC**; A Conversation Between Abigail Adams and Thomas Jefferson [January 1801], **UFC**.

74. AA to TBA, 3 February 1801, **UFC**; JA to AA, 16 February 1801, **UFC**.

75. **Aurora**, 11 March 1801.

76. **Washington Federalist**, 21 January 1801.

CHAPTER SEVEN. 1801–18

1. JQA to AA, 14 April 1801, **UFC**.

2. JA to William Tudor, 20 January 1801, **AP**, reel 123; JA to William Dexter, 23 March 1801, **Works** 10:580–81.

3. AA to TBA, 23 April 1801, **UFC**; AA to WSS, 3 May 1801, **UFC**.

4. JA to TBA, 12 July and 15 September 1801, **UFC**.

5. See Nagel, **Descent from Glory**, 56–135, for the complicated domestic situation at Quincy. In my judgment, Nagel's work on the Quincy

years is simultaneously invaluable and unreliable, in the latter case because he seems to have a vendetta against Abigail, and because he provides no documentation for his judgments.

6. AA to TBA, 26 April and 8 May 1803, **UFC;** a splendid summary of the legal transactions is in McCullough, **Adams,** 576.

7. AA to TBA, 12 July 1801, **UFC.**

8. AA to TBA, 12 June 1801, **UFC.**

9. AA to TBA, 12 June and 5 July 1801, **UFC;** JA to Thomas McKean, 21 June 1812, **Works** 10:16.

10. AA to JQA, 22 March 1816, **AP,** reel 430.

11. AA to TBA, 27 December 1801, **UFC.**

12. LCA, **The Adventures of a Nobody, AP,** reel 269.

13. JA to Benjamin Rush, 17 August 1813, in Alexander Biddle, ed., **Old Family Letters** (Philadelphia, 1892), 420.

14. JQA to JA, 19 November 1804, **UFC;** JA to JQA, 6 December 1804, **UFC.**

15. **DA** 2:253.

16. **DA** 1:xliv–xlvi.

17. **DA** 3:435–36.

18. AA to Mercy Otis Warren, 16 January 1803, **UFC.**

19. Mercy Otis Warren, **History of the American Revolution,** 3 vols. (Boston, 1805), 3:394–95.

20. JA to Mercy Otis Warren, 11 July, 27 July, and

3 August 1807, in Charles Francis Adams, ed., "Correspondence Between John Adams and Mercy Otis Warren," reprinted in **Collections of the Massachusetts Historical Society** 4 (1878), 354, 358, 411; Mercy Otis Warren to JA, 15 August 1807, ibid., 422–23, 449.

21. JA to Mercy Otis Warren, 27 July 1807, ibid., 354.

22. JA to William Cunningham, 27 February 1809, [Anonymous], in **Correspondence Between the Hon. John Adams . . . and the Late William Cunningham, Esq.** (Boston, 1823), 93; **Works** 10:310; JA to Nicholas Boylston, 3 November 1819, **AP**, reel 124.

23. The standard biography of Rush is David F. Hawke, **Benjamin Rush: Revolutionary Gadfly** (New York, 1971). The Adams–Rush correspondence is available in John A. Schutz and Douglas Adair, eds., **The Spur of Fame: Dialogues of John Adams and Benjamin Rush** (San Marino, Calif., 1966).

24. JA to Benjamin Rush, 29 November 1812, in Schutz and Adair, **Spur of Fame**, 254–55.

25. JA to Benjamin Rush, 22 December 1806, ibid., 72–73.

26. Benjamin Rush to JA, 4 June 1812, ibid., 233; JA to Benjamin Rush, 13 October 1810, ibid., 170; JA to Benjamin Rush, 26 March 1806, ibid., 52.

27. JA to Benjamin Rush, 14 May 1812, 8 January 1812, ibid., 216–17, 204.
28. JA to Benjamin Rush, 11 November 1807, 31 August 1809, ibid., 97–99, 152.
29. JA to Richard Rush, 2 May 1814, **AP**, reel 95.
30. JA to Benjamin Rush, 23 July 1806, in Schutz and Adair, **Spur of Fame**, 61.
31. AA to TJ, 20 May 1804, **AJ** 1:268–69.
32. TJ to AA, 14 June 1804, **AJ** 1:270–71.
33. AA to TJ, 1 July 1804, **AJ** 1:271–74.
34. TJ to AA, 22 July 1804, **AJ** 1:274–76, 279–80.
35. AA to TJ, 25 October 1804, **AJ** 1:280–82. The marginal note by John is printed at the end of this letter.
36. AA to LCA, 8 December 1804, **UFC**.
37. LCA to AA, 11 May 1806, **UFC**.
38. AA to JQA and LCA, 29 November 1805, **UFC**.
39. JA to JQA, 27 August 1815, **AP**, reel 122.
40. AA to AA(2), 23 May 1809, **UFC**.
41. AA to Caroline Amelia Smith, 2 February 1809, **UFC**; Benjamin Rush to JA, 20 September 1811, **AP**, reel 412.
42. AA to JQA, 17 November 1811, **AP**, reel 412.
43. AA to JQA, 17 November 1811, **AP**, reel 116.
44. AA to JQA, 13 September, 24 September, and 22 October 1813, **AP**, reel 116.
45. JA to Shelton Jones, 11 March 1809, **AP**, reel 118; JA to Francis Vanderkemp, 5 July 1814,

AP, reel 116; JA to Benjamin Rush, 15 January 1813, **AP,** reel 116.

46. JA to John Adams Smith, 15 October 1811, **UFC.**

47. JA to Benjamin Waterhouse, 16 August 1812, in Worthington C. Ford, ed., **Statesman and Friend: Correspondence of John Adams and Benjamin Waterhouse, 1784–1822** (Boston, 1927), 81; JA to Josiah Quincy, 9 February 1811, **Works** 9:630.

48. JA to Francis Vanderkemp, 27 December 1816, **Works** 10:235.

49. JA to Benjamin Rush, 25 December 1811, in Schutz and Adair, **Spur of Fame,** 200–202; Benjamin Rush to JA, 17 February 1812, ibid., 211; Benjamin Rush to JA, 16 October 1809, ibid., 156–57.

50. Donald Stewart and George Clark, "Misanthrope or Humanitarian: John Adams in Retirement," **NEQ** 28 (1955), 232.

51. Josiah Quincy, **Figures of the Past** (Boston, 1883), 79–80. It should be noted that this discussion of the Adams–Jefferson correspondence makes no pretense of being a comprehensive account. If this were a biography of John and not a book about the partnership between Abigail and John, the treatment of the Adams–Jefferson letters would be considerably expanded. See, for example, my **Found-**

ing Brothers, 206–48; **American Sphinx**, 235–51; and **Passionate Sage**, 113–42, for fuller treatments.

52. JA to TJ, 15 July 1813, **AJ** 2:358, where the quote is from Abigail's appended note.

53. TJ to JA, 21 January 1812, and JA to TJ, 3 February 1812, **AJ** 2:291, 298.

54. JA to TJ, 15 July 1813, **AJ** 2:358.

55. TJ to JA, 5 July 1814, and JA to TJ, 16 July 1814, **AJ** 2:430, 435.

56. JA to TJ, 1 May 1812, and TJ to JA, 27 May 1813, **AJ** 2:301, 324.

57. TJ to JA, 11 January 1816, **AJ** 2:458–61.

58. JA to TJ, 3 February 1816, **AJ** 2:458–61.

59. The key letters are: TJ to JA, 27 June 1813; JA to TJ, 15 July 1813; and JA to TJ, 14 August 1813, **AJ** 2:335–36, 358, 365.

60. TJ to JA, 28 October 1813, and JA to TJ, 16 July 1814, **AJ** 2:387–92, 437–38. The subject ignited all of John's long-suppressed convictions about human inequality and the intractable power of elites in all societies. Virtually all his letters during the summer and fall of 1813, twenty in total, deal with this fundamental disagreement between the two patriarchs.

61. AA to Elizabeth Smith Shaw Peabody, 10 February 1814, 29 December 1811, **UFC**.

62. While these glimpses into the day-to-day interactions of Abigail and John are partly conjec-

ture on my part, they are based on the few shreds of testimony from visitors and offhand observations in the couple's correspondence with each other.

63. AA to Elizabeth Smith Shaw Peabody, 18 July 1809, **UFC.**

64. The best biography of John Quincy is Lynn Hudson Parsons, **John Quincy Adams** (Lanham, Md., 1998). The quotation is the title for chapter 4, which covers his diplomatic career in St. Petersburg.

65. JA to JQA, 13 November 1816, and 26 November 1816, **AP,** reel 123.

66. JA to JQA, 10 August 1817, **UFC; AA** to Harriet Welsh, 18 August 1817, **AP,** reel 438; McCullough, **John Adams,** 620–21.

67. Will of Abigail Adams, 18 January 1816, **AP,** reel 429. You could develop an interpretation of Abigail's independence on the basis of this final statement, and Woody Holton has done so in his recent biography, **Abigail Adams** (New York, 2009), which strikes me as superb.

68. JA to JQA, 6 July 1816, **UFC.**

69. JA to TJ, 20 October 1818, **AJ** 2:529; John's remark is reported in Harriet Welsh to Louisa C. A. de Windt, November 1818, **AP,** reel 445.

70. See Nagel, **Descent from Glory,** 130–33, for an excellent account of the death scene and the quotation from Louisa Catherine; JA to

Francis Vanderkemp, 25 September 1819, **AP,** reel 124; JA to JQA, 10 November 1818, **UFC.**

EPILOGUE. 1818–26

1. JA to Caroline de Windt, 15 March 1820, **AP,** reel 124.

2. JA to LCA, 8 May 1820, **AP,** reel 124; JA to LCA, 29 January 1820, **AP,** reel 124.

3. LCA to JA, 16 April 1819, **AP,** reel 124.

4. LCA, **The Adventures of a Nobody, AP,** reel 269.

5. JA to Peter de Windt, 15 March 1820, **AP,** reel 124; JA to Elihu Marshall, 7 March 1820, **Works** 10:388–89.

6. JA to LCA, 21 October 1820, **AP,** reel 450.

7. JA to TJ, **AJ** 2:571–72.

8. TJ to JA, **AJ** 2:600–601.

9. JA to TJ, **AJ** 2:601–2.

10. TJ to JA, **AJ** 2:613–14.

11. JA to CFA, 3 December 1825, **AP,** reel 473.

12. Josiah Quincy, **Figures of the Past** (Boston, 1883), 61; Richard McLanathan, **Gilbert Stuart** (New York, 1986), 187; JA to Charles Carroll, 12 July 1820, **AP,** reel 123.

13. Quincy, **Figures of the Past,** 64–65.

14. Ibid., 80–82.

15. JA to LCA, 22 December 1818, **AP,** reel 123.

16. JA to JQA, 24 December 1818, **AP**, reel 123; JA to Benjamin Rush, 27 December 1812, in Alexander Biddle, ed., **Old Family Letters** (Philadelphia, 1892) 432.

17. JA to JQA, 24 December 1818, **AP**, reel 123.

18. JA to Alexander Johnson, 4 January 1823, **AP**, reel 124.

19. JA to JQA, 24 May 1815, **AP**, reel 122.

20. JA to TJ, 17 April 1826, **AJ** 2:614.

21. JA to TJ, 25 February 1825, **AJ** 2:610.

22. "The Diary of George Whitney," **AP**, reel 475.

23. John Marston to JQA, 8 July 1826, **AP**, reel 476.

24. There has been some suspicion that the reference to Jefferson was fabricated long after the fact, because it seems so melodramatic. But the written account of two witnesses soon after John's death confirms the remark. See Susan Boylston Adams Clark to Abigail Louise Smith Adams Johnson, 9 July 1826, A. B. Johnson Papers, Massachusetts Historical Society, Boston.

INDEX

Index

Index

Adams, Charles (son),
  42, 171, 211, 271,
  333, 355, 362
  alcoholism of, 68,
    264–6, 327, 329,
    343
  birth of, 25
  childhood of, 27, 52,
    54, 68–73, 90, 96,
    99, 107–8
  death of, 68, 345, 360,
    386
  education of, 151–5,
    264–6
  in Europe, 138, 147,
    149, 154–55
  voyage home of, 155
Adams, Charles Francis
  (grandson), 5, 401
Adams, George
  Washington
  (grandson), 357,
  363, 383, 399, 406
Adams, John
  Abigail's
    correspondence
    with, 5–10, 25, 45,
    50–5, 64, 70–2,

79–82, 100–8,
  113–15, 139–40,
  160–1
and Abigail's death,
  403–6
ambitions of, 13–15,
  100–1
assets brought to
  marriage by, 11–13
Atlantic crossings of,
  108, 112–15, 127,
  129, 136–40, 226
birth of children of, 6,
  25, 103–5, 323
Boston home of, 40
Boston Massacre
  defendants
  represented by,
  41–2, 148, 297, 340
Braintree estate
  purchased by,
  216–17, 228
and Charles's
  alcoholism and
  death, 264–6,
  327–8, 386
child-rearing practices
  of, 154–5, 211–12

Index

Index

A NOTE ABOUT THE AUTHOR

Joseph J. Ellis won the Pulitzer Prize for **Founding Brothers.** His portrait of Thomas Jefferson, **American Sphinx,** won the National Book Award. He is the Ford Foundation Professor of History at Mount Holyoke College in Massachusetts, where he lives with his wife and their youngest son.

AMERICAN CREATION

TRIUMPHS AND TRAGEDIES
AT THE FOUNDING OF THE REPUBLIC

LARGE
PRINT
RANDOM
HOUSE

JOSEPH J. ELLIS

PULITZER PRIZE–WINNING AUTHOR OF
FOUNDING BROTHERS and HIS EXCELLENCY